D1453035

BEHAVIORAL
PROBLEMS
IN
ORGANIZATIONS

Cary L. Cooper, Editor

University of Manchester
Institute of Science and Technology

PRENTICE-HALL, INC., ENGLEWOOD CLIFFS, NEW JERSEY 07632

59992

Library of Congress Cataloging in Publication Data

Main entry under title:
Behavioral problems in organizations.

Bibliography: p.
Includes index.
1. Organizational behavior. I. Cooper, Cary L.
HD58.7.B42   158.7   78-12451
ISBN   0-13-073080-7

Editorial/production supervision and
   interior design by Barbara Alexander

Cover design by Craig Wood Phillips, A Good Thing, Inc.

Manufacturing buyer: Harry P. Baisley

APPLIED MANAGEMENT SERIES
Cary L. Cooper, Editor

Printed in the United States of America

10   9   8   7   6   5   4   3   2   1

PRENTICE-HALL INTERNATIONAL, INC., *London*
PRENTICE-HALL OF AUSTRALIA PTY. LIMITED, *Sydney*
PRENTICE-HALL OF CANADA, LTD., *Toronto*
PRENTICE-HALL OF INDIA PRIVATE LIMITED, *New Delhi*
PRENTICE-HALL OF JAPAN, INC., *Tokyo*
PRENTICE-HALL OF SOUTHEAST ASIA PTE. LTD., *Singapore*
WHITEHALL BOOKS LIMITED, *Wellington, New Zealand*

Contributors

Cary L. Cooper (Editor), Professor of Management Educational Methods (a chair founded by the Foundation for Management Education), University of Manchester Institute of Science and Technology, England; Chairman-elect of the Management Education and Development Division of the Academy of Management. Professor Cooper is the author of nine books (e.g., *Theories of Group Processes* and *Understanding Executive Stress*) and over 60 scholarly journal articles.

Kenneth R. Brousseau, Assistant Professor of Management, Graduate School of Business Administration, U.S.C. Professor Brousseau is the author of numerous journal articles on job and work design.

Thomas G. Cummings, Associate Professor of Management, U.S.C. Professor Cummings is the author of several books on socio-technical systems and work autonomy (e.g., *Management of Work, Job Satisfaction and Productivity*).

Michael J. Driver, Professor of Management and Director of the Center for Career Research, U.S.C. Professor Driver is one of the leading national authorities on career development. He is the author of a large number of articles and books on this subject.

Milton G. Holmen, Professor of Management and Director of the Management Laboratory, U.S.C. Professor Holmen has written extensively on action research and is on the editorial board of the international journal, *Small Group Behavior.*

Mary Lynne Markus, Lecturer in Organizational Behavior, Case Western Reserve University.

James J. O'Toole, Associate Professor of Management, U.S.C.; former director of the Work in America program. Professor O'Toole's books on worker participation and the future of industrial life are among the classics in the field (e.g., *Work in Amercia, Work and the Quality of Life,* etc.).

Alan J. Rowe, Professor of Management and Director of the Management Decisions Systems Program, U.S.C. Professor Rowe is a nationally recognized figure in the field of effective decision making and has published widely.

Derek Torrington, Lecturer in Personnel Management, Department of Management Sciences, University of Manchester Institute of Science and Technology. Professor Torrington is one of the leading academics in the U.K. in the personnel management field. He has written numerous books (e.g., *Face to Face, Personnel Management,* etc.) and is a leading figure in the Institute of Personnel Management.

Contents

CHAPTER 1

Introduction

Cary L. Cooper

Today, many of the serious problems that industrial and public service organizations face center on human resources—problems linked to the "people" aspect of company life. These include issues of career development, personal work relationships, decision-making difficulties, the quality of working life, job satisfaction and stress, and so on. The solution to these and other behavioral problems has become a major effort of organizations through action research programs, personnel initiatives in organizations, organization development projects, and other approaches. It is the purpose of this volume to focus on some of the behavioral problems organizations are currently experiencing and some of the possible solutions or alternative strategies they may want to consider for their resolution.

Figure 1-1 is a diagrammatic representation of some of the sources and consequences of behavioral problems in organizations. Fundamentally, the effectiveness or ineffectiveness of work or organizational behavior is determined by the interaction of the

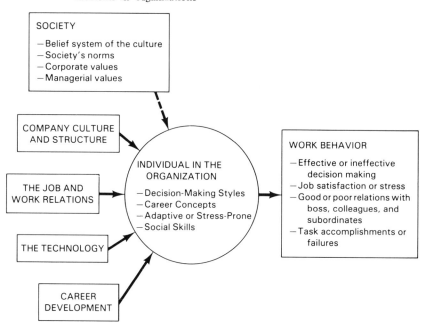

individual and his environment, or as Lofquist & Dawis (1969) label it, the *PERSON-ENVIRONMENT FIT.* The individual in an organization has a number of environmental influences acting upon him/her. The first two such factors are broad ones: First, the wider society or culture plays an enormous foundational role, albeit more indirectly—the attitudes and values imbued toward life in general and work in particular, standards of appropriate behaviors, the values of corporate life, and the like. Second, the culture and structure of the particular organization the individual works in have an even greater impact on him during working hours—its norms and values, level of support and trust, opportunities for autonomy and self-expression, and so forth. The interface of the individual with his culture and work subculture, although often neglected by organizational behavioral scientists, create behavioral and othe;problems that are important for us to understand, since they are potentially destructive but preventable, or at least amenable to change.

There are four other, more direct environmental factors that affect the individual at work: the job, the technological aspects of work, interpersonal relations at work, and career development prospects. These have a much more immediate and obvious influence on the individual and are critical to job satisfaction and performance (Cooper & Payne, 1978). None of the environmental factors (including the societal and organizational culture ones), however, influence behavior in a linear fashion; the extent and the nature of their impact depends on characteristics of the individual concerned as well—for instance, his or her personality predispositions, adaptability or stress proneness, decision-making style, career concepts, and social skills. Behavioral problems are kept to a minimum, for example, in a situation in which the individual's career concepts are consonant with the organization's career concepts. Similarly, effective decision making and harmonious work relationships can be achieved if, for example, a manager's "natural" decision-making style fits his subordinates' expectations and needs in a *particular* work culture. The successful fit of the individual and environmental factors is critical in effective organizational functioning; a misfit is responsible for many of the behavioral problems we find in organizations. We hope in this book to highlight some of these interactions and interfaces, to indicate how they can enhance organizational life or, at least, how the mismatch may create the conditions that lead to behavioral problems, and what can be done about them.

The book will start with an examination of the more global aspects of organizational behavior—namely, the interface between the individual and the corporate/managerial culture. Dr. O'Toole explores the "missing link" in organization phenomena, the influences of the cultural context of company activity. How does a firm's culture affect individual behavior? In what ways are organizational cultures dysfunctional, and can they be changed?

In the chapter that follows, Dr. Brousseau assesses the next most immediate interface, that of the individual and his or her particular job. He discusses a model of individual and job relationships, individual differences, and job enrichment, and proposes an approach to match the requirements of work and individual needs, which he terms "effective work system management." This entails work system diagnosis and design strategies that organizations should find exceedingly useful and stimulating. Dr. Cummings builds on Dr. Brousseau's chapter by examining the interface between the individual and the technological aspects of work. He provides us with a coherent theoretical account of the widely used "socio-technical approach" to organizations and describes how it can be used in organizational design to manage behavioral problems. He concludes with an example of the implementation of socio-technical ideas in a specific organizational context.

Dr. Driver focuses on an increasingly important topic in the field of organizational behavior, career management. He describes four different career concepts or patterns (transitory, steady state, linear, and spiral) and asks the perennial question, "How well does a given career concept fit that of a given organization?" A detailed examination follows of the match between an individual's and the organization's career concept on each of the four typologies. In addition, Dr. Driver discusses the direction of career change, the relationship of career concepts to life stage, and societal trends in career management.

The next two chapters explore the relations between certain characteristics of the individual at work—primarily his decision-making style and his ability to cope with pressure—and certain of the environmental factors illustrated in Figure 1-1. Drs. Driver and Rowe, for example, examine (in depth) management decision-making styles, arguing that an individual's "style predisposition" is not a necessary but sufficient condition for determining effectiveness in decision making. The authors ask and answer a host of conceptual and practical questions: (1) How do we know when a good decision has been made? (2) How does one find good decision makers? (3) How are jobs related to decision making in organizations? (4) How should decisions be shared with others? (5) How can organizations be designed to facilitate effective decision making?

Drs. Cooper and Torrington also examine an important topical issue, one that focuses on the individual and how he can be helped to cope with the stress of organizational existence. They examine the potential environmental stressors in organizations and then provide an account of how a company (or more specifically, how the personnel function) can begin to deal with them. Approaches to stress reduction and prevention are classified as either operational (short term) or influential (long term), and a detailed set of organizational prescriptions is posited.

And finally, Dr. Holmen devotes a chapter to an approach to organizational change that has been at the forefront of dealing with behavioral problems in organizations, *action research.* He attempts to explore answers to the following queries: (1) What is action research?

(2) What kinds of behavior problems does action research address? (3) With what kinds of organizations might action research work best? (4) What factors account for action research program effectiveness? This chapter is a very practical guide in helping organizations cope with behavior problems, as well as raising issues about action research as a change strategy—such as its possible dangers, how it can be evaluated, and so on.

REFERENCES

Cooper, C.L., *OD in the UK and US.* London: Macmillan; New York: Petrocelli, 1977.

Cooper, C.L., and Payne, R., *Stress at Work.* London & New York: Wiley, 1978.

Lofquist, L.H. and Dawis, R.V., *Adjustment to Work.* New York: Appleton-Century-Croft, 1969.

CHAPTER 2

Corporate and Managerial Cultures

James J. O'Toole

For nearly two decades, the corporation executive has been laid out on the headshrinker's couch. His fears have been probed by Freudians, his world view analyzed by Jungians, and his id (et cetera) massaged at Esalen and other centers of "humanistic psychology." He has suffered through scores of encounter groups to (1) find his Human Potential, (2) develop a hearty and healthy Primal Scream, and (3) pursue, *ad seriatim,* BFT, EST, TA, and TM. In an applied vein, organizational psychologists have dissected the manager's power needs, motivations, and leadership style with such quaintly named tools as "The Managerial Grid" (as opposed to the rack?), the Minnesota Multiphasic Personality Inventory (developed at the Mayo Clinic?), and the Leadership Behavior Description Questionnaire. In a more respectable intellectual tradition, psychoanalyst Michael Maccoby recently (1976) analyzed how William H. Whyte's Organization Man (1956) has now become the "heartless" Corporate Gamesman of the 1970s.

What are the implications of all this psychological tearing at the cerebral cortex of the corporate executive? For one thing, the implication is that the characters and personalities of executives are in large part responsible for corporate performance. From Abraham Maslow to Douglas McGregor to David McClelland and now to Maccoby, it has been assumed that individual managerial behavior is at the core of such problems as institutional inflexibility, bureaucratic behavior, resistance to innovation, insensitivity to employee needs, and social irresponsibility. This is Truth, by half.

THE MISSING HALF OF THE ANALYSIS OF ORGANIZATIONAL BEHAVIOR

The study of behavioral problems in private organizations has been dominated by psychologists. They have provided many invaluable insights into the processes of management, not the least of which is the now undeniable fact that human factors are singularly important determinants of success or failure in most organizations. But this finding is, alas, all too often not a guide for corrective action. That is, if individuals are defined as the cause of poor performance in the firm, one is often left with the near-impossible task of changing personalities or behavior to achieve effective organizational change.[1] Psychologists are not at all daunted by this imposing task. They assure all who will listen that personalities can be changed (or behavior modified). But layfolk are seldom willing to swallow this line; they know only too well that the state of the pedagogical art precludes teaching new routines to superannuated canines. Observation has taught us that few 50-year-old authoritarian managers ever become open and democratic, and that few aggressive Type A's ever become calm and introspective Type B's. Although we psychological civilians may all have witnessed heroic efforts on the part of friends to alter their behavior patterns, we've also seen the devastating

---

[1]Notable exceptions to this personality-based school of organizational psychology include Elton Mayo, Kurt Lewin, Warren Bennis, and my colleague Larry Greiner. Significantly, even the hard-line individualistic psychologists seldom practice what they preach. Instead of trying to change behavior, many are now using interview and testing techniques to *match* managers with jobs that meet their specific psychological characteristics. This is still personality-based, of course, and furthermore it seldom works; determining the person/ environment "fit" always falls far short of scientific accuracy.

onrush of recidivism ("When his real personality finally reemerged, it was with a vengeance").

Certainly, the personalities of corporate executives are of critical importance to the performance of most firms. But psychological analysis of organizational behavior is as *threatening* as it is important, because it places the burden of change squarely on the individual: There is something right or wrong, healthy or unhealthy, nurturing or destructive about *you*. In addition to the understandable reluctance on the part of managers to accept such a burden, the psychological focus can also be rejected as an incomplete and inadequate explanation of organizational behavior. The missing element is *the organizational context* in which managers find themselves. This is the half of the analysis concerned with the institutionalized social relationships that maintain the functioning of the corporation. This is the organization structure and ideology that make up the *culture* of the firm.

A focus on culture rather than personality permits the manager to get off the couch. This structural approach to the study of organizational behavior is rooted in the discipline of social anthropology. While psychologists are interested in *individual* differences in character and personality, social anthropologists focus on the *aggregate* behavior of whatever group (a tribe, nation, or firm) they are studying. An example helps to clarify the difference in levels of analysis: While the psychologist would be concerned with the difference in behavior between the personalities of, say, Stalin and Solzhenitsyn, the anthropologist would be looking for what the two Russians had in common. He might then find that the "national character" of Russians contained elements of authoritarianism, mysticism, and gloominess.

Stereotype is not the purpose of such analysis (although it can, unfortunately, degenerate to that level). Rather, the goal is to (1) identify the shared beliefs, ideas, customs, expectations, and symbols of a group; and (2) identify the principles of social organization that underlie the structure and functioning of that group. In brief, the anthropologist attempts to discover the (1) system of beliefs, and (2) system of actions, that characterize the group (Beattie, 1966). Taken together, these two mutually supporting systems constitute a group's culture. Thus, when one speaks of the culture of firm Z, one refers to that complexly interrelated whole of standardized, institutionalized, and habitual behavior that characterizes that firm only. The culture of the firm, then, is the unique behavior that binds its members together and differentiates it from other groups.

There is nothing normative about this definition. The culture might be good or bad, functional or dysfunctional, effective or ineffective, pleasurable or painful, all depending upon the criteria by which we choose to evaluate it. One of the major precepts of social anthropology is so-called cultural relativism—that is, there is no single, normative standard applicable to all cultures. What is good for the Mangbettu (to whom cannibalism was once a matter of course) is, simply, whatever the Mangbettu say is good for them. Although good anthropological practice thus precludes the normative evaluation of the culture of any particular firm by *outsiders,* even the corporate equivalents of the Mangbettu might want to evaluate their own behavior from time to time. Hence, I suggest below a tool—the Institutional Biography—for executives who might wish to analyze the cultures of their own firms. These suggestions are placed in the context of the following observations about the cultures of management.

Culture of Management at the Macro (National) Level

1. There is a dominant managerial culture that most American corporate executives share to at least some degree.
2. This dominant culture has changed in the last two decades, and is continuing to change.
3. The belief system of this culture is based on such values as economic efficiency, organizational growth, loyalty to the system, and camaraderie.

Culture of Management at the Micro (Firm) Level

4. Differences in the cultures of management between firms are varied and marked.
5. In some instances, a particular firm may find that its peculiar culture is dysfunctional for meeting its prevailing needs.
6. An organization can identify its own cultural characteristics and evaluate if they are functional or not.
7. An organization can alter its culture more readily than it can alter the personalities of its executives.

These seven assertions are developed in what follows.

THE DOMINANT CULTURE

The personal differences among corporate executives are manifest. For example, at one extreme, there are "Eastern-establishment" political liberals, who manage the entertainment and news industries of the nation; at the other end of the spectrum, there are the conservative middlebrows who manage the auto and steel industries. But political leanings, life styles, and industry type do not begin to exhaust the ways in which managers might be differentiated: levels of educational attainment, race, sex, age, cognitive styles, and performance records are just a few of the many other attributes that might be used. In short, managers in Exxon, IBM, and CBS might be as different from each other as Spaniards, Englishmen, and Italians.

Significantly, executives in large American corporations also have certain similarities, as Spain, England, and Italy all share in a common Western European civilization. Executives have these cultural similarities in part because most large corporations have certain *structural* similarities. They are almost all complex, hierarchical organizations run by professional managers who are the employees of absentee owners. Most executives also share common life histories: Data from a *Forbes* survey (1974) indicate that the typical corporate executive is a middle-aged man (a Midwesterner) who has spent most of his working life in one corporation, to which he came almost directly after graduation from Princeton or Yale.

In the late 1950s, William F. Whyte described how these similarities in background and organization environments conspired to produce a "modal type"—the security-seeking, bureaucratic, other-directed Organization Man, who eschewed innovation and risk and played it safe, "the company way." This submissive, conformist attitude was rewarded with warmth and security, high income, and promotions. Having grown up during the terribly insecure days of the Depression, the Organization Man took to the comfort of the corporation like a 6-month fetus takes to the womb.

When Whyte first published his study, his characterization was hotly denied by spokesmen for the corporate world. Interestingly corporate spokesmen today seem to admit the characterization was accurate at the time, and now argue only that organizations in the 1970s have "sent the grey flannel suit into mothballs" (Miller, 1977). Today, even Whyte's harshest critics seem to concede that there was, and is, a dominant managerial culture. The debate is only over the characteristics of the culture.

Change in the Structure

Maccoby now claims that Whyte's Organization Man has given way to a new breed of corporate cat, the Gamesman, whose

> character is a collection of near paradoxes understood in terms of its adaptation to organizational requirements. He is cooperative but competitive; detached and playful but compulsively driven to succeed; a team player but a would-be superstar; a team leader but often a rebel against bureaucratic hierarchy; fair and unprejudicial but contemptuous of weakness; tough and dominating but not destructive. [Maccoby; 1976, p. 100.]

Most of all, this puzzling fellow (who may even be a lady, in the liberted 1970s) views business as a game. The Gamesman's vocabularly is drawn from professional sports. He speaks of "the game plan," "making the big play," and "punting" when in trouble—all while trying to win "the money game," the "marketing game," or whatever game he happens to be playing. And that is the significant point: It does not matter what game he is playing, for Maccoby tells us that the Gamesman lacks all conviction. He is amoral, selfish, heartless, and uncommitted. The Gamesman is concerned only with his career. He will move anywhere and do anything, as long as he is progressing up the corporate ladder. Making or marketing Kepone is no different from making or marketing baby food. This amorality seems to derive from viewing his work as a game. A game, of course, is less significant than "real life." If work is only a game, then it is permissible to bluff (only a fool would show his hole card) and even permissible to cheat ("The best basketball and football players know that *holding* is part of the game"). Finally, the Gamesman is arrogant. He feels that he can run any organization, including the government (which is, after all, just another game, albeit with slightly different roles).

Where have we met this character? He is the recent Harvard M.B.A., the McKinsey man, the dynamic manager of the high technology corporation of the late 1960s. We met him at the Watergate hearings: the young wet-behind-the-ears functionary who "managed" the White House for President Nixon. (I recall meeting one of these young men shortly before the Watergate incident

12

reached epic proportions. I asked him if he planned to stay in Washington. "Of course," he replied, "where else could a 26-year-old M.B.A. have so much power?" Where else, indeed?)

No doubt, Maccoby has identified a real type. But has this Gamesman become the "typical" American manager? I suspect not. The high technology boom has abated a bit, and many of the small companies in this industry that were the Gamesman's stomping grounds have been swallowed up by big corporate bureaucracies. And the phenomenal growth that protected and nurtured the Gamesman in a few large companies is now a thing of the past. The boom-boom companies that would once tolerate his fierce competitiveness have now started to develop middle-age paunch and a slower pace that are fitting for those who now, too, are part of "the Establishment." Most Gamesmen now probably have two options: either to conform to the norms of mature firms, or to get out.

Here is the ultimate weakness of Maccoby's model: It is not personality that is the crucial variable in organizational behavior, it is culture. The systems of belief and action of giant corporations will usually wear down the maverick. One of the most important findings of American anthropologists has been that certain cultures are not conducive to certain personality types. Although all societies probably contain a random cross section of personalities, only certain behaviors are *rewarded*. Introspective and morose individuals do not flourish in societies that stress openness and gregariousness. Culture may not determine personality, but it greatly *influences* it. It is not so important, then, whether or not the Gamesman has overtaken the Organization Man. The crucial difference is how the *organization* has changed. Regardless of what kind of behavior is being rewarded, it is still the organization that sets the cultural norms to which young executives must adapt if they wish to succeed.

Indeed, one suspects that Maccoby's data (based on a sample of two companies, and some of it nearly ten years old) might not be all that reliable given the recent, rather rapid organizational changes in the high technology companies he studied. Today, the Gamesman may be out of step with the large, slow-growing companies in which he now finds himself. If this is true, then he is one of the most dissatisfied individuals in the corporate world. This is speculation. The direction in which the culture of management is changing is unclear; all that is known is that it is changing.

Characteristics of the Dominant Culture

Is there something that can be said with certainty about the characteristics of the dominant managerial culture in the late 1970s? If organizations shape managerial culture, as posited, then we might look at the *characteristics* of corporations for some clues. In general, large corporations have clearly become more complex in recent years: The financial resources at their disposal are larger; the size of their markets has expanded; capital requirements have soared; competition has increased; pace of change in the market has increased; technology is changing more rapidly; there are new pressures from labor, environmentalists, consumerists, and the government. . . . It's a new ballgame, as they say.

These changes suggest the need for a manager who is creative, fast-moving, flexible, and future-oriented. The ideal executive would seem to be one who is innovative and who can cope with uncertainty. It might seem, then, that entrepreneurs would be at a premium. But the structure and climate of large corporations is inhospitable to entrepreneurs. Hierarchical, bureaucratic companies are structured not to take risks but to avoid mistakes. Entrepreneurs quickly wash out of such environments. As the prevailing corporate wisdom expresses the problem, "Entrepreneurs are poor managers." If it is not the Organization Man, the Gamesman, or the Entrepreneur, who *is* running these complex organizations? One is tempted to answer in the psychological tradition by offering a category: the technocrat, the meritocrat, the bureaucrat, the specialist. . . .

But why this insistence on stereotype? The probable truth is that today's corporate managers are a diverse lot, with different personalities and characters. They are just people—liberal and conservative, intelligent and dull, aggressive and shy, authoritarian and caring, team players and loners. There is little analytical value in talking about them as individuals or in stereotyping them. Probably we would find (if we cared to make the effort) that corporate executives conform to the same personality types as a random cross section of the population. Perhaps the distribution would vary, but given the enormous number of executives (there are about 12 million of them in the United States), it is doubtful that even this difference would be significant. More important, to categorize is to run the risk of caricature. The temptation is to seize upon the modal personalities identified by psychologists and to see ourselves as "jungle fighters" or "gamesmen," and consciously or subsconciously try to adapt ourselves to fit the chosen archetype. More dangerously, the temptation is to stereotype others—"he's the typical bureaucrat"—and in so doing, close our eyes to the complexity of personality. Is anyone "the typical bureaucrat"?

The individual managers in question, then, are all different— but they still have the managerial culture in common. That is, corporate executives in general share a common belief system about corporate life. As a participant observer in several large organizations, I have attempted to identify the cultural characteristics (values, ideas, norms, symbols) common to corporate settings. The assumption guiding this enquiry is that a clear identification of what people value would be the most reliable indicator (predictor) of their behavior. For example, it is said that social and economic equality is the highest value to a Marxist. The Marxist will sacrifice all other values (liberty, efficiency, whatever) in order to attain equality. Contrariwise, a libertarian will sacrifice equality, the quality of the environment, full employment, and so on, to achieve *his* overriding goal—political and individual freedom. Managers tend not to be so absolutist or ideological as Marxists, libertarians, or others from extreme religious or philosophical camps. It rather seems that the managerial culture is characterized by a congeries of mutually supporting and complementary values, including the following.

Economic efficiency: A content analysis of speeches by business leaders will reveal a frequent use of such terms as "productivity," "consumer (market) sovereignty," "optimization," "least-cost," and "the most efficient allocation of goods and resources." If one can believe what businessmen say, they seem to value economic efficiency very highly. I recently undertook to informally measure the values of executives from thirteen major corporations, and learned that efficiency was, in this small sample at least, valued higher than nine other social objectives, including liberty, equality of opportunity, environmental quality, and full employment.

Growth: The behavior of executives indicates that growth is a significant goal in most large organizations. Indeed, it is probably their prime indicator of success, even more important than profit maximization. Of course, these two goals are often achieved simultaneously, but if a trade-off is necessary, the managerial culture often dictates the primacy of growth over profit. This is a quite logical ordering of preferences; after all, the primary beneficiary of profit is the stockholder, while the benefits of growth accrue to managers. Growth gives managers bigger empires, bigger pensions (through increases in stock value), and higher status (it is "better" to work for General Motors than for American Motors). Growth can be measured in terms of larger sales volume, more items produced, more employees, more branches, bigger market shares, and more operations in more countries. Granted, it is difficult to test the assertion that growth is prized higher than profit, but the measure of a "good year" in Detroit is that the number of cars sold exceeds the figure for the preceding year. Profits are important, too, but growth in sales is always reported first.

Loyalty to the system: Although there is a great degree of personal freedom in the corporate world (even executives of steel companies openly belong to the environmentalist Sierra Club), certain types of behavior are nevertheless taboo. Most important, the manager must never question the appropriateness of the current corporate system. The properly socialized manager simply does not express criticism of the prevailing forms of ownership and governance of the firm, of the competitive structure of his industry, or of the role of the corporation in society. In the same exercise that I referred to above, I found that corporate executives uniformly rejected *all* major alternatives to the status quo: greater free market competition, economic decentralization, greater government/corporate cooperation, or greater government regulation in the public interest. Significantly, the executives gave lip service to the values of free market competition, but resisted all suggested steps that would lead to its realization. (For this reason, I would not list "free enterprise competition" as a major value of the managerial culture.)

Camaraderie: There is a code of behavior that dictates that all interpersonal relations within the firm must be friendly and courteous, but not intimate. Everyone is called by his or her first name in American business. (As the lowliest cub reporter at Time Incorporated, I was once told to call Henry Luce "Hank" if I should ever run into him.) One must always show concern about the health, family, hobbies, and interests of one's co-workers. All meetings must be conducted in a climate of near-Victorian politeness and cordiality. Anger, hostility, and signs of weakness, fear, compassion, and love are taboo. A sense of humor is prized, as long as it is not cynical. Openness is valued, but it is always improper to question the appropriateness of the basic values of efficiency, growth, and loyalty. In short, this code of interpersonal behavior serves to shield the other, more basic aspects of the system of belief from attack from within.

This is far from an all-inclusive list of important corporate values (one might, for instance, reasonably include values of security, power, and stability), nor is the list rigorously taxonomic or scientific "truth." The list is merely suggestive. It serves only to shift the focus of analysis from individual to collective behavior. Its logical justification is that the values identified are consistent with, and complementary to, the structures of large American corporations. That is, it would appear that values of efficiency, growth, loyalty, and camaraderie would be, in general, *functional* for large, complex, hierarchical, and manager-run firms.

This general culture forms the basis for all the various specific cultures found in firms (as the Judeo-Christian culture is the bedrock on which all national cultures in Europe are built). It is useful to keep these general values in mind, then, as we move the level of analysis down to the firm, which is the prime level of interest of organizational behavior.

DIFFERENCES IN FIRM CULTURES

As no two managers are alike, it is obvious that no two corporations are identical. They differ by industry, product line, technology, size, age, nature of ownership, geographic location, and so forth. They differ in more subtle structural aspects as well— characteristics that have helped to define the culture of a particular firm:

> *Internal Stratification* - This can be measured by the height of the organizational hierarchy (e.g., flat with one or two levels of managers, or a pyramid with a dozen or more levels), and by the division of labor (the tasks performed by categories of workers, which includes horizontal as well as vertical stratification).
>
> *Roles* - This can be measured by the patterns of interaction, power, and status between the various horizontal and vertical strata in the firm. Certain behavioral expectations accrue to any set of formal roles: The

prescribed relationship of the secretary to the boss, the supervisor to the production worker, the president to the vice-president, the vice-president of marketing to the vice-president of finance are all measurable and vary between firms.

Associations and Networks - This is the pattern of informal social relationships in the firm. (Organizational psychologists study small-group behavior, which is the psychology of individuals in small groups. Anthropologists study patterns of influence, interaction, and association, focusing on the political functions of such networks.) This can be measured by who whispers what to whom.

System of Sanctions - This is a measure of how, when, and why people are rewarded or punished in a firm. It is the firm's "legal" structure. Negative and positive sanctions include money, status, acceptance, ostracism, promotion, and such perquisites as a new office and a company car.

Career Paths - This is a measure of the life history of the individual throughout his or her period of membership in the firm. It concerns where people are likely to start, the probabilities of where they will end up (and why), who is likely to exit early (and why), and how long each step in the hierarchy is likely to take (and why).

Structural Integration - As tribes can be organized by family, clan, or lineage, companies can be organized by product line, service function, or geographical region. The closeness or distance of the integration of these units, the patterns of group interaction, and the patterns of reciprocity among the various structural components differ between firms and are measurable.

All this definition, categorization, and measurement can lead to a sterile academic exercise. But such an analysis of structural differences can also lead to a better understanding of organizational behavior and the overall performance of the firm. For example, a pyramidal structure might inhibit creativity in a professional organization, or the lack of a well-defined career path might inhibit the recruitment of needed young executives, or the lack of structural integration might encourage uncooperative competition between organization units (or, conversely, it might motivate them through providing autonomy). Unfortunately, no general conclusion can be made about which structural factors are appropriate for which firms. What can be said is that the structure and system of beliefs may be inappropriate to a firm's needs at a given time. There is no law of anthropology that says that a system has to be in equilibrium. Unlike economics (which uses static models of systems), anthropology is dynamic. It recognizes that situations and environments often change in such a way that a once-appropriate culture might become dysfunctional to the long-term survival of an organization.

Dysfunctional Aspects of Managerial Cultures

The behavior of individuals changes when they are in groups. In organizations, people will often act in ways they would reject in their private lives. Work organizations employ sanctions to induce conformity to prevailing cultural norms that no one individual would be likely to adopt for his own behavior or the behavior of his family. The tyranny of organizational culture can be quite complete. Such cultural imperatives as order, efficiency, and loyalty will often be adhered to beyond the point of rationality, morality, or legality. (For example, those involved in the Watergate scandal and the recent cases of corporate bribery succumbed to organizational pressures that encouraged and rewarded unethical behavior of a kind that these people probably would have abhorred in their private lives.) Moreover, the culture of an organization may grow dysfunctional over time and prevent an organization from effectively pursuing its own goals—for example, when it leads to hostility to innovation, or to rejection of individuals or groups that could make a contribution to the firm. A firm will often select people who are compatible with the outmoded culture, or reject people and ideas that are needed to give vitality to the organization. Consider the following cases:

> A top executive of one of America's largest auto manufacturers suggested, in the 1960s, that his company should take the lead in developing small, fuel-conserving, safe autos. He argued that this would head off the market challenge by foreign manufacturers, provide American consumers with a real choice, and defuse criticism of the industry from environmentalists, consumerists, and the government. He was driven out of the firm shortly thereafter.

> At an executive conference in a large organization (100,000 employees), a top planner suggested that the basic strategy of the organization was based on some faulty assumptions. He said that the organization had not really defined its basic mission and that it should redo some crucial analyses before continuing to commit enormous resources to a major program. Within a year, he had lost his staff and

his title and was given a smaller office. Shortly thereafter, he left the organization. The organization floundered for three years while pursuing the strategy the planner had questioned. Finally, a new top-management team came in and adopted the planner's suggestions, which ultimately proved successful.

One of the nation's largest metal manufacturing firms chose as its chief executive a man with 40 years' experience in the firm. Starting on the shop floor, he had worked his way to the top of the company while earning a graduate degree in engineering. The man was chosen by his fellow executives (who had a working majority of the board of directors) because of (1) his familiarity with all aspects of the company, (2) his popularity with all his peers, and (3) his commitment to steady growth. Within five years, Japanese firms had won a major share of the company's market.

A leading manufacturing firm was highly centralized, and most important decisions were made at the top of the hierarchy. All the top executives belonged to the same golf club, where they often discussed important business while playing or dining. The club excluded Jews, Catholics, blacks, and women from membership. As the company entered the 1970s, it found it harder to recruit and to retain top young managers. Top management could not understand why the quality of its younger executives was not up to the standards of its competitors.

These cases are based on actual incidents in large American organizations. They exemplify some ways in which a prevailing culture in a firm can become dysfunctional. While a culture may once have been appropriate for a given era or stage in development of the firm, rigid adherence at a later time can limit the firm's ability to

Adapt to changing market conditions

Develop or accept new technologies

Tolerate new ideas

Respond sensitively to societal shifts

Meet the expectations of younger workers

Anthropologists have documented dozens of cases of once-successful cultures that literally fell apart when their environments changed. Because these tribes could not adapt to such influences as Christianity, a market economy, modern technology, urbanization, or an external (national) political authority, they disintegrated and left their people in chaos and anomie, a state sometimes called "culture shock."

Often, business organizations also have trouble adapting to environmental changes. For example, rigid adherence to economic efficiency may become socially dysfunctional in an era when society will no longer permit corporations to behave solely as industrial institutions. Businesses today are becoming social institutions, with many constituencies and many goals; in addition to pressures from stockholders to use capital efficiently, there are now pressures from consumerists, environmentalists, labor unions, and the government to produce safe and durable goods without damaging the environment and without wasting energy. Moreover, all these things must be accomplished while providing plentiful and satisfying jobs. Most corporations have been insensitive to these societal changes and have seen their public acceptance sink to an all-time low on public polls. Corporations have responded to changes in public sentiment with an "economic education" campaign designed to dismiss consumerist and environmentalist demands, or to discredit as "disloyal to capitalism" those who advance them. This misreading of the public interest stems in large part from the rigidity of the managerial culture, and it has perversely led to even greater public mistrust of corporations.

Internally, the dictates of the culture of industrial efficiency can be equally counterproductive. Until recently, the prime task of management has been to use capital and natural resources as efficiently as possible. But shortages of energy and changes in attitudes about the quality of work and the environment seem to have foreclosed many of the once-limitless options for the uses of capital natural resources. In the future, the prime task of management will probably be the development of human resources—if only because less than 40 percent of all workers in the United States are still engaged in the direct production of goods. Service and knowledge industries have only one resource—people. Unfortunately, the culture of economic efficiency often views people as the factor of production that should be traded off—that is, eliminated. And no American corporation has yet approached the development of human resources with the commitment with which almost all corporations approach the development of capital and natural resources. This rigid adherence to the managerial culture could, perversely, lead to a lowering of efficiency in the very corporations where efficiency is a leading goal.

Institutional inflexibility is a difficult problem to counteract, because patterns of behavior are rooted in past success and in observable truths. Economic or industrial efficiency was once an appropriate single goal for large corporations, and even today it is a reliable guideline for actions in the vast preponderance of instances. But few guidelines, no matter how honorable and long their lineages, are *always* applicable. "Honor thy father" is almost always a worthy precept—except when Dad is beating Mom with a baseball bat.

Sadly, corporations often respond to an external change by accentuating the very behavior that puts them out of phase with the environment. For example, when a company experiences problems assimilating the first woman or black manager it hires, it will often respond by recruiting whites who are quintessential caricatures of the traits that are most in conflict with the group that requires assimilation. It seems logical to recruit one's twins because "we all get along so well; we never have important disagreements." The process of twinning[2] accentuates the difficulty of change. Furthermore, selecting only people who are already compatible with the prevailing culture can be counterproductive when what is needed is a different perspective to give vitality to the organization. Twinning may be tolerable in small companies, but in large ones it runs against the pluralistic grain of the nation to whose needs the company is attempting to be responsive. Twinning does reduce conflict, but a certain amount of healthy conflict is the source of innovation and change in an organization.

Identifying the Culture of a Firm

If a firm is to alter its culture to cope with changes in the environment, it must first identify the prime characteristics of its culture. Through some kind of an analytical process, it could then be determined what aspects of the culture are functional and should be retained, and what aspects are dysfunctional and should be changed. One way of analyzing the culture would be to introduce a social anthropologist into the firm for six months or so, and ask him or her to write an ethnography of the corporation, much as the anthropolo-

[2]Twinning is the name of the process by which cattle farmers are seeking to double the size of their herds through either causing two eggs to be fertilized in the cow or causing a fertilized egg to split, thus producing identical twins instead of a single calf. In organizations, the process is done through recruiting.

gist would do as a participant observer in a primitive culture. As far as I know, this has never been done in a major American corporation. An alternative course would be to undertake a self-analysis of the culture for some unthreatening purpose.

Warren Bennis once suggested a tool that might be appropriate to this end.[3] Bennis argued that companies should prepare "institutional resumes" for recruiting purposes. He noted that a prospective employee usually knows very little about the firm that is interviewing him or her. (Significantly, in England they turn this phrase around: A prospective British employee "interviews a firm.") Bennis posited that a great deal of job dissatisfaction among young managers might result from a poor "person/environment fit." In short, many people choose the wrong places in which to work because of a lack of information, or misperceptions they develop during the recruiting process. Consequently, Bennis argued for greater "truth in recruiting." This might begin with the preparation of an institutional biography. This biography would be the basis for writing a firm's resume. Such an exercise could be a tool for identifying the managerial culture as well. Either or both processes could start by distributing the following kind of questionnaire to key executives in an organization:

Institutional Biography of Corporation Z

1. *Age*—Apart from the actual chronological age of the company, would you characterize Z as:

a. An infant	f. Young adult
b. A toddler	g. Adult
c. Prepubescent	h. Middle-aged
d. Adolescent	i. Old
e. Suspended adolescent	j. Senile?

2. *Health*—Apart from the financial health of the organization, would you characterize the state of health at Z as:

a. Robust	f. Remittently feverish
b. Sound	g. Declining
c. Better than can be expected, given Z's age	h. Infirm
	i. Paralyzed
d. Improving	j. Call the morgue?
e. Convalescing	

---

[3]Bennis made this suggestion at a Conference on Education, Work, and the Quality of Life conducted in Aspen, Colorado, in the summer of 1974.

3. *Key Events*
   a. Describe the three most pivotal events that have occurred since the founding of Z:
      1)   2)   3)
   b. What is the *best* thing that has occurred at Z during the past two years? Why?
   c. What is the *worst* thing that has occurred at Z during the past two years? Why?
4. *Qualifications*
   a. What distinctive competencies does Z possess?
   b. What competencies does it need to develop? Why?
5. *Characteristics*
   a. What five short, descriptive phrases or adjectives best describe Z?
   b. Circle the phrase/word you'd most like to change.
   c. Underscore the phrase/word you'd most like to preserve.
6. *Norms of the Organization*
   a. How much contact and interaction is required among people at Z?

1	2	3	4	5	6	7

   Virtually None   A Great Deal
   b. What amount of intimacy is appropriate at Z?

1	2	3 .	4	5	6	7

   Intimate, Informal   Distant, Formal
   c. To what extent are people encouraged to be collaborative and mutually supportive?

1	2	3	4	5	6	7

   Environment is   Environment is
   Collaborative, Supportive   Individualistic, Unhelpful
   d. How would you describe the decision-making climate at Z?

1	2	3	4	5	6	7

   Authoritarian   Participative
   e. To what extent is Z a place where people are happy with their work?

1	2	3	4	5	6	7

   Happy   Unhappy
   f. To what extent does ability count at Z, or is it *who* you know that is the key to rewards and promotions?

1	2	3	4	5	6	7

   What you know   *Who* you know

g. To what extent is Z open to new ideas?

1	2	3	4	5	6	7

Open   Closed

h. To what extent does Z accept employees with nontraditional life styles or views?

1	2	3	4	5	6	7

Open   Closed

i. To what extent are people encouraged to take risks?

1	2	3	4	5	6	7

Risk-Taking Rewarded   Play-it-Safe Rewarded

j. To what kinds of outside organizations do most managers at Z belong? (Circle no more than three.)

1) Country club   5) Church groups
2) Rotary club   6) Sierra club
3) Exclusive downtown men's club   7) Common cause
4) The Y   8) None

k. Who gets promoted at Z? (See Maccoby for description of types.)

1) The "Craftsman"   4) The "Gamesman"
2) The "Jungle Fighter"   5) The "Entrepreneur"
3) The "Company Man"   6) Other (Describe)

7. *Nature of Work*

a. What is the rhythm of life at Z? (Circle one.)

1) A 6-day, 12-hour grind   4) Seasonal
2) Typical 5 days a week, 8 hours a day   5) Relaxed
        6) Slow and dull
3) Intermittent periods of pressure and relaxation

b. To what extent is there attention to work *quantity?*

1	2	3	4	5	6	7

None   A Great Deal

c. To what extent is there attention to work *quality?*

1	2	3	4	5	6	7

None   A Great Deal

d. To what extent is *process* (bureaucratic, administrative processes) more important than the final *product?*

1	2	3	4	5	6	7

Product-Oriented   Process-Oriented

e. To what extent are there opportunities to learn on the job?

1	2	3	4	5	6	7

Learning-Oriented   Must Have All Skills
Organization   before You Start

8. *External Affairs*

a. How concerned is Z with the welfare of the local community?

1	2	3	4	5	6	7

Great Involvement   No Interaction

b. How concerned is Z with the welfare of its consumers?

1	2	3	4	5	6	7

Consumer-Oriented   "Let the Buyer Beware"

c. What is the typical image that outsiders have of Z?

1	2	3	4	5	6	7

Good Guys   Bad Guys

d. Why does Z have this image?

9. What do you think Z wants to be when it grows up?

Changing the Culture

From time to time, probably all firms should stand back and take a long look at themselves in a mirror. It is unimportant whether the mirror is the ethnographic description of the firm's culture undertaken by a participant observer, the findings of an institutional questionnaire, or the results of some other tool. What counts is that there is an open exploration of the culture of the group, followed by an open discussion of the results that were found. Benefits of such an analysis might well accrue to the individual, the firm, and the society.

The process of analysis of the culture can be threatening. ("Why don't we hire any Jews [Gentiles])?" "Why do we all wear flags in our lapels?" "Why don't we encourage entrepreneurial risk-taking?") But such questions are probably *less* threatening than the related probing that the psychologist would direct at an individual, or that would come out in a T-group.

Of course, *people* are the problem. But some problems must be addressed *indirectly* to be successfully resolved. It is hard to imagine a policy for change that would be more frustrating or futile than one based on changing people, since there are only two ways to change people in an organization: fire them, or alter their personalities. From time to time, one reads of studies that conclude that "the schools can be improved only if there are better teachers," or that "local governments would be more effective if they had more talented administrators," and, one would like to add, the world would be a better place if there were fewer sinners. The fact is that most organizations are stuck with the people they have. In most instances, wholesale firing is not in the cards. Moreover, there is no guarantee that there is a sufficient supply of better people "out there" to serve as replacements. Certainly, a company *can* make personnel changes at the margin. The trick is to alter the systems of action and belief in the firm so that these new people can be effective when they join the firm. This doesn't mean trying to make the old-timers into people they aren't. It means altering the rewards and norms to tolerate the old behavior while at the same time encouraging the new behavior. That way, no one is unduly threatened.

The anthropological approach to organization change thus begins with an analysis of the structures and sanctions that encourage and discourage certain kinds of behavior. If bureaucratic behavior is rewarded at Z, then it is bureaucratic behavior that Z is likely to get in response. If it is decided that bureaucratic behavior is unwanted, then the reward system at Z can be altered. This is not easy to do, but it is much less threatening than singling out bureaucrats and trying to change their personalities. Culture (structure) is simply easier to change than personality. One hopes, in the long run, that behavior may even change to meet the new culture of the organization. The assumption is that few, if any, people are born with solely bureaucratic personalities. If bureaucratic behavior is no longer sanctioned, then other aspects of the individual's personality might emerge. This approach is unlikely to be foolproof. People do have differing needs, wants, and personalities. All that is suggested is that an attempt to train people to become less bureaucratic, while leaving the structural rewards for bureaucratic behavior untouched, is not likely to be effective. Moreover, any approach that singles out *people* for change when it is the *institution* that is determining their behavior is patently unjust.

Such a process of cultural change should not be confused with Skinnerian conditioning. Culture change is an open and participative process, not a manipulative one. It is a pluralistic process, not a monolithic one (that is, it is not necessary for *everyone* to go along with *all* the changes in the culture). Ultimately, cultural change attempts only to alter the *way* things are done. The individuals involved may well remain nasty or loving, selfish or generous, hostile or kind. They remain free to go to the shrink on their own time if they don't like who or what they are. They (and we) may even find that they really aren't so crazy after all.

REFERENCES

Beattie, John, *Other Cultures*, London: Routledge & Kegan Paul, 1966.

Maccoby, Michael, *The Gamesman: The New Corporate Leaders*, New York: Simon & Schuster, 1976.

Miller, Arjay, "Review of Maccoby's *The Gamesman*," *Wall Street Journal*, Jan. 27, 1977, p. 16.

"Stereotypes, Statistics and Some Surprises," *Forbes*, May 15, 1974, pp. 118-25.

Whyte, William H., Jr., *The Organization Man*, New York: Simon & Schuster, 1956.

CHAPTER 3

Toward Effective Work System Management

Kenneth R. Brousseau

During the past two decades, research in the area of work design has generated a number of important findings, which have begun to reshape notions about relationships between people and their jobs and about the role of work as a part of human experience. In some cases, these findings have been used to suggest ways in which jobs can be designed to enhance organizational effectiveness and the quality of life people experience at work. For the most part, however, the knowledge derived from this research exists in bits and pieces and has yet to be organized into a coherent set of recommendations for the effective management of work systems in organizations. Accordingly, the purpose of this chapter is to present some suggestions for effective work system management based on a brief survey of the major highlights of research on work design and individual-job relationships.

RESEARCH PERSPECTIVES

Scientific Management

Although in recent years, concern with the consequences of various strategies for designing work has attracted an increasing amount of attention in academic, business, and government circles, job design has long been considered an important determinant of organizational effectiveness. Perhaps the earliest serious research in this area can be traced to the work of Frederick W. Taylor (1911) and his colleagues, who founded the so-called "scientific management" movement during the opening decades of this century. Essentially, the thrust of this movement was to reduce work functions to sets of highly simplified and routine tasks. Each task, which by itself required minimal skill or creative thought, was then assigned to a particular person as his "job." Usually, each job was accompanied by a highly specific and detailed set of instructions dictating the precise procedures the person was to use in carrying it out.

The general rationale underlying this approach to work design was that simple and repetitive jobs could be performed by virtually anyone, regardless of intelligence, skills, or abilities. By standardizing performance procedures, wasteful and inefficient work methods could be eliminated, and workers could be dealt with essentially as low-cost, interchangeable extensions of the machinery employed in the production process.

Although the scientific management movement originated in the United States, where it was applied initially to the design of industrial, mass-production jobs, its influence has subsequently been felt around the world. Jobs designed either explicitly or implicitly according to the principles of scientific management are evident in many, if not most, organizations today. And, as can be seen by the armies of white-collar clerical employees who perform highly simplified and standardized tasks, such jobs are by no means limited to the realm of blue-collar industrial work.

From Job Enlargement to Job Enrichment

Despite the pervasive and lingering influence of scientific management, the past couple of decades have seen the debut of several innovative approaches to work design that differ drastically from that of Taylor and his colleagues. In large part, these new approaches have arisen in response to research evidence demonstrating that simple and routine jobs often result in undesirable consequences for individuals and dysfunctional consequences for organizations (for instance, Blauner, 1964; Davis, 1957; Friedmann, 1961; Kornhauser, 1965; Walker and Guest, 1952). More specifically, the evidence indicates that, for many people, jobs designed along the lines prescribed by scientific management lead to low job satisfaction, absenteeism, high turnover, and low-quality work performance. In effect, these findings drew attention to the previously neglected consideration that human beings differ significantly from machines, and illustrated the fact that many people possess needs and motives that cannot be satisfied through the performance of simplified and fragmented jobs.

As a consequence of these findings, researchers began to explore various ways to design more satisfying and motivating jobs. For many, the most promising solution appeared to lie in a loose collection of job design strategies that came to be known as "job enlargement." As implied by its name, the essential thrust of job enlargement was to make jobs "larger," consisting of a greater number and variety of activities instead of one or a few simple tasks. Unfortunately, however, this general approach tended to lack a clear-cut theoretical foundation and design methodology. Ideas about what kinds of tasks and activities to include in a job, or how their properties relate to individuals' motives and needs, remained vague at best. Consequently, some of the early attempts to apply job enlargement in organizations produced results that were either negligible or ambiguous (Hulin and Blood, 1968).

The so-called two-factor theory developed by Frederick Herzberg and his colleagues (Herzberg, Mausner, and Snyderman, 1959) represents one of the first attempts to cut through the confusion surrounding job enlargment. Essentially, the major contribution of Herzberg's theory was its identification and clarification of relationships between certain human needs and various facets of work situations. More specifically, Herzberg separated the characteristics of the work situation into two major clusters, which he called "motivators" and "hygiene" factors, each of which supposedly relates in different ways to employees' needs. In particular, he suggested that motivators (such as opportunities for achievement, recognition, responsibility, advancement, and personal growth), which reflect the nature of the work itself, as opposed to hygiene factors (such as physical working conditions, pay, supervision, company policy, and relations with co-workers), which reflect the nature of the work setting, have the power to tap "higher-order" needs such as those for self-actualization or self-realization (Maslow, 1954). Based on his theory and research, he argued further (Herzberg, 1968) that the best way to design jobs to enhance satisfaction and work motivation (as opposed to merely reducing job *dissatisfaction*) is to manipulate the motivator factors so as to provide maximum opportunities for the satisfaction of higher-order needs.

To differentiate his approach from job enlargement, which he viewed as merely a technique for making a job "structurally bigger" without fundamentally altering its motivational properties, Herzberg called his strategy "job enrichment." From his point of view, the primary advantage of job enrichment over other job design methods or attempts to satisfy and motivate employees by manipulating hygiene factors (which he claimed could only reduce job dissatisfaction) is that it makes the work itself *intrinsically* satisfying and motivating, rather than simply an instrumental means for obtaining extrinsic rewards.

Characteristics of Enriched Jobs

Although several empirical studies have cast doubt on the validity of some of the basic tenets of Herzberg's two-factor theory (Graen, 1968; Hinton, 1968; House and Wigdor, 1967), application of his methods has resulted in a number of successful job enrichment experiments in the United States, particularly those conducted at AT&T (Ford, 1969, 1973). Nevertheless, a couple of troublesome issues have tended to limit the usefulness of his approach to job design.

First, although Herzberg's job design methods place central importance on the manipulation of motivators, they provide little guidance for translating these factors into specific job characteristics. This makes it particularly difficult to identify the specific ways in which a job might be redesigned most effectively to enhance its potential to satisfy and motivate the people who perform it.

Recently, however, considerable progress has been made toward the development of methodologies for assessing the degree to which jobs possess certain characteristics that importantly influence job satisfaction and work motivation. Most notable of the research in this area is that of Richard Hackman and Greg Oldham, who have developed a concise theory of work motivation and a set of diagnostic tools for assessing a job's "motivating potential" (Hackman and Oldham, 1975, 1976). Building upon the work of earlier researchers (for example, Turner and Lawrence, 1965; Hackman and Lawler, 1971), their research indicates that five "core" job characteristics influence three "critical psychological states" (experienced meaningfulness, responsibility, and knowledge of results) individuals experience as they perform their jobs. In turn, the degree to which individuals experience the three psychological states influences the ways in which they respond to their jobs in terms of job satisfaction, internal work motivation, quality of performance, and attendance. From this perspective, the extent to which a job is "enriched" or has a high motivating potential depends upon the degree to which it possesses the following five characteristics:

> *Skill Variety* - The extent to which a job requires a variety of activities involving the use of a number of different skills and talents.
>
> *Task Identity* - The degree to which a job involves performing a "whole" piece of work from beginning to end with a visible outcome.
>
> *Task Significance* - The extent to which results of one's performance of a job importantly affect the lives or work of other people—whether in the immediate organization or in the external environment.
>
> *Autonomy* - The degree to which a job provides the opportunity to exercise personal discretion in determining how and when to perform the work.
>
> *Feedback* - The extent to which the process of performing a job results in direct and clear information about one's performance effectiveness.

According to the theory, skill variety, task identity, and task significance contribute most directly to how meaningful people perceive their jobs to be; autonomy contributes most directly to experienced responsibility; and feedback determines knowledge of results. Therefore, to have the *potential* to be intrinsically rewarding, a job must rate high on both autonomy and feedback and on at least one of the other three dimensions that contribute to experienced meaningfulness. As Hackman and Oldham point out, however, whether or not such a job will actually be experienced as personally rewarding depends upon who will perform it.

Individual Differences

This brings up a second problem with the Herzberg approach to job design: It does not specify who would be likely to respond most positively to enriched jobs. In fact, one of its underlying assumptions seems to be that there are no significant differences in the ways in which people respond to the characteristics of their jobs. Ironically, this is a weakness it shares with the scientific management approach to job design. Like Taylor before him, Herzberg appears to assume that there is a one best way to design jobs.

Contrary to this notion, however, the results of a number of studies, beginning with those reported by Turner and Lawrence (1965) and Blood and Hulin (1967), show that individuals' responses to enriched versus simple, routine jobs vary substantially. Consequently, in developing their theoretical model of work motivation, Hackman and Oldham propose that the strength of an individual's needs for personal growth and development influence his responses to the characteristics of his job. In particular, they propose that people who have strong needs for personal growth respond more positively to enriched jobs than do those whose growth needs are comparatively weak. This notion has received empirical support from several studies (Brief and Aldag, 1975; Hackman and Lawler, 1971; Zierden, 1975). In addition, a number of researchers have found that other personality characteristics, such as work values (Robey, 1974; Wanous, 1974), active (versus passive) orientation, and emotional well-being (Brousseau, 1976), similarly influence individual's responses to the properties of the jobs they perform.

As Hackman (1977) points out, these findings show that there is no one universally good way to design jobs. Job enrichment is apt to work much better for some than for others. Therefore, if a job is to lead to beneficial outcomes for individuals and the organization, it must be designed to "fit" the personalities of those who will perform it. From this point of view, the research evidence suggests that people who are relatively free of emotional depression and who desire strongly to take an active part in developing their skills, abilities, and other personal qualities are most likely to perform effectively and derive personal benefits from complex and challenging jobs.

Effects of the Work Context

One of the strongest features of Herzberg's theory is that it places primary importance on the role of the work itself, as opposed to that of the features of the work setting, in determining employees' work responses. Yet it appears that in emphasizing the importance of the work, he may have underestimated the importance of the organizational context in which the work is performed. As a number of authors have argued (Katzell, Yankelovich, et al., 1975; Sirota and Wolfson, 1972), the effectiveness of a work system can be enhanced or diminished by the nature of the broad organizational context in which it is imbedded. Beyond this general notion, however, little was known about the specific ways in which individuals' work responses might be affected by the context of their work.

Recently, research in this area has begun to provide insights into this issue. For example, a study conducted by Oldham and his colleagues (Oldham, Hackman, and Pearce, 1975) shows that employees' attitudes toward certain features of the work context can greatly influence the way they respond to the characteristics of their jobs. Their findings indicate that attitudes toward such contextual factors as pay, job security, and relationships with supervisors function in much the same way as growth needs in moderating individuals' responses to the kinds of jobs they perform. People who are satisfied with these factors tend to respond with more enthusiasm and greater performance effectiveness to enriched jobs than do those who are less satisfied with the work context. Although these findings do not dispute Herzberg's assertion that the work itself most directly influences employees' work responses, they do show that so-called "hygiene" factors can substantially affect the particular way an individual reacts to the content of his job.

Significantly, Oldham et al. also report that contextual attitudes interact with individuals' personalities in moderating responses to job characteristics. People respond most positively to enriched jobs when they have strong needs for personal growth *and simultaneously* are satisfied with the overall work context. In contrast, those who possess relatively weak growth needs and also feel dissatisfied with contextual factors tend to react *negatively*—in some cases, markedly so—to enriched jobs. As the authors point out, these findings strongly imply that prior to conducting work redesign projects, individual differences in needs and potential sources of dissatisfication should be carefully assessed. Failure to do so could detract in important ways from the ability of individuals and organizations to reap the benefits of improved job designs.

Effects of Work on Personality

Although the findings described above shed light on the factors that determine individuals' behavioral and attitudinal re-actions to their jobs, they provide little insight into the ways in which their orientations toward work might change over time. In particular, they do not indicate whether individuals' personality characteristics—including those that moderate their work responses—are susceptible to change as a function of their work experiences. This is an important issue with profound implications for the design and management of work systems in organizations.

During the past ten to fifteen years, researchers have accumu-lated a substantial body of evidence indicating that certain features of work have the potential to influence personality in important ways. For example, in a study of blue-collar workers in the auto industry, Arthur Kornhauser found consistent relationships between the amount of skill required by jobs and various indices of em-ployees' mental health. Workers employed in low-skill jobs, com-pared to those in relatively high-skill jobs, more frequently reported low self-esteem, high anxiety, few friendships, low levels of satisfac-tion with life, and an absence of an active or goal-directed orienta-tion to life. Similarly, in a series of studies based upon a representa-tive sample of over 3,000 adult males in the United States, Melvin Kohn and Carmi Schooler (Kohn, 1969; 1971; Kohn and Schooler, 1969, 1973) found significant relationships between certain charac-teristics of individuals' jobs and a number of facets of their psychological and emotional functioning. In particular, they report that freedom from close supervision and "substantive" job complex-ity are positively associated with strong values for self-direction, favorable self-images, interests in the intrinsic (versus extrinsic) benefits of work, and intellecutal flexibility. In addition, several other researchers have reported evidence linking job characteristics to leisure activities and sociopolitical attitudes (Meissner, 1971; Torbert, 1973).

Although striking parallels between these findings and those of numerous other researchers have appeared in the literature (see reviews by Argyris, 1973; Kasl, 1974), conclusions about the casual influence of job experiences have been constrained by the cross-sectional nature of most of the research in this area. For example, as several authors (for example, Hulin and Blood, 1968) have pointed out, the observed relationships between jobs and personality might simply reflect the fact that different types of people find their way into different kinds of jobs and occupations, either through their own choices or the selection processes of organizations.

Recently, however, the results of several longitudinal studies have provided convincing support for the notion that work experiences have the potential to influence personality. For instance, in a study of 116 engineers, scientists, and managers employed by a large petroleum-products firm in the United States, Brousseau (1976, 1977) found significant relationships between the "richness" of individuals' jobs and changes that took place in their personalities over an average period of six years. Specifically, he reports that the higher people's jobs scored on task identity and task significance (two of the Hackman-Oldham "core" job dimensions), the more likely they were to develop increasingly active orientations toward their lives and to become increasingly free of emotional depression. Similar evidence supporting the job-effects notion has been reported by Kohn and Schooler (1977), based on analyses of longitudinal data collected in a follow-up survey of a sample of individuals originally interviewed for their earlier research. Using highly sophisticated analytical techniques, they were able to show conclusively that, although individuals' levels of intellectual flexibility influence job choices, further development of this dimension of psychological functioning is directly affected by the complexity of one's job experiences.

Taken collectively, these findings indicate the important ways in which individuals can be affected over a period of time by their work. In particular, they show that the richness and complexity of a person's job can influence his values, motives, thinking ability, and emotional well-being. These findings become especially significant in the light of the fact that some of these personality characterisitcs must inevitably play a central role in determining the overall quality of an individual's life. And, as can be seen, they include a number of characteristics that the findings discussed earlier have shown to mediate the way a person responds to his job in terms of job satisfaction, work motivation, and performance effectiveness.

In essence, evidence on the impact of work on personality demonstrates the dynamic, rather than static, character of relationships between individuals and their jobs. Therefore, the possibility must be recognized that a job that is designed to fit a person's current needs, motives, and capacities may differ substantially from the sort of job for which he would be best suited in the future. From this perspective, it becomes important not only to assess people's personalities and abilities prior to conducting work redesign projects, but also to consider the possible ways in which the individuals might be affected by changes in job designs in the long run.

A DYNAMIC MODEL OF INDIVIDUAL-
JOB RELATIONSHIPS

When pieced together, the research findings discussed so far describe a model of job-person relationships that is not only more complete, but fundamentally different from, those that have guided the design and management of work systems in the past. As Lawler (1974) has pointed out, for the past half century, the study of behavior in organizations has been characterized by two distinctly different points of view. One of these is founded on the basic notion that people differ substantially from one another and respond in a diversity of ways to similar kinds of work situations. The other operates on the dual assumptions that similarities between individuals are more important than whatever differences exist, and that most people respond similarly to a particular kind of work situation. As might be guessed, these two viewpoints have resulted in markedly different approaches to work system management.

The first, or "individual differences," perspective implies that one of the central tasks of work system management involves achieving a good "fit" between the individual and his job. In practice, this has typically led to attempts to create a good job-person fit by matching individuals to jobs, rather than the reverse. That is, the types of jobs that exist in an organization have tended to be seen as fixed, thereby placing primary emphasis on the development of techniques for selecting and placing people in available job "slots." In contrast, the second viewpoint (as reflected in some of the early approaches to job design discussed above) has resulted in efforts to identify the one best way to design jobs. In effect, this has involved attempts to "fit the job to everyone."

As different as these two points of view are, each is represented in the model implied by the findings discussed in this chapter—albeit in modified form. That is, the model recognizes that there are substantial individual differences in employees' responses to their jobs, but it also recognizes that, because certain general principles govern people's work responses, some kinds of jobs tend to be "better" than others.

To be more specific, most of the studies of job satisfaction and work motivation that have revealed individual differences in work responses have shown that, whereas some people respond to complex and challenging jobs with a great deal of enthusiasm, others remain rather indifferent to such jobs. Said otherwise, correlations relating indices of job richness to job satisfaction and work motivation have generally been found to be positive, although they are significantly *more* positive for some groups of people than for others. Although a couple of studies (Turner and Lawrence, 1965; Blood and Hulin, 1967) have reported negative correlations between job richness and desirable work responses, thereby indicating that some people react against enriched jobs, the more recent research suggests that this should not necessarily be construed to mean that the individuals themselves are predisposed to respond negatively to challenging jobs. More specifically, the research on the influence of employees' contextual attitudes suggests that people are not likely to respond negatively to enriched jobs unless, in addition to lacking strong desires for challenging jobs, they also feel dissatisfied with the organizational context in which they perform their jobs. In the context of a different organizational setting, these same people might simply fail to respond to enriched jobs with much enthusiasm, rather than being actively repelled by them.

This suggests that when people become actively interested and involved in their jobs, it is because their jobs are complex and challenging, instead of simple and routine. Although this point of view recognizes that people's responses to complex work differ in magnitude, it does not include the extreme individual-differences notion that some people are most highly satisfied and motivated when they perform rich jobs, while others are most satisfied and motivated when their jobs are simple and repetitive. It may well be that some people prefer nonchallenging jobs. Such a preference, however, is more likely to reflect a lack of interest in intrinsic work rewards than an active interest in simple and routine work. The needs and motives that are of greatest immediate importance for these people are not likely to be satisfied through the work itself, regardless of how challenging or nonchallenging, complex or simple, their jobs happen to be.

Aside from these issues, the model implied by the research described earlier differs from traditional models of job-person relationships in one fundamentally important respect: It is a dynamic, rather than fixed, model. In this respect, it is founded on the basic notion that relationships between individuals and their jobs can, and often do, change over time. This feature of the model reflects the research evidence demonstrating that people's personalities are susceptible to modification as a function of the kinds of jobs they encounter and experience as they proceed along their career paths.

Neither of the traditional views explicitly recognized this possibility. The individual-differences point of view more often than not appeared to assume that, after maturity, "you are what you are—for life." On the other hand, the "generalist" model seemed to assume that, since people are basically alike anyway, changes that might take place in them over time are of little consequence.

In contrast, the present model explicitly recognizes that personality change that results from work experiences (or, for that matter, other life circumstances) can influence individuals' work orientations in important ways. For example, it is possible—if not probable—that a person who, because of weak growth needs, is indifferent to challenging work will progressively acquire a greater interest in actively furthering his personal development *and* in having jobs that contribute to this process if his job experiences gradually increase in complexity and challenge. The extent to which such changes in the individual are likely to occur depends, of course, upon the initial strength of his developmental needs and related personality characteristics, in combination with the sequencing and pacing of changes in his work experiences. In other words, it depends upon the fit between the individual and his work. In this case, however, the fit must be dynamic and developmental.

The model also recognizes the possibility that, under certain circumstances, an individual's development can move in the reverse direction. Confined to a simple and restrictive job, a person who initially possesses an active interest in his personal growth may, over time, acquire a more passive orientation toward his further development. The probability of this sort of change taking place, however, is less clear than in the preceding case. This is because, possessing an active or proactive orientation to begin with, such a person might struggle more. For instance, he might attempt to make his job more interesting and challenging. Failing this, he might look for a better job elsewhere. Failing this, he might attempt to compensate for his understimulating job by involving himself in more challenging activities off the job. Failing this, however, he may change in the direction suggested above.

For some, these notions may seem difficult to accept, departing as they do from past views of relationships between individuals and their jobs. Nevertheless, they are implied clearly by the findings described earlier. This is not to say that everyone undergoes radical personality change over the course of his working life. For a variety of reasons, many people, at an early stage in their careers, become "locked" in jobs or work situations that do not change in important ways over time. If the type of situation in which a person lives and works remains fixed, his own personal qualities also are likely to remain fairly constant after initially adjusting to his circumstances. If and when his situation is altered, however, the possibility is introduced that the person himself may change.

SUGGESTIONS FOR EFFECTIVE WORK SYSTEM MANAGEMENT

Just as the model described above differs from past views of job-person relationships, so does the approach it implies for effectively managing work systems. Most clearly, it implies that effective management of work systems is a dynamic, continuous process involving several different kinds of activities. In particular, the activities include assessment (collection of data on the current state of a work system), evaluation (interpretation of assessment data), design (planning improvements in the system), and implementation of changes. The order in which these activities are mentioned defines a management cycle. Because work systems are likely to exist in a more or less continuous state of flux (owing to changes in the external environment, in technology, within individuals, in the composition of the work force, and in jobs and work methods), the completion of one cycle should mark the beginning of another. In many respects, the recycling of the management process is the feature that differentiates the present approach most clearly from work system management strategies of the past.

If an organization can accept the need for this continuous and dynamic approach, it will have taken a significant step toward creating a more effective work system. This is not to say that the management of work systems can ever be an easy process. Quite the contrary, many difficult issues and problems are guaranteed to make the process a complicated one (Hackman, 1977; Katzell, Yankelovich et al., 1975; Mankin, 1978). What all these problems are, and how they might be solved, cannot be dealt with or even anticipated within this chapter. Therefore, the reader should recognize that the following discussion is intended only to sketch the rough outlines of what a dynamic approach to work system management might entail.

Work System Assessment

Assessment is, and will always be, a most crucial element in the design and maintenance of an effective work system. Without a thorough assessment of the existing features of a work system (for instance, job characteristics, individuals' personalities and abilities, the features of the work context), attempts to improve the system must proceed in the dark. In some cases, incomplete or inaccurate information about the system could lead an organization to implement ineffective changes; in other cases, it could conceivably result in disruptive and detrimental changes. Moreover, as indicated above in the context of a dynamic work system management program, assessment becomes *re*assessment as data are collected to evaluate the results of changes in the system and the need for further changes.

Assessing jobs. A good place to initiate an assessment effort is with the collection of data on the nature of the jobs, which currently characterize the way work functions are organized in the system. This information is needed (in conjunction with other assessment data) to evaluate the fit between individuals and their work, to plan work redesign activities where needed, and (in the long run) to determine whether past activities have created the particular job or work designs intended.

Over the years, researchers have devoted considerable effort to the development of methodologies for measuring job properties. For the most part, these methods have focused primarily on the assessment of job *requirements*. That is, they have been designed to collect information about the specific kinds of knowledge, skills, and abilities they demand for effective performance. Since some of these methods are applicable to the assessment of virtually any job (for example, see Fine, 1955; McCormick, Jeanerret, and Mecham, 1972), they can play a useful role in identifying the particular qualifications people need to perform each of the jobs in the work system. Used effectively, this can be highly useful information for enhancing and maintaining the job-person fit.

Nevertheless, simply knowing what people must be *able* to do to perform effectively is not enough. The findings reviewed earlier clearly indicate that it is also important to know what features jobs possess that potentially determine a person's *desire* to perform effectively.

This is an issue that few job assessment methods have been designed to address. With the increased understanding of relationships between job characteristics and individuals' needs and other personality characteristics, this situation has begun to change. Consequently, an increasing number of researchers have turned their attention to the problem of measuring the motivational qualities of jobs. As mentioned previously, the recent work of Hackman and Oldham in this area has been especially productive. In particular, they have developed a set of tools, including a paper-and-pencil instrument called the Job Diagnostic Survey (JDS), for assessing the extent to which a job possesses each of the five "core" job dimensions described earlier. Applied to specific job categories, scores on the five JDS dimensions can be used to construct an index of the "motivating potential" of each of the jobs surveyed.

Used in conjunction with techniques for assessing the skills and abilities requirements of jobs, instruments like the JDS can provide a great deal of useful information needed to gain an accurate picture of the work design features of the work system. It should be recognized, however, that the kinds of job characteristics assessed by the JDS indicate only a job's motivating *potential*. Whether or not that potential becomes reality and leads to beneficial outcomes for the organization and individuals depends, of course, on the characteristics of the people who perform it. This brings us to the issue of individual assessment.

Assessing individuals. In a sense, the assessment of individuals should focus on two sets of variables similar to those measured in jobs: "technical" qualifications, and personality characteristics that influence predispositions to respond positively to "enriched" work. As has been the case with research on job assessment methods, most of the work in this area has focused on the development of techniques for matching individuals with the abilities requirements of jobs. Consequently, once it is known what jobs require for competent performance, a number of methods are available for assessing the related dimensions of knowledge, skills, and abilities in individuals (see Dunnette, 1976; Fleishman, 1975; Owens, 1976).

In the past, the tendency has been to use these kinds of techniques to assess a person's qualifications for a *particular* job or position. In conducting a thorough assessment program, however, these techniques should not be used in so limited a way. More specifically, in recognition of the possibility that an individual may be qualified—or at least, potentially qualified—to perform a number of different kinds of work, his qualifications in terms of a variety of skills and abilities should be assessed. This is where the job assessment data can be very useful. In assessing all the jobs in the current work system, it is likely that a considerable range of job requirements will have been identified. Therefore, the potential exists for assessing the extent to which an individual possesses the various skills and abilities needed to perform any job in the system. If this is done, the possibility of making inaccurate assumptions about what individuals can or cannot do, based on such indirect criteria as previous work experience or education, can be avoided. In addition, this information could indicate a number of ways for improving the fit between an individual and his work that might otherwise go unnoticed. And, as discussed later, information about a wide array of individuals' current skills and abilities is essential to accurately anticipating the ways in which the work system may need to be altered to adjust to developmental changes in employees' skills and abilities.

By now, it should be evident that, in addition to assessing skills and abilities, the assessment effort must also address those aspects of people's personalities that determine their orientations towards complex and challenging versus simple and routine work. As indicated earlier, a number of personality characteristics are likely to be involved here. For example, higher-order-need strength, active versus passive orientations, and emotional well-being have all been shown to influence responses to the motivating features of jobs. In addition, Driver's (1977) recent research on career "concepts" suggests that the way in which a person thinks about and would like to pursue his career can strongly influence the strength of his desire for complex and rich work experiences.

Over the years, psychologists have developed an enormous number of devices for measuring personality, as can be seen by briefly leafing through any recent volume of Buros's *Tests in Print.* Unfortunately, however, none of these devices has been designed for the specific purpose of measuring the particular facets of personality that moderate people's reactions to the motivating potentials of their jobs. Consequently, scales that might be useful for this part of the assessment program are scattered here and there among the mass of available personality inventories.[1] This is where skilled psychometricians can provide a useful service for organizations by helping to identify and develop techniques for measuring those aspects of personality that are particularly important to the conduct of a well-rounded assessment program.

In addition to utilizing paper-and-pencil measurement methods, assessment programs should also be designed to include personal interviews with employees. Conducted by trained counselors or experienced clinical psychologists, personal interviews could be particularly useful for collecting in-depth information about individuals' personalities and valued abilities that is needed to "fine-tune" the work system. Moreover, in viewing assessment as the foundation of an ongoing work system management program, interviews could also double as counseling sessions in which people receive feedback of assessment information and are encouraged to participate in making important decisions about jobs and career

---

[1] The reader should note that the Hackman-Oldham Job Diagnostic Survey includes two scales for measuring growth need strength. This, however, is only one of the potential moderators of an individual's work responses. Measures of other personality dimensions are needed.

directions based on potential opportunities in the work system and their own unique and developing needs, values, skills, and abilities.

Assessing the work context. Another target for assessment is the organizational context surrounding the work system. As discussed previously, individuals' attitudes toward the work context can influence their work responses in important ways. In particular, the potential benefits available from enriched types of jobs can be substantially reduced if people are dissatisfied with contextual factors, perhaps because the "demands" of a challenging job are perceived as just another cause for resentment when one's energies are already being consumed in coping with problems in the work context (Oldham et al., 1975). To avoid these kinds of situations, information about jobs and individuals must be supplemented with information identifying sources of dissatisfaction originating in the organizational context surrounding the work system.

There are a variety of potential "sore spots" in the work context of any organization. Punitive supervisory practices, conflicts with co-workers, uncomfortable working conditions, and job insecurity are just a few examples. Many others can be traced to the organization's reward system. Often, dissatisfaction with rewards results not so much because available rewards are too limited, but because the system fails to recognize individual differences. That is, organizations frequently make the mistake of assuming that employees all basically desire the same kinds and amounts of rewards, when in fact marked individual differences in preferences may exist (Lawler, 1971; 1977; Nealy, 1963).

The possibilities that a number of sources of dissatisfaction exist in a work context and that individual differences characterize contextual dissatisfaction have several implications for how the assessment effort should be conducted. First, the assessment program should be designed to cover as wide a range of issues as possible. Whether by questionnaire or interview (perhaps in conjunction with the individual assessment program), or a combination of the two, attempts should be made to gather information that is detailed and specific. Questions like, "How satisfied are you with the organization?" will not suffice. A better approach is to use a mix of "structured" questions (addressing a range of specific issues) and "unstructured" questions (to allow people to point out unanticipated problems). In addition, it may prove highly useful later on to obtain individuals' suggestions about how problems in the work context might be eliminated.

In analyzing the data, it should be kept in mind that simply averaging responses by all employees to particular questions may result in an oversimplified picture. Averaged responses can point out features of the work context that are dissatisfying for most employees, but they can completely hide the fact that certain factors are sources of satisfaction for some and sources of dissatisfaction for others. Therefore, evaluation of the work context should be based on average *and* individual responses, with particular attention given to the possibility that attitudes toward factors in the work situation are moderated by employees' demographic and personality characteristics (Nealy, 1963).

Assessing work system output. The actual output of the present work system represents a final area to be investigated by a work system assessment program. As used here, *output* refers to the more or less immediate consequences of the work system in terms of individuals' performance effectiveness, work motivation, job-related satisfaction, and attendance. As discussed later, information on these variables is needed to help interpret various aspects of data collected in other parts of the program.

Data on job satisfaction and work motivation are relatively easy to collect, since these variables have been the focus of substantial research for some time. For instance, the Hackman-Oldham JDS includes scales for measuring internal work motivation, general job satisfaction, and growth need satisfaction. Information concerning attendance is also comparatively easy to collect, since in most organizations it can be obtained readily from company records.

In comparison, however, collection of meaningful performance data represents a more difficult task. In large part, this is because many organizations tend to rely on rather dubious performance evaluations, such as "annual performance ratings" made by supervisors. These ratings are commonly based on very little objective information and can easily be distorted by a supervisor's subjective perceptions and personal attitudes toward his subordinates. Recently, I was provided with an example of how "bad" such ratings can be when several of my colleagues reported that the annual performance rating used by a large company was found to be related *negatively* to "hard" data on individuals' performance effectiveness.

For many organizations, a good deal of thinking will have to be devoted to identifying valid performance criteria. Often, this will entail, perhaps for the first time, thorough consideration of the *raison d'être* of many jobs. In and of itself, however, this can be a beneficial process, since it will force an evaluation of the logic of the existing work system.

In some cases, the problems of performance evaluation are made especially difficult because of the time frame in which the work is performed. For example, many R&D projects cannot be fully evaluated for months, or even years. In cases where reasonably objective data simply are not available, it is probably better not to attempt a performance appraisal at all than to rely on subjective reports.

Work System Diagnosis and Design Strategies

After data have been collected in all the areas discussed above, the resulting information can be used to generate ideas for improvements in the work system—that is, if a thorough evaluation of the data indicates that changes in the existing system are needed (at the present time) or are feasible. In this respect, diagnosis and design go hand in hand.

Building a supportive work context. One of the first areas for diagnosis and design involves establishing a work context that will support the changes that might need to be made in the work system itself. As indicated earlier, there are many possible sources of dissatisfaction in the work contexts of most organizations—far too many, in fact, to attempt to identify specific solutions for them in this chapter. There are, however, some general comments that can be made about establishing a supportive work context.

First, many sources of contextual dissatisfaction can be eliminated simply by heeding employees' recommendations for improvements. This is a far better approach than making guesses about what would or would not satisfy their needs and preferences. If the assessment data are sufficiently detailed, solutions to a variety of problems may be easy to identify. In addition, acting upon people's recommendations for solving personally important problems would have the beneficial effect of contributing to the trust between employees and management that is required to effectively bring about changes in the work system.

Another point worth making is that contextual dissatisfaction can often be reduced substantially by introducing sufficient flexibility into an organization's policies and practices to allow the features of the work context to respond to individual differences. Examples are such possibilities as relaxation of restrictive dress codes, or providing employees with the opportunity to choose the kinds of rewards they, as individuals, will receive for their participation in the organization. A good example of this kind of flexible approach is that of TRW Systems Corporation, where employees are presented with a sort of "cafeteria plan" of fringe benefits. Within broad limits, people decide for themselves which of the benefits they will receive (Lawler, 1977).

However an organization chooses to address these issues, the most important requirement is that there be a genuine commitment to make *significant* improvements in the work context where the need is indicated. Otherwise, there is little reason to proceed with changes in the work system itself when, ultimately, they are likely to become bogged down or to fail completely because of the absence of a supportive organizational context.

Toward individualized work. After progress has been made in the development of a supportive work context, the next logical step toward a more effective work system involves the use of assessment data to diagnose the current closeness of fit between individuals and their work. Here, the objective is to find ways to maintain, enhance, or create "individualized" work that fits well with as many aspects of individuals' skills, abilities, and personalities as possible. Of course, what is "possible" will in part be determined by the "technical" features of the work system (technology, production schedules, and so on). Nevertheless, because work system management is a continuous process, where existing conditions seriously limit design choices an organization must remain on the alert for ways to deal with, or eliminate, those factors that are obstacles to flexibility.

In diagnosing job-person relationships and searching for possible improvements, assessment data should be used to identify not only those areas in the system where the match between individuals and jobs is poor, but also those areas where the match is good as it stands. In this respect, analytical methods that have been developed for personnel selection and placement purposes (see Dunnette, 1966; 1976) can serve a useful service. Although in the past these methods typically have not been applied to the problem of matching individuals' needs and related personality characteristics with the motivational properties of jobs, there is no inherent reason why they cannot be extended to deal with this issue too.

As useful as these analytical tools have the potential to be, care must be taken to use them in ways that are consistent with the long-term requirements of effective work system management. In the past, this has seldom been the case. In particular, because most applications of selection and placement techniques have been based on a static model of individual differences, they have usually focused on filling an available position with a person whose current skills and abilities qualify him to perform it, without giving further consideration to how the person himself might change later on.

The present approach to the design and maintenance of an effective work system—one that results in effective performance and high job satisfaction, both now and in the future—requires a different use of these analytical t ools. Instead of addressing the problem in terms of the narrow issue of filling existing jobs with qualified employees, the techniques could be used more productively to identify the kinds of work for which an individual is currently suited (both in terms of his abilities and the needs of his personality), the types of work for which he might be suited in the future, and the kinds of work experiences that would be most likely to contribute to the further development of his capacities and his personal well-being.

Approached from this perspective, improvements in a work system might entail a combination of job redesign, reallocation of personnel among existing jobs, and career counseling and planning activities. Accordingly, neither current job assignments nor current job designs should be considered sacred. For example, assessment data might indicate that, in certain cases, the match between people and their work might best be enhanced simply by reassigning them to different jobs that already exist in the system and by opening up opportunities for movement to other types of jobs later on. In addition, the data might indicate that, for others, none or few of the existing jobs are adequate, either because the jobs do not fit their qualifications well, or because the jobs do not meet the needs of their personalities, or both. In such situations, the need for work redesign is indicated. Or the data might indicate that the dynamic fit between an individual and his job might be maintained effectively by leaving him in his present job and providing him with the opportunity to redesign it periodically to fit developments in his needs and abilities.

Regardless of the particular form of improvements in the work system, it should be kept in mind that there are several ways in which people can be mismatched with their jobs. A situation in which a person's skills and abilities are insufficiently developed to meet the demands of his job is one example. This is the type of mismatch that selection and placement methods have most commonly been used to eliminate or to avoid altogether. Consequently, the tendency has been to fill a job with a person who scores *highest* on tests designed to assess those skills and abilities that are required by the job. The problem here is that this practice can lead to a situation in which a person is overqualified for his job. And overqualification can be just as severe a problem as underqualification (Hackman, 1977).

Another type of mismatch occurs where a job is insufficiently rich and challenging to satisfy the needs of an individual's personality. This is the type of situation job enrichment strategies have most commonly been designed to remedy. Consequently, the tendency has been to design jobs to be as challenging and complex as circumstances will allow. Although this practice assures that jobs will not be experienced as too restrictive or monotonous, for some people it could result in a situation where the job is experienced as too challenging and stimulating. This also represents an inadequate job-person fit, although in some ways it is probably the least serious, as discussed previously.

What all this points to is the need to develop rather sophisticated procedures for "fine-tuning" the fit between the person and the job. This is where work system output data, in conjunction with data on the characteristics of jobs and individuals, can be put to good use. Through careful analysis, these data can be utilized to identify the specific levels or strengths of each of a range of skills, abilities, and needs that characterize those who perform best and derive greatest satisfaction from particular jobs (the characteristics of which are also known). In this way, measures of job requirements and motivational characteristics of jobs can be calibrated with measures of the corresponding abilities and personality characteristics in individuals. By conducting these kinds of analyses, a great deal of valuable information could be obtained. For example, it might be found that for certain ability requirements, a very narrow margin for error characterizes a proper job-person fit, whereas other ability requirements are surrounded by a comparatively wide zone of indifference. Or it might be discovered that certain personality characteristics play a substantially more important role than others in determining the closeness of fit between a person and his job. Insights like these can significantly reduce the probability that changes designed into a work system would eliminate one kind of mismatch only at the expense of creating another.

The work-function block. As indicated above, there is a variety of options available for enhancing the effectiveness of a work system that may or may not entail work redesign. Usually, however, at some point in the life of a work system management program, the need will arise to reorganize or redesign work functions. On such occasions, there are a number of strategies from which to choose. Each of these strategies will have its own special advantages and disadvantages, depending primarily upon the organization in which it is applied. Since a number of publications discuss the details of various contemporary approaches to work design (for example, Cummings & Srivastva, 1977; Hackman, 1977; Katzell, Yankelovich, et al., 1975), the following discussion is limited to some general comments about a new method for attacking the problem of work design and allocation that could be used in conjunction with other design strategies.

One of the more important issues involved in work design relates to the way in which the term "job" is conceptualized. In any organization, jobs are likely to vary substantially from one another in a variety of ways. Some may entail performing only one or two simple tasks; others may involve many different kinds of activities. Nevertheless, no matter how limited or how varied a job may be, it usually has an identity that distinguishes it from other jobs. Said otherwise, a person's "job" usually refers to a more or less specific set of activities, operations, and duties that characterize the way he spends his time at work.

In some important respects, thinking about jobs in these terms imposes unnecessary rigidity on the way in which work systems are managed. Instead of defining jobs in terms of particular functions and activities, a better approach may be to conceive of jobs as being defined by the general characteristics of the work a person is qualified and willing to do. For example, rather than defining a person's job as typing, filing, and/or bookkeeping—all of which are specific activities—we might think of his job as potentially involving any activities that require specific amounts of data-processing skills, cognitive complexity, and manual dexterity, and that involve particular amounts of variety and autonomy. This way of conceptualizing jobs has several important advantages for effective work system management.

In particular, it would provide increased flexibility in organizing and allocating the work that must be accomplished in an organization. That is, rather than dividing up work into jobs that are performed by particular individuals, work functions and processes could be organized into tasks and activities that constitute what might be thought of as "work-function blocks." The resulting blocks could each be categorized in terms of their requirements and motivational properties and then allocated to any individuals who happen to be available and whose qualifications and personalities fit with the blocks' properties. However, the particular block allocated to an individual would not necessarily define his job in the traditional sense, since he might perform entirely different blocks on different days, or perhaps on the same day.

The concept of a work-function block proposed here is in some respects similar to the "work module" concept proposed by Robert Kahn (1974). A work module, as defined by Kahn, is a "time-task unit," consisting of the smallest allocation of time to a given task that is sufficient to be "economically and psychologically meaningful." As a means of defining and organizing work, he suggests that modular work design would allow individuals to construct their own jobs by deciding how many and which modules to perform on any given day.

Although work-function blocks could be used in a similar fashion, as defined here, they differ from work modules in that they would be neither time-specific (that is, they would not be limited to the *smallest* amount of time required to be experienced as meaningful) nor necessarily limited to one task. For example, whereas one particular work-function block might involve only one task requiring two hours on the average to complete, another block might consist of several interlocking tasks that compose a whole work process, requiring an average of two weeks to complete. Similarly, several "mini" blocks, each consisting of one or two tasks of comparatively short time duration, could be combined to construct a "macro" block involving the production of a particular piece of work from beginning to end. Consequently, work-function blocks could be divided and combined according to the requirements of production processes and the qualifications and personalities of individuals.

From this point of view, the process of maintaining the fit between a person and the type of work he performs is freed of several of the limitations imposed by the traditional task- or activities-centered conception of jobs. Although the specific activities and duties of an individual's job might differ from day to day, the properties—the abilities requirements and motivational character-istics—of his job could be held constant. Or they could be allowed to vary as the person's abilities, needs, and other personality character-istics change over time. For example, he could begin his tenure with the organization by performing relatively simple mini work-function blocks, and then, by gradually sampling increasingly "enriched" blocks, eventually move on to highly complex and challenging macro blocks.

As can be seen, this approach to work system management fits well with the dynamic model of individual-work relationships described earlier in this paper. It provides a means for establishing a work system that potentially can be designed to fit the abilities and needs people bring with them to the work situation, and to respond flexibly over time to changes that take place in individuals and in the composition of an organization's work force.

CONCLUSION

In contrast to past practices, the present approach to work system management does not rely exclusively on traditional selection and placement methods or on conventional work redesign strategies. It is a substantially more eclectic and integrated approach that utilizes a blend of traditional and contemporary work system management methods, as well as some new conceptual tools. And, most impor-tant, it is based firmly on the implications of a large body of research literature.

By no means, however, is the approach to the design and management of work systems outlined in this chapter meant to be the "final word." There are many issues involved in managing work systems that this chapter has not addressed. In part, this is because the actual problems that might be encountered in implementing some of the suggestions discussed above are difficult to anticipate at this point. One of the few things that *is* clear, however, is that a great need exists for further research to generate answers to a number of lingering questions before the definitive approach to work system management can be identified. In the meantime, however, the ideas presented in this chapter are intended to provide some useful guidelines for creating synergistic work systems that benefit organizations and their members as individual human beings.

REFERENCES

Argyris, C., "Personality and Organization Theory Revisited," *Administrative Sciences Quarterly,* 18 (1973), 141-67.

Blauner, R., *Alienation and Freedom.* Chicago: University of Chicago Press, 1964.

Blood, M.R., and C.L. Hulin, "Alienation, Environmental Characteristics, and Worker Responses," *Journal of Applied Psychology,* 51 (1967), 284-90.

Brief, A.P., and R.J. Aldag, "Employee Reactions to Job Characteristics: A Constructive Replication," *Journal of Applied Psychology,* 60 (1975), 182-86.

Brousseau, K.R., "Effects of Job Experience on Personality." Technical Report No. 14, School of Organization and Management, Yale University, January 1977.

_____, "Effects of Job Experience on Personality: A Theoretical and Empirical Investigation" Unpublished doctoral dissertation, Yale University, 1976.

Cummings, T.C., and S. Srivastva, *Management of Work: A Sociotechnical Systems Approach.* Kent, O.: Comparative Administration Research Center, Kent State University (distributed by Kent State University Press), 1977.

Davis, L.E., "Job Design and Productivity: A New Approach," *Personnel,* 33 (1957), 418-429.

Driver, M.J., "Career Concepts: A New Approach to Career Research." Paper delivered at Western Academy of Management Meetings, Sun Valley, Idaho, March 1977.

Dunnette, M.D., "Aptitudes, Abilities, and Skills," in M.D. Dunnette, ed., *The Handbook of Industrial and Organizational Psychology,* Chicago: Rand-McNally, 1976.

————, *Personnel Selection and Placement*. Belmont, Calif.: Wadsworth, 1966.

Fine, S.A., "Functional Job Analysis," *Journal of Personnel and Industrial Relations,* 2 (1955), 1-16.

Fleishman, E.A., "Toward a Taxonomy of Human Performance," *American Psychologist,* 30 (1975), 1127-49.

Ford, R.N., "Job Enrichment Lessons from AT&T," *Harvard Business Review,* January-February 1973, 96-106.

————, *Motivation through the Work Itself.* New York: American Management Association, 1969.

Friedmann, G., *The Anatomy of Work.* New York: Free Press, 1961.

Graen, G.B., "Testing Traditional and Two-factor Hypotheses Concerning Job Satisfaction," *Journal of Applied Psychology,* 52 (1968), 366-71.

Hackman, J.R., "Work Design," in J.R. Hackman and J.L. Suttle, eds., *Improving Life at Work.* Santa Monica, Calif.: Goodyear, 1977.

Hackman, J.R., and E.E. Lawler, "Employee Reactions to Job Characteristics," *Journal of Applied Psychology Monograph,* 55 (1971) 259-86.

Hackman, J.R., and G.R. Oldham, "Development of the Job Diagnostic Survey," *Journal of Applied Psychology,* 60 (1975) 159-70.

————, "Motivation through the Design of Work: Test of a Theory," *Organizational Behavior and Human Performance,* 16 (1976), 250-79.

Herzberg, F., "One More Time: How Do You Motivate Employees?" *Harvard Business Review,* 46 (1968), 53-62.

Herzberg, F., B. Mausner, and B. Snyderman, *The Motivation to Work.* New York: Wiley, 1959.

Hinton, B.L., "An Empirical Investigation of the Herzberg Methodology and Two-Factor Theory," *Organizational Behavior and Human Performance,* 3 (1968), 286-309.

House, R.J., and L. Wigdor, "Herzberg's Dual-Factor Theory of Job Satisfaction and Motivation: A Review of the Evidence and a Criticism," *Personnel Psychology,* 20 (1967), 369-89.

Hulin, C.L., and M.R. Blood, "Job Enlargement, Individual Differences, and Worker Responses," *Psychological Bulletin,* 69 (1968), 41-55.

Kahn, R.L., "The Work Module: A Proposal for the Humanization of Work," in J.J. O'Toole, ed., *Work and the Quality of Life.* Cambridge, Mass: M.I.T. Press, 1974.

Kasl, S.V., "Work and Mental Health," in J.J. O'Toole, ed., *Work and the Quality of Life.* Cambridge, Mass.: M.I.T. Press, 1974.

Katzell, R.A., D. Yankelovich, et al., *Work, Productivity and Job Satisfaction.* New York: The Psychological Corporation, 1975.

Kohn, M.L., "Bureaucratic Man: A Portrait and Interpretation," *American Sociological Review.,* 36 (1971), 461-74.

_____, *Class and Conformity: A Study in Values.* Homewood, Ill.: Dorsey, 1969.

Kohn, M.L., and C. Schooler, "Class, Occupation, and Orientation," *American Sociological Review,* 34 (1969), 659-678.

_____, "Occupational Experience and Psychological Functioning: An Assessment of Reciprocal Effects," *American Sociological Review,* 38 (1973), 97-118.

_____, "The Reciprocal Effects of Substantive Complexity of Work and Intellectual Flexibility: A Longitudinal Assessment." Unpublished manuscript, National Institute of Mental Health, Bethesda, Md., 1977.

Kornhauser, A., *Mental Health of the Industrial Worker,* New York: Wiley, 1965.

Lawler, E.E., "The Individualized Organization: Problems and Promise," *California Management Review,* 17 (1974), 31-39.

_____, *Pay and Organizational Effectiveness: A Psychological View.* New York: McGraw-Hill, 1971.

_____, "Reward Systems," in J.R. Hackman and J.L. Suttle, eds., *Improving Life at Work.* Santa Monica, Calif: Goodyear, 1977.

McCormick, E.J., P.R. Jeanerret, and R.C. Mecham, "A Study of Job Characteristics and Job Dimensions as Based on the Position Analysis Questionnaire (PAQ)," *Journal of Applied Psychology Monograph,* 56 (1972), 347-68.

Mankin, D., *Toward a Post-Industrial Psychology: Emerging Perspectives on Education, Work, Technology and Leisure.* New York: Wiley, 1978.

Maslow, A., *Motivation and Personality,* New York: Harper & Row, 1954.

Meissner, M., "The Long Arm of the Job: A Study of Work and Leisure," *Industrial Relations,* 10 (1971), 239-60.

Nealy, S., "Pay and Benefits Preferences," *Industrial Relations,* 3 (1963), 17-28.

Oldham, G.R., J.R. Hackman, and J.L. Pearce, "Conditions under Which Employees Respond Positively to Enriched Work," *Journal of Applied Psychology,* 61 (1976), 395-403.

Owens, W.A., "Background Data," in M.D. Dunnette, ed., *The Handbook of Industrial and Organizational Psychology,* Chicago: Rand-McNally, 1976.

Robey, D., "Task Design, Work Values, and Worker Response: An experimental Test," *Organizational Behavior and Human Performance,* 12 (1976), 264-74.

Sims, H.P., and A.D. Szilagyi, "Job Characteristics Relationships: An Experimental Test," *Organizational Behavior and Human Performance,* 17 (1976), 211-33.

Sirota, D., and A.D. Wolfson, "Job Enrichment: What Are the Obstacles?" *Personnel,* May-June 1972, 8-17.

Taylor, F.W., *The Principles of Scientific Management.* New York: Harper, 1911.

Torbert, W.R., *Being for the Most Part Puppets.* Cambridge, Mass.: Schenkman, 1973.

Turner, A.N., and P.R. Lawrence, *Industrial Jobs and the Worker.* Boston: Harvard Graduate School of Business Administration, 1965.

Walker, C.R., and R.H. Guest, *The Man on the Assembly Line.* Cambridge, Mass.: Harvard University Press, 1952.

Wanous, J.P., "Individual Differences and Reactions to Job Characteristics," *Journal of Applied Psychology,* 59 (1974), 616-22.

Zierden, W.E., "The Person, the Manager, the Job: Interactive Effects on Job Related Satisfactions." Unpublished doctoral dissertation, Yale University, 1975.

CHAPTER 4

A Socio-Technical Systems View of Organizations

Thomas G. Cummings

Mary Lynne Markus

It is probably safe to say that socio-technical systems theory is the most extensive body of conceptual and empirical work applying the systems perspective to organizations today. From its British origins at the Tavistock Institute of Human Relations in London, the socio-technical approach has spread to a number of industrialized countries in a little over two decades (Trist and Bamforth, 1951; Rice, 1958; Trist et al., 1963). Yet in spite of its increasing importance, relatively few people understand fully the socio-technical view of organizations or its implications for organization design. This chapter is intended to provide a basic understanding of the premises underlying the socio-technical approach, a theory of organizations derived from them, and the implications of this theory for organization design.

PREMISES OF SOCIO-TECHNICAL THEORY

Socio-technical systems theory is based on two fundamental premises: (1) that an organization comprises a combined, socio-plus-technological whole; and (2) that this whole must relate effectively to its environment if it is to survive and grow. The first assumption suggests that whenever human beings are organized to perform tasks, there is a joint system operating, a socio-technical system. This system consists of two independent yet related parts, social and technical. The former component includes the people who perform the organization's tasks and the relationships among them, and the latter comprises the tools, techniques, and knowledge required for task performance. The social and technological parts are independent by virtue of the different laws governing their behavior. Social systems—individuals and work groups, for instance—follow predominantly biological and psycho-social principles; technical systems, on the other hand, operate according to mechanical and physical laws. Nevertheless, the two components are related, since they must act together to accomplish tasks. Hence the term *socio-technical system.* The hyphen between the words *socio* and *technical* represents the relationship that must occur between the two independent parts if a goal is to be achieved. The term *system* signifies that this association results in an organized whole.

The example of two loggers operating a double-handled saw illustrates this simple but important premise. In this socio-technical system, the social part consists of the loggers and their interpersonal relationship, and the technical component is the saw and the knowledge of how to operate it. Biological and psycho-social principles govern the two-person social system, whereas mechanical laws determine the operation of the saw. Because of these different laws, the two components may be considered independent; but they must work together to cut a log into smaller segments. Thus, the social and technical parts are independent yet related, forming an organized system.

The second premise underlying socio-technical theory implies that an organization must interact with its environment to survive and develop. Organizations have traditionally been viewed as closed to their surrounds. Thus, only activities and interactions taking place within the organization were considered as important variables, while the environment was seen as a given or constraint. This "closed system" perspective fails to account for the simple observation that materials and information continually enter the organization from outside. These inputs are transformed by the organization's social and technical parts into goods or services that are returned to the environment. This two-way exchange allows the organization to replenish itself and the environment to gain needed resources.

In relating to the environment, an organization is open to a variety of external influences. A scarcity of raw material, for example, may spur developmental activity that drastically alters the organization's future. Less frequently observed, however, is the obverse process, whereby the organization affects its environment. The development and marketing of a new product, for instance, can change the needs, habits, and consumption patterns of people throughout the world. Given this interpenetration of organization and environment, one cannot be understood except in the context of the other. This necessitates viewing organizations as open socio-technical systems.

A SOCIO-TECHNICAL THEORY
OF ORGANIZATIONS

A theory of organizations is derived from the two premises discussed above. Briefly stated, effective organizations are those that optimize both the *internal relationship* between their social and technological components and the *external relationship* with their environment. Each of these associations presents different problems to the organization, however.

The Internal Relationship:
Joint Optimization

Starting with the social and technical interface, the major issue is how to optimize the outputs of both parts. Since organizations are composed of social and technological components, it follows that they produce two kinds of outcomes: products, such as goods and services, and social and psychological consequences. The example of the loggers and the two-handled saw illustrates this point. The production outputs of this system are felled trees and small log segments. Other outputs, just as "real," are the human emotions derived from teamwork, the fatigue of strenuous labor, and the psychological experience of rhythmic activity in the out-of-doors.

A major shortcoming of traditional theorists has been to concentrate on one or the other kind of output. Engineers and economists, for instance, have tended to focus on material and economic outcomes, either ignoring social results or regarding them as unintended consequences of the rational functioning of the firm. Social scientists, on the other hand, have concentrated primarily on social and psychological outputs almost to the exclusion of economic results. Each perspective fails to realize that in a functioning organization, the social system cannot be separated from the technical part. Put differently, social consequences cannot be divorced from material outcomes.

Given the interdependence between the social and technical parts, the only way to optimize the overall operation of the organization is to jointly optimize its independent yet related parts (Emery, 1966). *Joint optimization* refers to a relationship between the social and technical components such that each functions optimally according to its own laws without interfering with the other. This results in an organization in which the task requirements of the production system and the social-psychological needs of workers are jointly satisfied. A jointly optimized relationship in the logging example would require matching the two-handled saw technology with pairs of physically fit workers who enjoy team activity. Matching the saw with workers who are less physically fit or who desire independent forms of work would probably result in poorer performance and attitudes. If such workers made up the available work force, a different technology, such as a chain saw, would be more likely to result in joint optimization.

Suboptimal performance results when either component is optimized independently of the other. Thus, for example, when an engineering improvement fails to take into account the needs of workers, savings from increased production are sometimes offset by the costs of increased absenteeism and turnover. Conversely, many human relations programs aimed at developing the social system fail to produce significant increases in productivity because they ignore the technical side. Socio-technical systems theory avoids the pitfalls of either of these approaches taken separately. By considering the interaction between the social and technical components, this more integrative theory accounts for the joint optimization of both social and material outcomes.

The External Relationship: Open-System Properties

A jointly optimized socio-technical relationship is necessary but not sufficient for organizational effectiveness. Since we are dealing with open socio-technical systems, the organization and environment interface must also be considered. This requires knowledge of open-system properties and how they apply to organizations. These properties enable the organization to be both independent of its environment and interdependent with it. A certain degree of independence is necessary if the organization is to exist as an autonomous entity, yet interdependence with the environment is required to provide needed resources and outlets for products and services.

The first open-system property refers to the exchange of materials and information with the environment: the *import-transformation-export cycle.* Most organizations have a number of such cycles operating, each associated with a different part or subpart of the firm. A packaging line, for instance, imports finished product and packaging materials, transforms them via its social and technical components into packaged goods, and exports these back to the environment. Each piece of equipment on the line also engages in a similar although more restrictive cycle of events.

Given the multitude of exchange processes occurring in a typical organization, it is necessary to identify the *primary task* or that conversion process the organization needs to accomplish if it is to survive (Miller and Rice, 1967). Identification of the primary task is a practical measure that allows the organization to sort out from among its many import-transformation-export cycles those that are critical for survival and those that are merely ancillary. This helps the organization to focus its social and technical resources on the appropriate task and to identify those environmental exchanges necessary for survival. In a hospital, for example, environmental exchanges associated with preparing food, laundering linen, and treating patients occur simultaneously. Unless medical treatment is defined and accepted as the primary task, members will experience ambiguity as to whether they work in a restaurant, a laundry, or a hospital. Depending upon the choice, necessary environmental exchanges may vary considerably.

The second characteristic of organizations as open systems is the *boundary*. This serves two related functions: to differentiate the organization from its surrounds, and to regulate environmental exchanges. These functions enable the organization to operate as an independent entity while engaging with its environment. Organizations are typically differentiated or bounded on the basis of territory, technology, and time (Miller, 1959). A hospital, for instance, may be separated from the community it serves by the distinctness of its medical tools and knowledge, by the location of its buildings and grounds, and by the hours it is in operation—for instance, patients remain in the hospital around the clock, whereas visitors are present only at specified times.

Beyond separating the organization from its environment, boundaries also selectively filter information and materials entering and leaving the system. The criteria for establishing the types and rates of imports and exports are determined, in large part, by the social and technical components associated with the organization's primary task. If these components are flexible, a wide range of imports may be converted into similar exports, or similar imports may be transformed into a variety of exports. Some hospitals, for example, admit only a limited range of patients, whereas others with more comprehensive services treat the full range of medical problems.

The third open-system property concerns *regulation or control*. Organizations, like all open systems, maintain themselves in relatively steady states while exchanging with their environment and performing work. They accomplish this by maintaining an orderly balance among their components and between themselves and their environment. When disruptions occur, from within or outside the system, they are counteracted to restore as nearly as possible the original balance.

Regulation involves a negative feedback process whereby information about deviations from a preferred steady state is fed back to the organization so that it can mount a corrective response to negate such disruptions. Effective regulation is based on four characteristics: (1) a set of desired states or goals; (2) information about the actual degree of goal achievement; (3) a variety of regulatory responses appropriate to different disturbances; and (4) the ability to choose a correct response and enact it before the cause of the disturbance changes.

The final property of open systems is their ability to achieve a desired steady state from a variety of initial conditions and in different ways. Referred to as *equifinality,* this property enables organizations to adapt continually to environmental changes while keeping their basic form intact. Equifinality represents the process of growth and development in the organization. It suggests that organizations are not constrained totally by their initial structure. Rather, there is *choice* in how the organization continually redesigns itself and responds to its environment. The tendency is to develop toward greater complexity and size in order to relate to a wider range of external conditions. This provides organizations with a certain stability and constancy of direction in spite of changes in the environment. Thus, for instance, an organization may increase its advertising or cut prices to attain a larger share of the market; it may evolve matrix structures or specialized product lines to engage with an increasingly differentiated market.

In summary, socio-technical systems theory suggests that effective organizations must optimize both their social and technical relationship and their relationship with the environment. The social and technical interface requires that neither of the two components be treated independently of each other; rather, the relationship must be such that the technological requirements and needs of workers are jointly optimized. The organization and environment relationship is accomplished by providing organizations with open-system properties: an import-transformation-expert cycle appropriate to the organization's primary task; differentiated boundaries for protection and environmental exchange; steady state regulation; and the capacity for organizational choice and change.

IMPLICATIONS FOR ORGANIZATION DESIGN

The Socio-Technical Relationship

The most striking difference between socio-technical theory and other views of organizations is that it regards both the social and technological systems as operant variables. This has far-reaching implications for organization design. Foremost among these is that neither component is regarded as a fixed constraint to which the other must adapt. This frees designers to examine both parts as action levers for change. Depending upon the situation, however, the primary change target may be either the social system or the technology, or both. When the cost of modifying technology is prohibitive—in the steel industry, for example—redesigning the social component to match technological requirements is often the only feasible strategy. When a new facility is starting up, more flexibility is possible. Here, both the social and technical systems can be modified jointly during the intiial design state. Walton's (1972) description of the design of a new pet-products factory is a good illustration of this alternative. A third strategy is currently being tried in the Norwegian shipping industry (Herbst, 1975; Johansen, 1978). Designers there feel that the social and psychological requirements for crews who spend months at sea are more critical than the technical problems associated with ship design. Accordingly, they have specified a desired social system and are designing new ships to facilitate the emergence of the preferred social structure.

Regardless of the change target, socio-technical designs aim toward a jointly optimized social and technical relationship. This includes two dimensions: structure and process. *Structure* refers to the spatial arrangement of the social and technical components; *process* is concerned with the modification of structure to account for social and technical change. The tendency is to start with an initial structure that approximates the desired work system and to redesign continuously to match relevant social and technical changes.

In designing socio-technical systems, both structure and process are considered simultaneously. For clarity of presentation, however, structure is discussed here first. The problem is to design an initial structure appropriate to the situation. This includes at least three structural elements: role differentiation, task dependence, and goal dependence (Cooper and Foster, 1971). *Role differentiation* refers to the breakdown of tasks by position or the division of labor by role occupant. The issue is how much task variety and complexity should be included in a particular job. Greater differentiation of roles leads to jobs of limited complexity and challenge. For many individuals, this may result in lowered motivation. *Task dependency* represents the interrelation of tasks on which two or more people work together. The problem is to reduce the disruption potential of certain "key" tasks. Thus, for example, in a sequence where one task feeds several subsequent tasks, the design problem focuses on the one task that is most likely to disrupt the overall task cycle. *Goal dependency* involves the existence of a common objective for more than one individual. Since mutual goals require reciprocal supporting behaviors among workers, the question is how to group reciprocal roles to achieve integration around a common goal.

When organizations become increasingly differentiated along the structural dimensions discussed above, they tend toward greater segmentation, hence greater need for external control and coordination. The typical bureaucratic structure illustrates this condition. Here the organization is segmented into its simplest components, which are joined like building blocks into a predictable task sequence. Each level of this structure requires an external control system that coordinates the separate parts and regulates sources of variance from goal attainment. Since the control units generate their own variance and coordination problems, additional control levels are needed, and so on. This results in a hierarchy of control, each higher level regulating the next lower level. The primary disadvantage of highly segmented organizations is a slow rate of adaptability to change, since people are limited to a set of predetermined responses prescribed by others. Narrowly specified jobs also tend to thwart the social and psychological needs of workers.

To overcome these problems, socio-technical designers have developed more adaptive organization structures, responsive to both the social and the technical sides of work. Referred to as *self-regulating work systems,* these designs take full advantage of the open-system properties of organizations by segmenting the organization into relatively whole task groups where people regulate their own behavior (Herbst, 1962; Cummings, 1976; Cummings and Griggs, 1977). The focus of design is on interdependent task groupings, and the locus of control is located within the work unit rather than external to it. This reduces considerably the need for external control, thus decreasing the number of hierarchical levels required for task performance.

Self-regulating work systems are adaptive to change. Members are able to control variance from goal attainment by adjusting their behavior to respond to emergent conditions. At least three factors are necessary for self-regulation: whole task, boundary control, and task control (Cummings and Griggs, 1977). *Whole task* refers to the extent to which the work system's task is relatively autonomous, forming a self-completing whole. This provides workers with a sense of task identity, facilitating responsible autonomy around an overall task (Turner and Lawrence, 1965).

Boundary control may be thought of as the extent to which individuals can influence environmental relationships. Relevant considerations for controlling these exchanges include a well-defined work area that employers can identify as their own territory (Rice, 1958); an adequate variety of skills, which frees workers from having to rely on others for task performance (Herbst, 1966); and responsibility for boundary control decisions, such as quality assurance, which reduces employees' dependence on external boundary regulators, such as inspectors. The combination of these dimensions provides work groups with the necessary independence to maintain a distinct identity while relating selectively to the wider environment.

Task control concerns the extent to which group members can regulate their internal activities toward task achievement. This requires freedom to adjust work activities and patterns of interaction to meet changing task and environmental demands (Herbst, 1962). Similarly, discretion over production goals is needed if employees are to modify their output to adapt to novel situations, such as unpredictable breakdowns and stressful working periods (Emery, 1963). A final condition for task control is relevant and timely feedback of results. This provides the knowledge necessary for goal-directed behavior (Herbst, 1962; Emery, 1963).

The above-mentioned conditions for self-regulation serve as useful criteria for designing jointly optimized work systems. Specifically, the whole task dimension underscores the need to enact work system boundaries at points of task discontinuity. This assures that interdependent tasks will be grouped together into common units. The boundary control factor directs attention to those external conditions that may intrude on task performance. When employees have some control over these elements, they possess the necessary physical and social independence to operate as a fully functioning system. The task control dimension identifies the freedom and feedback required for responsible autonomy. Given sufficient discretion and knowledge of results, employees are able to control variance from goal attainment as close to its source as possible. This frees managers from having to concentrate on issues of worker control and allows them to focus on the more relevant tasks of developing the work system and relating it to the wider environment.

Whereas self-regulating work systems structure the social and technological relationship, the method of design accounts for the process of socio-technical change. Referred to as *developmental system design,* socio-technical practitioners specify only the minimal conditions needed to create self-regulating structures (Herbst, 1966). These include whole task boundaries and properties for boundary and task control. The remaining design variables, such as the allocation of workers to tasks and the specification of interaction patterns, are left free to vary with the control needs of the system. This design process differs considerably from the traditional method of specifying completely the organization's structure. The latter form of design assumes that an organization is predominantly a technological system that can be constructed mechanically and then implemented in one step. Developmental system design, on the other hand, recognizes that social organization cannot be created mechanically, but that rather, the social component goes through a series of growth stages as it develops toward maturity. Thus, socio-technical systems are not created; they create themselves, given an initial self-regulating structure and a succession of suitable environments that maintain and feed the growth process (Herbst, 1966).

Developmental system design recognizes that social systems develop differently from technical systems. Human systems are capable of both biological and symbolic growth. They can take ideas, expand on them, and transform them. In other words, they can increase their store of knowledge and skills through learning. Hence, social systems *appreciate* in their capacity to learn and act. Technological systems do not possess this self-generating capacity; they are dependent upon people for their creation and development. Since people appreciate with time, they outgrow existing technology. Hence, technology *depreciates* in the hands of those who use it.

What this implies for work structuring is that the final design of the social component can rarely be implemented in one step, but will need to evolve through a series of growth stages. The technical design must be such that a workable socio-technical system exists at each stage. This results in a series of socio-technical designs, each representing a viable work system, each geared to the developmental needs of the social system.

The Organization-Environment Relationship

Designing the socio-technical relationship focuses primarily on the internal structure and dynamics of the organization. Since we are dealing with organizations as open systems, however, effective environmental exchanges must also be considered. Although this issue has been discussed indirectly in terms of the whole task and boundary control properties of self-regulating work systems, it is addressed more directly here in reference to two major elements corresponding to the structure and process respectively of the organization and environment relationship: boundary management and open-systems planning.

Organizations relate to their environment through a boundary that both differentiates the system from the environment and regulates exchanges with it. *Boundary management* is an attempt to enact organizational boundaries to protect the organization from external intrusions and to mediate environmental relations (Cummings and Srivastva; 1977). This enables the organization to remain relatively independent from its surrounds, while selectively relating to them. This is a pertinent point, for organizations must have some certainty or control over these conditions affecting task performance. To achieve this control, the organization's primary task must be sealed off from unnecessary disruptions. This requires organizational boundaries that clearly differentiate the primary task from other activities outside the system.

As mentioned earlier, three criteria provide such differentiation: time, territory, and technology. *Time* refers to a discontinuity in the time span of task performance. A factory, for example, may separate itself from other organizations in its environment, such as hospitals and restaurants, by the hours it is in operation. *Territory* involves a discontinuity in the spatial arrangement of organizational components. One company's territory can usually be distinguished from another's by the location of buildings, fences, and signs.

Technology implies a differentiation in the tools, techniques, and methods of doing used in task performance. Thus, a steel mill can easily be differentiated from a university by virtue of the different technologies employed.

These criteria are useful for differentiating the organization from its environment. Their use may be enhanced, however, by four additional strategies for protecting the organization: buffering, leveling, anticipating, and rationing (Thompson, 1967). *Buffering* involves the placement of import and export components at the organization's boundary. These components—raw materials and finished product inventories, for example—provide the primary task with both a continuous supply of imports and a stable market for exports. *Leveling* seeks to reduce external fluctuations by smoothing out import and export exchanges. Thus, for instance, maintaining alternative sources of raw materials and offering discounts during slack sales periods help to smooth environmental exchanges. *Anticipating* protects the organization through forecasting and adapting to environmental conditions. Since this strategy is relatively uncertain, it is usually employed when external forces cannot be buffered or leveled adequately. Finally, *rationing* includes the allocation of task performance to selected exchanges only. This tactic is used whenever the organization's primary task cannot meet current demands. The allocation of emergency medical services to selected patients during a community disaster illustrates this form of organizational protection.

Whereas the criteria and strategies above differentiate and protect the organization's primary task from external influences, the organization must also exchange materials and information with its environment if it is to survive. To carry out these exchanges, organizations must regulate their imports and exports. This involves the placement of boundary control units at those locations where the organization is interdependent with its environment. These components—purchasing and quality assurance, for instance—regulate both the types and rates of imports and exports. To avoid unnecessary confusion, boundary control units should be located at clear points of discontinuity for the organization. Since we have already discussed the need for boundaries to protect the organization from external disruptions, it is apparent that boundaries that protect the organization are also likely to provide the differentiation needed to control exchanges. Thus, boundary protection is a prerequisite for boundary regulation; the former provides the differentiation required for the latter.

The foregoing discussion has concentrated primarily on the structural aspects of the organization and environment relationship. Turning to more process-oriented issues, it is apparent that the organization must manage not only its boundary, but the environment itself if the system is to be assured of a suitable milieu. Referred to as *open-systems planning,* this process attempts to map the organization's environment and to plan for a desirable future and ways to bring it about (Clark and Krone, 1972). Since the focus is on the environment as an independent entity, attention is directed outward to those forces affecting the organization's survival and growth.

Open-systems planning is based on the premise that individuals appreciate or value certain parts of their world as important and other aspects as relatively inconsequential. These appreciations, based on judgments of reality and value, determine in large part how people relate to their environment. A person who appreciates the ecological fabric of life, for instance, is likely to relate to his environment quite differently from one who does not. Applying this conception to organizations suggests that organizational members must share a common appreciation of their environment if they are to formulate and implement plans for achieving common objectives. Indeed, a major source of organizational conflict is competing views of reality among role occupants and subunits of the firm.

Open-systems planning is a practical method to help organizational members understand and influence their environment. The technique starts with employees' perceptions of the organization's (or work group's) primary task. This serves as the focal point for identifying the relevant task environment. Each segment or domain of the environment is mapped out in terms of its current impact on task performance. Members then discuss how they presently act toward and, hence, value those domains. From these data about the current environment, they can begin to map out how they want to engage with the environment in the future. Plans for influencing the environment in these valued directions constitute the last step of this process.

Initial experience with open-systems planning suggests that well-developed communications skills and a variety of environmental data increase the success of this method. Open and direct forms of communication enable employees to confront and work through the differences in perception that invariably arise. This increases the likelihood that members will effectively resolve their discrepancies into a sufficiently agreed-upon view of reality, hence permitting collaborative action toward a common environment. Data from a variety of environmental domains—that is, economic, physical, political, and social spheres of the environment—provide a comprehensive evaluation of the task environment. This information allows people to discover how parts of the environment are interconnected. Such knowledge is necessary to project the likely primary and secondary effects of anticipated courses of action.

Open-systems planning differs from traditional forms of planning in a significant way. Rather than forecasting a future that may or may not happen, the focus is on visualizing alternative futures and on taking action to bring them about. This represents an active rather than a reactive stance toward the environment. It recognizes that an organization must plan and act in the present if the future is to unfold favorably. This, of course, raises the ominous issue of manipulating the environment in ways that are unfavorable to the wider society. The best that can be said here is that the very process of engaging people in the analysis of their environment gives rise to the realization that its parts are richly interconnected. This ecological perspective leads to the sobering conclusion that, if organizations are to survive, they must enhance rather than depredate their wider environment.

The Implementation of Socio-Technical Principles

Heretofore, we have discussed the implications of socio-technical theory for designing both the socio-technical and the organization-environment relationships. This raises the more pragmatic issue of how to implement such designs in an actual organization. Socio-technical designers have evolved a change strategy responsive to the practical needs of organizational members (Cummings and Molloy, 1977; Cummings and Srivastva, 1977). Based on the use of operational experiments in selected parts of the organization, this approach seeks to devise and test appropriate designs under relatively protected conditions. This experimental process reduces the disruption potential of organizational changes and leads to designs tailored to the situation. Although it is beyond the scope of this paper to discuss the strategy thoroughly, its more salient features are outlined below.

Socio-technical experimentation involves a collaborative process whereby workers and managers jointly participate in the change program. This reduces people's resistance to change and provides for realistic designs tailored to the needs of the organization. Participation is legitimized in the organization through a formal sanctioning process. Members from the highest implicated levels in the organization agree to protect the experiment from unnecessary disruptions, such as demands for increased production. This provides experimental members with the necessary freedom to analyze their work system and to explore new ways of working. Employees are also afforded job and wage security during the experiment, thus reducing the likelihood that redesigns will adversely affect their livelihood.

After sanctioning the experiment, organizational members analyze the experimental system. This provides knowledge of its current operation and of its design needs. Two analytical models have been devised for this purpose, one appropriate for production systems and the other for more service-oriented units (Foster, 1967). The models examine the social and technological aspects of the workplace as well as relevant environmental exchanges. A major feature of socio-technical analysis is the detection of key variances from goal attainment and of how well the social system controls them. These analytical data provide the basis for subsequent design activities.

Socio-technical designs are developed and tested under experimental conditions. Employees try out new methods and behavior as they explore design alternatives. It is important to note that socio-technical designs emanate from the experimental process rather than from preconceived ideas about what is "right" for the work system. This evolutionary process tailors the design to the situation, thus avoiding the pitfalls of applying standardized or packaged programs to contexts that may be inappropriate.

Once socio-technical designs are brought up to normal operating conditions, the experimental process ends. The strategy now is to disseminate relevant results to other organizational units, hence instituting wider organizational change. The success of this diffusion process depends on how well the experimental system continues to show good results, is sufficiently visible and clearly convincing, is accountable in the organization, provides know-how for implementation, and is supported by powerful groups in the organization. To the extent that these conditions are satisfied, socio-technical experimentation is a powerful strategy for organizational improvement and change.

CONCLUSION

The socio-technical systems view of organizations is a significant step toward understanding how people, technology, and environment interact for productive achievement. It represents a promising integration of the social sciences and engineering on the one hand, and of organizational theory and open-systems theory on the other. This integration is sorely needed if we are to understand the whole organization rather than its limited parts. Indeed, if the realities of organizational life are embedded in the interaction of people, technology, and environment, then traditional segmented approaches are doomed to fail.

FIGURE 4-1

	SOCIO-TECHNICAL RELATIONSHIP	ORGANIZATION-ENVIRONMENT RELATIONSHIP
ORGANIZATION STRUCTURE	Self-Regulating Work Systems	Boundary Management
ORGANIZATION PROCESS	Developmental System Design	Open-Systems Planning

Beyond its power of conceptualization, socio-technical theory is an innovative strategy for designing and managing organizations. Figure 4-1 summarizes this approach in terms of organizational structure and organizational process as one dimension, and the socio-technical and the organization-environment relationships as the other. Managers must be concerned with all four quadrants if organizations are to function effectively.

Self-regulating work systems are an attempt to structure the social and technical relationship for joint optimization. *Developmental system design* is the process for achieving this integration. *Boundary management* protects the organization from external disruptions and mediates environmental exchanges. *Open-systems planning* generates alternative futures and ways to bring them about.

Each of these concepts focuses management practice on relevant organizational issues. Like all ideas, their use is primarily in how well they capture the essence of reality. In an age dominated by organizational complexity and change, the socio-technical systems approach may well mirror the image of the times.

REFERENCES

Clark, J., and C. Krone, "Towards an Overall View of Organizational Development in the Early Seventies," in *Management of Change and Conflict,* J. Thomas and W. Bennis, eds. Baltimore: Penguin Books, 1972.

Cooper, R., and M. Foster, "Socio-Technical Systems," *American Psychologist,* 26 (1971), 467-74.

Cummings, T., "Socio-Technical Design: Toward Self-Regulating Organizations," paper delivered at the Joint National Meeting of ORSA/TIMS, Miami, Florida, 1976.

Cummings, T., and W. Griggs, "Worker Reactions to Autonomous Work Groups: Conditions for Functioning, Differential Effects, and Individual Differences," *Organization and Administrative Sciences,* (1977), 87-100.

Cummings, T., and E. Molloy, *Strategies for Improving Productivity and the Quality of Work Life,* New York: Praeger, 1977.

Cummings, T., and S. Srivastva, *Management of Work: A Socio-Technical Systems Approach,* Kent, O.: The Comparative Administration Research Institute of Kent State University (distributed by the Kent State University Press); 1977.

Emery, F., "The Democratisation of the Work Place," *Manpower and Applied Psychology, 1 (1966), 118-29.*

_____, "Some Hypotheses about the Way in Which Tasks May Be More Effectively Put Together to Make Jobs," Tavistock Institute of Human Relations, Doc. T. 176, 1963.

Foster, M., "Analytical Model for Socio-Technical Systems," Tavistock Institute of Human Relations, Doc. 7, 1967.

Herbst, P., *Autonomous Group Functioning,* London: Tavistock Publications, 1962.

_____, *Socio-Technical Design,* London: Tavistock Publications, 1975.

_____, "Socio-Technical Unit Design," Tavistock Institute of Human Relations, Doc. 899, 1966.

Johansen, R., "A New Ship Organization," in *Stress at Work,* C.L. Cooper and R. Payne, eds., London & New York: Wiley, 1978.

Miller, E., "Technology, Territory, and Time: The Internal Differentiation of Complex Production Systems," *Human Relations,* 12 (1959), 243-72.

Miller, E., and A.K. Rice, *Systems of Organization,* London: Tavistock Publications, 1967.

Rice, A.K., *Productivity and Social Organization: The Ahmedabad Experiment,* London: Tavistock Publications, 1958.

Thompson, J., *Organizations in Action,* New York: McGraw-Hill, 1967.

Trist, E., and K. Bamforth, "Some Social and Psychological Consequences of the Longwall Method of Coal Getting," *Human Relations,* 4 (1951), 3-38.

Trist, E., G. Higgin, H. Murray, and A. Pollock, *Organizational Choice,* London: Tavistock Publications, 1963.

Turner, A., and P. Lawrence, *Industrial Jobs and the Worker,* Boston: Harvard University, Graduate School of Business Administration, 1965.

Walton, R., "How to Counter Alienation in the Plant," *Harvard Business Review,* 12 (1972), 70-81.

CHAPTER 5

Career Concepts and Career Management in Organizations

Michael J. Driver

INTRODUCTION

"One if by land, two if by sea"—so went the immortal instructions of Paul Revere before his ride that heralded the opening of the American Revolution. But what was to show if the British came both by land and by sea? Three lanterns?

At the present time in American history, another revolution seems to be massing strength. It is a "career revolution" (see Driver, 1976a). The revolutionaries are the young, women, and minorities seeking meaningful work; the "middle-aged" facing crises of meaninglessness; and the elderly, increasingly disturbed with policies of enforced retirement and "leisure worlds."

I wish to acknowledge the extremely valuable assistance of Dr. Dianne Sundby in editing this chapter at a conceptual level. I wish to also thank Mr. Bruce Prince for his help in locating material and his very useful syntheses of some research in this area (Prince, 1977).

The major targets of the revolution are organizations, and within those organizations it is the managers who will bear the brunt of the attack. And the attack is not coming from just one side. Unlike Revere, who had the British coming only one way, today's manager faces a two-sided assault—from within the organization as well as from outside. It is a genuine "three-lantern" problem. Employees are increasingly dissatisfied with the state of work in this country, and this dissatisfaction is showing up in production and cost figures and even occasionally in sabotage (see O'Toole et al., 1973). There is an increasing demand for organizations to cope more effectively with career discontent within these ranks. One estimate alone suggests that productivity might increase by as much as 45 percent with proper changes (Walton, 1973). Nor is this dissatisfaction restricted to blue-collar or white-collar levels. In one recent study, Schein (1972) found the most dissatisfaction among top managers! In a Gallup poll, 70 percent of professionals (usually thought to be most satisfied—see O'Toole et al.) reported that they could increase productivity by 70 percent.

At the same time, the number of people seeking new work—or more precisely, new careers—is also on the rise. The latest U.S. census (1970) reports an average of 6-7 job changes for the "average" person. Dunnette et al. (1973) report turnover levels approaching 50 percent, and Athos et al.'s study of new MBAs' job turnover (reported in Kotter, Faux, and McArthur, 1977, p. 380) found a truly alarming level of 62 percent job shifts within six months of hiring. Nor are these changes merely within job families. The latest figures report that the average person changes career area at least once (see Goldstein and Delaney, 1974), and data from within organizations suggest that a large majority of blue-collar workers would choose a different occupation if they could; a smaller majority of white-collar workers (57 percent) felt the same way (see O'Toole et al.). Tarnowiewski (1973) reports that even the supposedly satisfied manager and professional group is indicating career-change interest at a 49 percent level.

In response to this massive career demand, a whole host of new phenomena are appearing—mainly to aid the career-seeking individual. In one of the best regarded of these aids—Richard Bolles's *What Color Is Your Parachute?* (1977)—there is a section 24 pages in length listing a "selection" of career-aid books and articles, approximately 186 titles. Courses and seminars on career development are mushrooming around the country, from college classrooms to hotel conference halls. In April 1977, a major conference called in Washington to discuss the problem featured speakers ranging from Willard Wirtz, former secretary of HEW, to the author of the best selling "career crisis" book, *Passages.*

What lies behind this "revolution"? Its cause is clearly complex. In a later section of this chapter, a more detailed look at causality will be essayed. For now, a few points seem worth stressing:

1. There is now a far greater obsolescence rate of knowledge and skills—forcing new learning and even abandonment of fields.

2. Computerization and automation, although not causing mass unemployment, have forced changes in types of work needed.

3. Education has drastically changed the outlook of youth (and in today's world, those in their 30s and 40s are included in this group). Yankelovitch (1972) documents major changes in youth values concerning work—especially with regard to "meaningful use of self" and absence of blind, robotlike obedience. Studies of cognitive styles (i.e., habits of thought) have shown marked decreases in the kind of rigid simplistic cognitive styles of the past (Jacobson, 1974). This can be traced in current research to the ever-enlarging impact of college education (Driver, 1977a; Driver and Sundby, in prep.).

4. The failure of the radical "communal economics" solution (e.g., communes) of the 1960s has brought home the need to rely on oneself.

5. The recent period of unemployment and recession frightened many into seeking help in finding keys to economic stability or safety, not to mention issues such as success or self-realization.

For these reasons and a host of others, the revolution is upon us. People are seeking aid. Most are actively trying to build careers rather than fall back on welfare.[1] Where do they turn? Bolles and other sources cite absolutely dismal statistics about the success of most current career placing systems. Private employment agencies, Bolles says, place about 5 percent of their applicants. The U.S. Employment Service was found to place 59 percent, but a 30-day attrition rate reduced placement effectiveness to about 20 percent. Clearinghouses and ads in papers seem to produce equally bleak

---

[1]There are excellent data (e.g., O'Toole et al.) that absence of any work—including avocations—is unwanted and damaging to most Americans.

results. More positive are executive recruiters and college placement systems. But data on the *effectiveness* of executive recruiter placements are largely nonexistent, and data on the effectiveness of college placement (62 percent failure reported by Kotter, Faux, and McArthur, 1977) are very alarming.

At present, Bolles calls the plight of career searchers a "national tragedy." He notes that when we add in the waste of people grimly hanging onto jobs that underemploy them, out of fear of the search process, the dimensions of the tragedy approach a disaster.

The situation is not only poor in the placement area; it is very weak in the counseling and career "development" area as well. Bolles, for instance, suggests a bold, ego-building procedure of locating your own favored skill, researching a company that needs that skill, and presenting yourself as just the problem solver they need. Excellent advice for a multicompetent, self-aware person with high research skills and little shyness. But how well can it work for those with little self-insight or serious distortions in self-image? What about the anxious or shy security seeker?

Other self-help books (for instance, Kotter et al., 1977) make a more concerted effort to use established psychological measures— such as the Strong-Campbell Interest Blank—as "reality checks," but even here, the ability of all people to accurately assess their interests and abilities is doubtful.[2] It is my view that ultimately, people must develop their own careers, but that in most cases, expert help is needed to:

1. Assess oneself accurately—especially with respect to long-term development tendencies.
2. Learn how to make desired or needed changes.
3. Size up industries, companies, bosses, and jobs.

Despite the deficiencies in the present system, an army of career seekers—armed with self-help books, advice from friends, perhaps a course or seminar, and maybe even some counseling—is descending on managers from within and from outside corporate walls.

---

[2]This opinion is based on over five years' personal experience in teaching a career course and three years as director of USC's MBA Core Program.

The manager is the main target! Why not personnel? Let me quote Bolles:

> The personnel department in most companies they[3] say is at the bottom of the social and executive totem pole; it rarely hears of middle-high level vacancies even within its own company; when it does know of the vacancies it rarely has the power to hire . . . therefore avoid this department like the *plague.* Professors in some graduate business schools are predicting that personnel departments are either on the way out or on the way to drastic restructuring.[4] [Bolles, 1977, p. 141.]

All the evidence on salary and function seems to support Bolles' view. Even at the lowest entry level, supervisors often relegate personnel to a paper-filing agency rather than the decision maker on hiring and promotion. The process has gone so far that many firms even send managers rather than personnel people out to interview.

Despite the barrage of aids for the individual career seeker, there is an odd lack of material aimed at helping the organization and its managers cope with the career issue. (One recent exception is Hall's *Careers in Organizations,* 1976.)

The purpose of this chapter is to offer a preliminary cognitive "map" of the career area for people in a management position. It is also an open invitation to researchers from all fields to join in the corrections and additions that are obviously going to be needed in any such map. The reason I offer a map and not a solution to the career revolution problem is that I do not see any one "solution." I see no panacea such as MBO or Assessment Centers offering even a hope of a total solution. My belief is that management needs a conceptual roadguide—a descriptive model in the career area from which a variety of situation-specific solutions can be built.

This approach is based on the failure of monolithic bureaucratic solutions of any type to deal successfully with organizational work-related problems (see Wilensky, 1966). There is a deep-rooted tendency in American behavioral science thought to assume that "all

---

[3]Experts such as Albee, Crystal, Haldane, Harper, Kent, Miller, Miner, Shapiro, Snelling, Townsend, Uris—references are in Bolles.

[4]Time has come for a drastically needed upgrading of personnel as an "expert" field via certification programs comparable to CPA or the newer CFA in the finance field (Driver, 1977b).

men are created equal"—in all ways. This faith is then used to argue that appropriate and generalized situational changes can equally improve all people within a system. Faith in the power of the environment is massive.

Unfortunately, most current thinkers on social psychological issues (such as work and careers) have begun to realize that situations do not affect all people equally—that there are enduring personality traits that affect how a person reacts to a situational intervention.

For instance, Sheppard and Herrick (1972) found that dullness in work was not uniformly disliked; those highest in need to achieve (a basic personality factor) found routine most oppressive. Reif and Luthans (1972) found that job enrichment was not well received by people with strong social-interaction or security needs. O'Toole et al. (1973, p. 85) state that "some workers apparently prefer mechanically paced highly structured jobs and claim some satisfaction in their very regular and mindless (but predictable) triviality."

It is clear that people are different—and I favor the view, "different strokes for different folks." I wish to defer to later sections the thorny issue as to whether those who reject challenge, enrichment, participation, achievement, and growth are "sick" or defective. For the moment, let me simply agree with O'Toole et al. (1973, p. 111) that "simple remedies (e.g., job enrichment, job rotation, management by objectives) . . . have failed because there is no single source of job dissatisfaction."

Since people do differ in motives, abilities, and even—as I shall show—their very conceptions of what a career means, I propose to develop a multidimensional map of career patterns, focusing on individual differences.

The focus is on *careers,* not jobs or work—a subject that was dealt with by Brousseau earlier. My interest in career as a focus is that career is an inclusive idea that in its broadest meaning defines one's total identity (see Hall, 1976). It includes not only one's job but one's avocations, hobbies, and social activities. It is deeply rooted in the issue of family and particularly the "identity-career patterns" of the spouse (Van Maanen and Schein, 1977; Bailyn, 1970; Rapoport and Rapoport, 1971). Certain strange-appearing career patterns may be understood only be examining nonwork factors—for example, a "happily" adapted person in a "dead-end" job may in fact see his career as centered on a key hobby, such as Boy Scout leader, or on his family.

The focus on career is somewhat challenging at this point, since researchers are at present in dire need of comprehensive theories of careers (see Van Maanen and Schein, 1977). The map offered here, then, is a first effort to develop a framework for theory. It is based on more than a decade of research on decision-making styles (that is, information-processing habit patterns).[5] From an analysis of different information-processing patterns in people emerged the idea underlying the present model: *That individuals differ in the informational structure underlying their career concepts.*

I assume that each person has some concept in mind when the term *career* is used, but that in some cases the concept is very simple or confused, and in others, it may be a very elaborate, long-range plan embracing not only one's job but one's family and hobbies as well.

Based primarily on Decision Style Theory, four basic Career Concept Types are proposed:

1. *Transitory*—No clear pattern
2. *Steady State*—Lifetime occupation
3. *Linear*—Steady progression in a career ladder
4. *Spiral*—Planned search for increasing self-development

These concepts will be further developed in the next section. An effort will be made to show how each concept type differs not only in cognitive properties (that is, rigidity) but also in motivation—in what Schein terms "anchors" (Schein, 1968, 1977). It will be assumed that sociological models of role learning and psychological theories of stages of human development are very intimately linked to Career Concepts (see especially the three sections beginning with "Related Career Typologies.")

Career Concept Theory can take two forms, each to be briefly developed herein. *Form One* can be termed the "Consistency" view. The assumption here is that career concepts, once formed, are generally stable over a lifetime. *Form Two* can be termed the "Dynamic" view. It suggests that career concepts continuously evolve during a lifetime, owing either to work or other social learning

---

[5]E.g., Driver, 1962; Driver, 1965; Schroder, Driver, and Streufert, 1967; Driver and Streufert, 1969; Bryson and Driver, 1972; Alawi, 1973; Boulgarides, 1973; Driver and Mock, 1975a, 1975b.

(see Brousseau, 1977) or to an inner dynamic of human development (Jung, 1931; Maslow, 1962; Gould, 1972).

Both approaches can be useful in an organizational setting. The "Consistency" approach would suggest answers to such questions as:

1. Does a person's "career concept" fit the prevailing career culture of an organization?[6]

2. Does a person's career concept fit the prevailing selection system in an organization? (E.g., a Transitory may be viewed as "confused" by an interviewer looking for clear purpose.)

3. Does a person's career concept fit the reward and control system in an organization? (E.g., a Steady State person might find promotion—a Linear reward—a penalty.)

4. Does the person's career concept fit the nature of the job? (E.g., a Linear person might find a highly enriched job in a factory organized via democratic autonomous work groups—see McWhinney, 1973; Walton, 1974—to be utterly alien to his career concept.)

The "Dynamic" model can also address interesting issues:

1. Can one use a person's general age or life stage to imply his/her probable Career Concept?

2. Can one build manpower planning on a foreseeable change in employee career concepts?

3. Can one build more effective employee development programs, given a knowledge of the direction of career concept change an employee is experiencing? (E.g., for a Linear person trending toward a Spiral pattern, intensive self-awareness counseling would be helpful, but it might be of little value for a Steady State person transitioning into a Linear path—for whom skill training might be more useful.)

4. If the general trend of employees is toward a given Career Concept, should one plan in advance appropriate changes in organization structure and strategy? (E.g., if the "trend" is to a Spiral pattern, more horizontal mobility and participative management, as well as more emphasis on creative quality rather than volume production, can be anticipated.)

---

[6]Organizations may evolve implicit or explicit Career Concepts, which reinforce individuals with matching concepts.

The implicit hope of this chapter is that the reader will begin to examine his own Career Concepts and those of people around him. Given a better understanding of Career Concepts, there is real hope that both managers and employees can learn a most critical function—i.e., a regular, cooperative manager-employee interaction on career development, as advocated by Schein (Van Maanen, Schein, and Bailyn, 1977) and many others.

The payoffs should include:

1. A possible decline in welfare costs. As will be seen, economists identify a "secondary labor market," which in my view is essentially Transitory in Career Concept and which, because of tragic misunderstandings by Steady State or Linear organizations, is often rejected for work, creating a massive welfare problem.

2. Possible increases in satisfaction with work quality—which is hardly altruistic. "One cannot serve shareholders effectively if he does not act to make business itself an agent for human growth and fulfillment." (S. Harmon, cited in O'Toole et al., 1973, p. 23; see also Seashore and Taber, 1976, on the links between job satisfaction and profit.)

3. Increased productivity in terms of either more reliability, more quantity, or more creativity. (See the sources above on unused productive potentials; also O'Toole et al.)

4. Decrease in the tragedy and cost of inadequate placement, assignment and promotion.

5. Greater potential for organizations to appropriately develop personnel as needed to foster their own growth, stability, movement, or creative self-renewal. (See Gardner, 1965.)

6. Greater consonance of business practice with popular opinion in America on the role of business. (E.g., a Harris poll in 1973 reported that in 1972, 85 percent of all Americans in a national sample felt business and companies should lead in "enabling people to use their creative talents fully." [Carson and Steiner, 1974, p. 15])

FOUR BASIC CAREER CONCEPTS

In the paper entitled, "Career Concepts—A New Approach to Career Research" (Driver, 1977c), I indicated that it was the very lack of agreement among researchers about the meaning of the word *career* that led to the notion that this lack of uniformity (for example, see Hall, 1976, pp. 2-3) might itself be of vital importance in studying and mapping career patterns. Perhaps one of the most crucial factors in understanding or developing careers is to first comprehend the concept each person has of his or her career.

Research on concepts in psychology has taken two directions: content and structural. The content approach is more obvious—in the Career Concept case, content would refer to the field of choice and perhaps the underlying motives, interests, or values lying behind vocational choices. The work of Roe (1956), Holland (1959, 1966), and Super (1957) exemplifies this approach as well as the practical research behind the Strong-Campbell Vocational Interest Blank (Strong, 1943; Campbell, 1966a).

Although this type of career content work is very valuable, it has deliberately not attempted to deal with structural issues. In the psychology of concepts, structure refers to the pattern within a concept—and includes such factors as:

1. Differentiation—i.e., Number of dimensions of different parts in a concept
2. Integration—Modes of connection among parts in a concept
3. Flexibility—Capacity of relationships among parts to change (see Driver, 1962; Schroder et al., 1967; and Vinacke, 1974)

With respect to Career Concepts, structural variables would point attention to factors such as:

1. How much information is or was used in developing the Career Concept?
2. How many different career directions can a person forecast, given his or her level of career information?
3. How open to new information and change is the information structure underlying the Career Concept?
4. How pervasive is the Career Concept—i.e., does it include work alone, or does it extend to other life areas?

Many of these structural questions are closely related to issues dealt with in Decision Style Theory (Driver and Mock, 1975a, and also Chapter 6 in this volume), which makes several basic assumptions about conceptual structure:

1. That people learn consistent and pervasive "styles" of processing information.[7] These styles lead to the formation of typical concept structures in a given person.

2. That two primary structural dimensions characterize a style:

   a. *Amount of information* used (i.e., level of differentiation in concepts)

   b. *Degree of focus* in thinking (i.e., at the simplest level, the distinction between integrating all parts in one way versus multiple ways)

These two dimensions are used to describe a fourfold typology of Decision Style, as seen in Table 5-1.

TABLE 5-1   Basic Decision Styles

		Amount of Information Used	
		Satisficing	*Maximal*
	Uni	Decisive	Hierarchic
Focus			
	Multi	Flexible	Integrative

The *Decisive* style is seen as one in which enough data are used to arrive at firm, focused decisions. In *Decisive* thinking, enough information is used to develop a workable, stable concept, which is then rarely reexamined.

The *Flexible* style of thought also sets up concepts with "just enough" data, but is constantly open to reinterpretations as new data become available. The *Hierarchic* style usually formulates very elaborate concepts based on maximum data use. Long-range contingency planning is often involved; tactical patterns may alter, but the basic focus of the concept remains fixed.

---

[7]This is quite controversial. Some experts maintain that conceptual structure or style is not consistent or pervasive (see Warr, 1970).

Integrative thinking also involves use of maximum data, but the information is simultaneously used to formulate different integrations of a concept. Like the Flexible style, the Integrative style is also open to constant change in structure.

Translating style into Career Concepts, we can make the suggestion that each Decision Style may give rise to a unique Career Concept structure:

1. The Decisive style would seem to favor a Career Concept in which a profession or career is selected—possibly on external authoritative advice[8]—and held onto for life. Since the Decisive style is so highly prevalent among late adolescents (Driver, 1977a), it is probable that most Decisive Career Concepts are formed early in life—during high school or possibly college years.

2. The Flexible style would favor a continuously open Career Concept— possibly based on personal contacts and opportunities—which lacks any obvious pattern or focus, but rather seems to lead to an extremely varied work pattern. Time of choice would become almost meaningless, as the Concept would keep changing.

3. The Hierarchic style would lend itself to a very careful career plan with a long-range time horizon. Extensive use of information, particularly in written and in research formats, would be employed. For various reasons having to do with a tendency toward self-oriented authority, counseling does not seem well liked for this style.[9] The style also suggests that the Career Concept would have some single long-range objective of a rather lofty or impressive nature.

4. The Integrative pattern would be quite unusual. Much information of the sort used by a Hierarchic would be used, but also, personal experience—trial and error—would be valued. A complex, multidimensional plan would evolve stressing increasing complexity and awareness on a wide variety of fronts—work and nonwork. Research has found this style most creative (Raynolds, 1972) and most in touch with their own unconscious. Hence, a unifying symptom of their apparently spiraling work or life pattern might be a slowly evolving, ever more complex concept of self (see Jung, 1954).

We can summarize these structural features and the tie-in between Career Concepts and Decision Styles in Table 5-2. With

---

[8]See Driver, 1960.
[9]See Driver, 1976a.

TABLE 5-2 Basic Structural Characteristics of Career Concepts

Career Concept	Information Use	Focus	Direction of Change in Pattern	Time of Choice	Breadth of Concept	Most Likely Decision Style
Transitory	Minimal; Contacts	Changing rapidly	Usually lateral	Continous	Work or other	Flexible
Steady State	Minimal; authority	Constant for life	None	Youth	Work or other *	Decisive
Linear	Maximal research	For life	Upward	Youth	Work, hobbies, and family*	Hierarchic
Spiral	Maximal research and personal experience	Cyclic	Periodic lateral moves, inward building	5-7 year cycle	Work, hobbies, and family	Integrative

*This is very tentative and is based purely on deduction from structural theory—i.e., greater integration in Hierarchic vs. Decisive style. Intuitively it seems that the Hierarchic with its extreme focus might ignore real family needs, whereas the Decisive might more effectively compartmentalize family and work, thus giving family more real time and concern.

respect to the Transitory Concept, note that I see direction of change in Table 5-2 as often "lateral." This dimension of "direction" in the table actually has little meaning in a Transitory Concept, since life is lived for "now," and minimal attention goes to comparisons with past or future. Yet on examination, I doubt whether many Transitory Concept people would show any pattern other than a generally lateral shift across jobs.

Note also the "work" focus under "Breadth of Concept" in Table 5-2. This is conjectural. Some Transitory Career Concepts may focus on an avocation—say, musical skills, or family—but the thought here is that an integration of all life areas is not expected in this concept. An example might be the rather disastrous family pattern of Woody Guthrie, as portrayed in *Bound for Glory.*

On the Steady State concept, the Direction notation "none" may be misleading. One can imagine a fairly steady maintenance of necessary skills in a chosen field—be it electrician or physician. I can also see that a constant pressure for security, self-esteem, and money might require certain changes. But the essential idea is identity with a fixed, esteem-building work role.

A related point is that it may take a trial or training period to attain a "Steady State." In a craft or profession, years of training and upward movement may be needed, but once the desired role is attained, it is held for life. A similar point holds for the determined push of certain very Decisive business executives (see Grimsley and Jarrett, 1975) to the role "executive," which then becomes a lifelong role definition.[10]

A final point on this concept concerns work. It may well be that the Steady State person moving to his or her desired role is an oblivious "workaholic." However, once arrived, the Steady State person often shifts interest to hobbies or family. He may also compartmentalize work and family and give equal time to both (see note to Table 5-2).

The Hierarchic pattern is more likely to set perfectionistic, "long-term achiever" goals.[11] The career pattern here is most likely to involve a steady upward mobility through managerial, professional, or political levels. Hobbies and family may often be "orchestrated" to support this upward surge (which may result in neglect of real family needs). A critical factor separating this pattern from the Steady State is its nearly insatiable upward pattern. This is most evident in certain political careers—such as that of Woodrow Wilson. These Linear patterns often seem to be formulated early in life (as with Wilson), although sometimes the concept could evolve later, say, in college.

The Spiral path is so named because it seems a nonrandom pattern of career change, often apparently lateral (from a Linear view), possibly even downward. Yet there does seem to be an inner pattern of self-growth that I feel can be symbolized by a Spiral leading outward towards ever-widening self-awareness. The movements on this path seem oddly cyclic (5-7 years), although the intervals may decrease as one goes through successive changes. Movement in this career path usually involves an integration of family, hobbies, and work.[12]

It is increasingly obvious that as each concept is discussed, content issues intrude on pure structure. Motives such as achievement, esteem, and self-development have already been tied to particular career concept structures. Perhaps this is inevitable. Per-

---

[10]See Driver, 1977d, on types of achievement need. For the "Steady State," achievement is a means; for Linears, it is an end.

[11]See Driver, 1977d.

[12]I must express a great debt to John Gardner and Richard Gunther for clarifying these ideas in words and by the example of their lives.

haps certian values by their very nature adhere to certain structures, whereas other values show no relation to conceptual structure (see Boulgarides and Driver, 1977). At this stage in model building, it seems valuable to make a preliminary effort to tie content to structure in Career Concepts.

As a starting point, Schein has developed a very useful set of career anchors (Schein, 1968, 1977). He views a career anchor as a basic value or motive in forming the direction of a career. Table 5-3 contains a list of his career anchors, with which I have tried to tie in motives and Career Concept linkages.

TABLE 5-3   Career Anchors, Motives, and Career Concepts

Career Anchor	Motive(s)	Career Concept
Security	Family-Hobbies Fun Fear	Steady State
Identity	Esteem Self-realization	Steady State Spiral
Technical Competence	Achievement Esteem	Linear Steady State
Managerial Competence	Achievement Esteem	Linear Steady State
Entrepreneur	Achievement Variety	Linear Transitory
Autonomy	Independence Self-realization	Transitory Spiral
Service	Respect, Acceptance Generative*	Steady State Spiral

*In the sense of wanting to develop others, be a mentor, as developed by Eriskon (1968).

What Table 5-3 suggests is that perhaps subtypes based on motivation within each Career Concept would be useful. For instance, at least two subtypes of Transitory emerge:

1. An independent, non-entrepreneurial, relatively passive type who drifts from job to job—whose major need is freedom to move on.
2. An entrepreneurial active type who keeps innovating new activities, yet gets out as soon as stabilization sets in.

The difference here might be captured by focusing on independence versus innovative variety as motives, or perhaps more simply on passive versus active Transitory concepts.

Within the Steady State type, a similar active-passive dimension emerges:

1. A relatively passive (at work) security seeker who has
   a. Invested energy in family or hobby, or
   b. Decided to have fun in a sport or social sense, or
   c. Developed a deep-seated fear of failure.
2. A more active type who, like the Decisive, energetic manager described by Grimsley (1975) and Graves (1977), drives to the level desired and maintains his/her position by constant energetic updating of skills.

On the one hand, we have passive Steady States motivated by hedonism, duty, or fear, and on the other hand, active types motivated by esteem and a sense of identity and competence.

The Linear subtypes could possibly break on an active-passive dimension (as will be seen later), but from Table 5-3 emerges a very key distinction between Technical Linear careers—such as professors or scientists, building via theories and ideas and seeking recognition from peers—and People Linear careers—for instance, managers or entrepreneurs, building via increased power and organizational scope. This distinction within Linear careers becomes most crucial in discussing career stages (Thompson and Dalton, 1976) and trends in interest patterns (McLaughlin and Tiedeman, 1974).

There seems to be an active-passive break in the Linear type as well. This is the distinction between the Linear who is still actively moving up (or hopes to) and the Linear who was blocked or "plateaued" and has retreated from failure by leaving his field in what seems like a downward spiral, or tailspin, ending in absolute failure.

Schein's anchors do not suggest any particular subdivision of the Spiral type, since all presumably seek Identity, Autonomy, and possibly Service.[13] However, some work by Rapoport (1970) suggests a very interesting difference within Spiral patterns. In discussing mid-career adaptations in England, Rapoport distinguished between "metamorphic developer" and "tangential" reactions.[14] The meta-

---

[13] At a later point, however, it may be found that some Spiral careers are service-oriented, some relationship-oriented, and some self-oriented at different life stages.

[14] He also identifies an "incremental developer" who resembles our People Linear type.

morphic developer moves creatively within an organization. The tangential spins off to new areas. Perhaps a useful subdivision of Spiral patterns is:

1. An Internal Spiral—who stays within an organization or professional field, yet moves around creatively in search of self-development.
2. An External Spiral—who more dramatically switches organizations and fields in the same search.

This array of "subtypes" is not intended as theory at all; what is hoped for is an increasingly more detailed mapping of career patterns so that managers and researchers—and all of us—can better understand where we are and where we want to go.

Each Career Concept has its own unique problems as well as advantages, which the careerist and managers must recognize and try to cope with. For instance, the Transitory, although "free and enterprising," may suffer from what Erikson (1968) calls "identity confusion." If Erikson is right, this is a serious problem, and organizations—not to mention society—should try to adapt means of easing the identity crises through acceptance of this concept's validity or via helping the Transitory to "find an identity."

The Steady State person may be full of pride of place, or quietly and desperately suffering from lack of growth and development, especially in duller routine occupations (see O'Toole et al.). If so, can we make this concept more acceptable, as it once was in medieval guild times? (See Driver, 1977c.) Or should we "develop" Steady Staters into achievers and self-actualizers?

The Linear pattern can lead to immense success but also to a great variety of crises, such as plateauing, being advanced beyond absolute competence limits, neglect of total self, alienation of family, and so on. Again, should organizations provide supportive mechanisms for such crises, or should Linears be "defused" into Steady Staters or self-renewed as Spirals?

Spirals perhaps have the greatest self-contentment but possibly also the worst woes, if we can assume a basically Linear or Steady State value system in American organizations. Being mistaken for failures or classed as "crazy" is among their headaches. Can we adjust organizations to fit this concept (see McWhinney, 1973), or should these types be resocialized?

In the following section, no final solutions are offered;

rather, we shall explore what managers might do to improve matters, given knowledge of Career Concepts by all concerned.

APPLICATIONS OF BASIC CAREER CONCEPTS FOR MANAGEMENT—THE CONSISTENCY VIEWPOINT

The basic idea in the consistency viewpoint is that Career Concepts, once formed via social learning, are relatively stable cognitive phenomena. Work already cited on interest/value "content" stability (for instance, Strong, 1943; Campbell, 1966b) and even behavioral stability (Richards, Holland, and Lutz, 1967), as well as data on intelligence stability (Kagan and Freeman, 1963) and cognitive style stability (Gallagher, 1964; Leach, 1967), suggest that many people do develop consistent cognitive patterns, especially past adolescence. This is not to deny:

1. Momentary random fluctuations due to acute situations—e.g., effect of pain

2. Systematic shifts in patterns over definable situational dimensions—e.g., decision styles are seen to shift systematically and characteristically for a person as environmental stress or "load" changes (see Driver and Mock, 1975a; Driver and Rowe, Chapter 6 in this volume)

3. Developmental trends over long periods of adult life—e.g., Owens, 1966; McLaughlin and Tiedeman, 1974

In respect to the first issue, random fluctuations, one simply expects these to occur seldom and to cancel each other out in effect over time. The second issue poses more serious questions. It suggests that as situations change on measurable dimensions (such as success-failure, information load), Decision Styles will shift in a manner characteristic of each type of person (Streufert and Streufert, 1969; Streufert, 1969; Streufert, Suedfeld, and Driver, 1965; Driver and Mock, 1975b). This may mean that Career Concepts undergo systematic shifts as work or family situations change. For example, Spiral or Linear concepts may tend to give way to Steady State Career Concepts, given excessive stress (say, failure, or chronic overload). The closeness of Career Concept shift to Decision Style shift constitutes a much needed area of research.

The final issue—long-term developmental trends—will be examined in later sections. For now it suffices to say that some people may show developmental trends, but for those who do not—who have "stabilized" a Career Concept—the following applications will make most sense.

The basic application idea recommended here is based on a contingency concept. I do not at this point see any innate universal superiority of one Career Concept over the others; as noted in the preceding section, each has problems and advantages. Rather, I would suggest that the critical application idea is *how well a given person's Career Concept fits that of a given organization.* Where fit is good, both person and organization should gain in satisfaction and output indices.

But this idea assumes that organizations have something like Career Concepts. Table 5-4 offers a preliminary sketch of how organizations might be categorized in terms of the four Career Concepts.

A Transitory organization is by nature likely to be loose, temporary, entrepreneurial; formal procedures are at a minimum, people are "used" for a quick gain, and even a central location may be absent.

In contrast, both Linear and Steady State organizations would be classic pyramid structures with tight controls and central locales. Contrasts would include stress on vertical movement and decreased control upward in Linear organizations, versus widely dispersed "equalized" units of great stability in Steady State systems.[15]

Spiral organizations would seem fairly rare as total systems in current society—yet certain high-technology or artistic organizations (public and private) may show many Spiral patterns (see Jenkins, 1973; Walton, 1975). Within Linear or Steady State organizations, one may find departments that operate in a Spiral mode.

It will be obvious that these factors are intended to serve as preliminary guides. Research will be needed to confirm these patterns and add or subtract from this set. Also, it is clear that most organizations will not fit exactly into one pattern; however, most should show a predominant pattern.

---

[15]It is tempting to speculate that Steady State is more often found in government, but I believe many examples can be found in more economically stable areas of the private sector as well.

TABLE 5-4 Career Concept Culture Factors in Organizations

Career Concept	External Focus	Organizational Form	Control of Rule Systems	Assignment Policies	Job Description	Reward	Place of Work	Attitude toward Employee
Transitory	Temporary; entrepreneurial	Temporary teams	Loose	"Right man in right place"	None	Quick ROI: high autonomy; tolerance of lateness	Not necessarily central; could be home	Means to easily foreseen temporary end
Steady State	Maintenance of needed service/product	Pyramid (horizontal)	Strict	Permanent[a] specialty grades	Precise	Security; quality of product; service; respect	Central office; plant	Paternalistic long-term concern
Linear	Increasing production of product/service to market satiation; shift to new areas as needed for growth	Pyramid (vertical)	Decreases with success level of employee	Upward mobility (up or out)	Less rigid as pyramid climbed	Achievement; power; recognition; status	Central office; plant	Skill training for increased success
Spiral	Production of goods/services which simultaneously express creative capacity of employees and needs of society; Constant reassessment of both factors; cyclic shift of output based on reassessments[b]	Matrix; permanent autonomous teams; "link pin" system four plans[c]	Self-determined	Rotation; expansion of job skills horizontally	Evolving based on shared data	Creativity; interpersonal closeness; generativity (training others)	Central or dispersed	Development of employee to maximum growth of capacity—done with concern for whole society's needs

[a]Preliminary assessment and apprentices phases.
[b]See McWhinney, 1973.
[c]Likert, *The Human Organization*, 1961.

A final note on organizational analysis: The Career Concepts of key managers may be as important as or more so than all the factors in Table 5-4. Even in an overwhelmingly Steady State organization, a new CEO with a strong Linear Concept may "turn around" rewards and policies either overtly or covertly so as to reform the system in his image.

Given that organizations can be viewed in this manner, the following procedures would be suggested for managers:

1. Determine Organizational Career Concept Culture (using Table 5-4 factors and key leader analysis). This may require care, since certain departments or units may have unique cultures distinct from the whole organization.

2. Determine the employee's Career Concept.

3. Assess the fit between person and organization.

4. If the fit is poor,[16] consider:
   a. Training the employee to adapt
   b. Changing certain local policies to facilitate the functioning of a "non-fit" employee

At present, there appear to me to be no really fine-tuned tools for organizational Career Culture analysis beyond Table 5-4. Likert (1961, 1967) has developed a questionnaire for measuring certain aspects of organization patterns that might prove somewhat helpful (especially his System 4 as it approaches the Spiral patterns). Lawrence and Lorsch (1969) and Morse (1970) have also built a questionnaire for measuring organizational differentiation and integration, which gives useful data on time frames and structure. Waters, Roach and Batlis (1974) have assembled an even more comprehensive set of organization climate variables—some of which relate to Career Concept issues (see also Dessler, 1976, Chap. 8).

However, at this point, managerial judgment, using a framework like Table 5-4, talking with other people in the organization (especially top executives), and examining the career fates of varied people seem like the best route to organizational Career Concept analysis—until better measures emerge from research.[17]

---

[16]This is especially critical where unions or other factors limit the choice of hiring or retention.

[17]Currently, some of our research is leading toward a usable Organizational Career Concept Climate Questionnaire.

As to employee Career Concepts, the best recommendation at this point is to seek expert assistance. There are in existence measures of Decision Style (see Chapter 6), motivation tests, and even some preliminary versions of a Career Concept Questionnaire (see Driver, 1976b). Proper use of tested instruments and interviews by trained interviewers have proved to be the best way of identifying Career Concepts accurately in our present experience.

In the near future, a single questionnaire being currently developed may prove useful without the attendant battery of objective measures and interviews. The utility of this approach will be reported subsequently.

If outside help cannot be obtained, the next best route is to talk to employees about their plans and needs. Using a somewhat structured approach employing issues raised earlier (under "Four Basic Career Concepts") may be more useful than a purely non-structured discussion. It may be helpful to have a person write out his "Career Decision-Making Story" under appropriate conditions of mutual trust. Finally, one can experiment with policy or training measures in a trial-and-error manner—which can be rather time-consuming and unproductive.

One approach to be wary of, in my view, is the use of résumés. Perhaps a career history showing retention of a single job is clear evidence of a Steady State concept, and perhaps a steady rise in a single organization suggests a Linear pattern, but most career histories can be very deceptive. A pattern of job shifts might result from Transitory or Spiral concepts; or it might even be the track of a Linear person in a downward spiral. Even an upward pattern can be deceptive—it might be a Steady State pattern still in an apprentice role. A nonmoving pattern could disguise a strong Spiral or Transitory whose real focus is on an avocational rather than a job area. At present, the safest course would seem to be to use résumés only as a backup to expert analysis or one's own interviews. In the future, more research may reveal how résumés can be more effectively utilized.

One final way of gauging a Career Concept might be the use of a person's age, life stage, or organizational stage. These ideas will be developed in later sections.

Despite difficulties in present methods, a manager or employee with some practice and training should be able to get a fair idea of the fit or lack of it between a person and an organization.

The next phase would be to try to reduce any gaps. The method of training people or developing different Career Concepts will be discussed later. For now, the focus is on what organizational changes can be made to better accommodate a person of a given Career Concept. Possible solutions appropriate to each type or organization depicted in Table 5-4 will be briefly presented.

I   *Transitory Organizations*

  A. *Transitory Career Concept Individual* - In a Transitory organization, the matching Career Concept should be most at home— although even here, the more passive Transitory may need some relaxation on punctuality and other demands that even Transitory organizations may make. (See below.)

  B. *Steady State Career Concept Individual* - This individual would be very uncomfortable in a Transitory organization; the lack of structure, security, and identity would be appalling. Yet Transitory organizations may need Steady State craftsmen or professionals for periods of time. Two suggestions come to mind:

  1. Create "buffered" departments with more structure, role identity, etc., for Steady Staters.

  2. Provide guaranteed "outplacement" for Steady Staters when their role—or the organization (task group)—is finished. An example of this is the careful career counseling and placement of engineers by certain aerospace firms during the early 1970s' squeeze. The atmosphere and effectiveness in these Transitory state systems[18] was very good. Rehiring in current improved times is very easy for these firms. In contrast, I have noted that firms in similar conditions with no such outplacement policy were characterized by intense production-inhibiting anxiety, and rehiring is also far more difficult.

  C. *Linear Career Concept Individual* - If anything, the misfit here with a Transitory system is more acute than for the Steady States. There is no future, nowhere to go over the long haul. Short-term achievement will seem meaningless. One possibility, however, is to provide for the ultimate transfer of power to Linear Career Concept people in a Transitory organization that is moving out of an entrepreneurial stage into a more stable stage. (See section below, "Applications of Career Concept Theory—The

---

[18]These firms themselves were most likely Linear in form, but their space projects in many respects have a Transitory flavor.

Dynamic View.") This transfer could be by sell-out of ownership, franchising, or simple delegation of power. Many organizations go through such stages (see Greiner, 1967). It might make sense to offer Linear personnel required during the Transitory phase the specific option of this kind of organizational vertical movement. Another type of Linear concept might be more technical (see above). For this type, one could offer:

1. A major chance for technical achievement in the present short-run effort (perhaps ceding patent or copyright control).

2. Professional outplacing into another venture where further building on technical advancement is again possible.

D. *Spiral Career Concept Individual* - When the Transitory Organization's goal fits this person's self-search, the lack of structure, etc., should prove of low concern. However, if the Transitory organization is bent on some noncreative, exploitive venture and/or flagrantly "uses" people, the Spiral type will be alienated. A solution would be to use their creative bent by insulating them from distractive time pressure and by defining the purpose of the organization in a more creative manner (see McWhinney, 1973).

II. *Steady State Organizations*

A. *Transitory Career Concept Individual* - Here, a primary problem will be a feeling of being "trapped," or of being labeled "disloyal."[19] The Transitory is also seen as ill-disciplined and "immature." Lateness, absenteeism, etc., are a real problem for Steady State organizations needing Transitory workers.

One obvious solution is the use of temporary hiring agencies. But the problem really lies at a much deeper level. Piore (1970) has identified what are in fact two labor markets. The primary market is well paid, has good conditions, and is usually employed; in our terms, it would seem to consist largely of Steady State and Linear people.

The secondary labor market is the exact opposite—low pay, poor conditions, and chronic unemployment except in certain firms that deliberately use these people. The secondary labor force is most often the young and the poor. In our terms, they share a Transitory Career Concept—probably mainly a passive one. They are tardy, absent, very unpredictable, often liking to work away from central sites.

---

[19]For example, some firms have a policy of never rehiring people who have left (i.e., "deserted").

I agree with Piore that these Transitory people are "...not intrinsically bad. It fits the needs of the young ... and matches the preferred life styles of those who don't want to be tied down to a job" (p. 173).

I would concur with many of Piore's recommendations for these Transitory people. Steady State organizations should build in "Transitory subunits" with more flexible time patterns (such as Flexitime), more flexible work rules, perhaps even more flexibility as to work sites (work at home?). It may not even be necessary for government to offset inefficiency costs of such arrangements. Flexitime alone has shown itself capable of increasing the effectiveness of many people (Golembiewski, 1974). Another possibility would be to provide for voluntary job rotation for Transitory people; to permit extended leaves of absence—even indefinite leaves—with an opening to return.

This may sound chaotic to a Steady State or even a Linear person, but if it is kept within limited units and/or is not given over and above Steady State benefits (see below), it might prove quite workable.[20] It would also go a long way, in my view as well as Piore's, in solving some of the chronic welfare problems in this country.

B. *Steady State Career Concept Individual* - The fit here is maximum—yet problems do occur. These usually have to do with incorrect initial placement in a field. Data on the effectiveness of current placement methods (see Bolles, 1977; Kotter et al., 1977) indicate that misplacement is severe. Methodology is often the culprit. In the rush to abandon testing, following EEOC assaults, interviewing has come to the fore as a prime selection device. Yet its adequacy as an effective placement device—except in the hands of an occasional highly gifted person or well-trained clinical psychologist—is highly questionable (see Porter, Lawler, and Hackman, 1975, pp. 137-38 and 144-147). Interviewer bias, interviewee role playing, and inadequate data all contribute to some colossal errors. Even when both are trying to be honest, lack or distortion of self-concepts in interviewees or poor empathy by interviewers can lead to poor results.

Psychological assessment, as I prefer to call testing, is fortunately not deceased. In a recent article (Hogan, DeSoto, and Solano, 1977), it is argued that EEOC may actually have greatly aided

---

[20]It is therefore obvious that Transitory "concessions" should be made available with no acceptance pressure to Steady State employees, who will probably largely ignore them.

psychological assessment by eradicating invalid, overgeneralized, and misused measures from industry. However, when measures are properly validated, they can serve as very effective placement tools. What is clear is that the reliance on one measure (such as an IQ test) for a vague set of jobs is ludicrously inappropriate. On the other hand, a battery of measures covering aptitudes, cognitive styles, and personality can lead to very effective placement decisions (see Hall, 1976) if clearly tied to a particular kind of work (see Gough, 1976; Driver, 1977a).

As progress continues to be made on measures of work demands and rewards and parallel batteries of skills and motives (see Hackman and Suttle, 1977; Driver, 1977a). I suspect that psychological assessment will continue to resurge effectively in placement.

Even more promising is the combination approach known currently as "assessment centers" (see Byham, 1970). Growing out of the wartime OSS situational testing, this procedure combines psychological measures, interviews, group sessions, and simulated situations in an intensive process. The success of these intensive efforts seems high, yet cautions need to be sounded. There is a tendency to discount "professionals"—psychologically trained experts—and allow managers to run these centers. A danger of personal and corporate culture bias and inexpertness may begin to creep in.

More promising yet in my view are either independent or quasi-independent assessment centers,[21] staffed by measurement and interviewing experts and by specialists in the demands and rewards of particular vocations or professions. Combinations of clinical assessment and psychological measurement seem to offer optimal validity (Campbell, Dunnette, Lawler, and Weick, 1970). This validity should be enhanced when "faking" is reduced to a minimum by locating assessment and placement in noncorporate settings.

One final point on placement: Can "educational certification" serve as a shortcut to effective placement? Many firms, Steady State or otherwise, deal with placement via educational requirements. While the matter is still very controversial, the overall usefulness of past performance in predicting the future (see Hall, 1976, especially p. 115) suggests that education may in fact be an overmaligned tool for placement.

---

[21]That is, loosely coupled with a university.

Much research has shown major aptitude, cognitive style, and personality differences between high school dropouts, high school graduates, and college graduates (Trent and Medsker, 1968; Gough, 1966; Dressel and Lehman, 1968; Feldman and Newcomb, 1969; Barton, Cattell, and Vaughn, 1973; Tseng, 1972).

Recently we have verified major differences in "profile" between educational levels (Driver, 1977e). This is not to say that all college graduates show a "college profile"; nor is any given education level optimal for all work. Our results clearly show that some occupations better suit the high school than the college profile.[22] This is simply because whether by selection, training, or both, a person at a given educational level generally exhibits certain aptitudes, styles, and personality aspects that are useful in particular occupations.

As with data from psychological measures, interviews, or assessment centers, background data such as education do seem very relevant to optimal career placement when the connection or selectivity of the education level for aptitudes, styles, and personality are related to effective occupational performance by actual analysis. Clearly, the arbitrary use of educational level when not related to an occupation via such analysis is questionable.

In sum, considerable progress on effective placement or career choice (of crucial importance in Steady State cases) is being made and can be effectively used as the gap between research and personnel/management narrows (see Hall, 1976; Kotter et al., 1977).

C. *Linear Career Concept Individual* - In a Steady State organization, the Linear person is very likely to feel blocked, trapped, underchallenged. A solution may be to set up Linear units within a larger Steady State system—with specifically Linear procedures such as Management by Objectives (MBO) and special recognition for achievement. Another route might be to encourage the Linear person to seek achievement outside the organization—in educational movement, civic groups, sports—while maintaining a "pseudo-Steady State" position inside. Again, one might consider options previously discussed, such as taking on a more Linear role, as the organization moves into a more dynamic Linear mode (that is, via anticipated economic changes) or offering "outplace-

---

[22]The connection of education to Career Concept is as yet unknown.

ment" after a period of technical achievement. Finally, one might consider allowing Linear types to "spin off" a totally Linear aspect of the parent organization under a franchise or diversification, holding-company format.

D. *Spiral Career Concept Individual* - Here again, there will be felt a sense of being "locked in," and perhaps they will resent emphasis on quantity versus quality, output versus inner growth. Solutions here resemble those for Transitory Career Concept people: Permit Spiral subunits within the Steady State systems,[23] allow some Spiral persons to move horizontally to new jobs (without threatening the security of the majority Steady Staters). More uncommon Spiral options might be to permit sabbaticals for periods when the Spiral needs to reexamine issues, intensive group and personnel counseling aimed at enhancing self-awareness, and specific means of reentry for a Spiral rejoining the organization.

III. *Linear Organizations*

A. *Transitory Career Concept Individual* - Here, a strong sense of inadequacy, of being a "bum," will develop. One compromise for more active Transitory people might be to build in incentives for innovation or for cross training. Otherwise, the points made in conjunction with Piore vis-à-vis the Steady State organization hold with equal force here. Loosening up, tolerating Transitory people within Linear systems (which I believe are numerically most common) could greatly ease our welfare burden.

B. *Steady State Career Concept Individual* - This person in a Linear organization undergoes the well-known pressure to "move up" beyond his level of desire or competence (the "Peter Principle"); alternatively, he may feel "left behind" and a "failure," as documented by Thompson and Dalton, 1976. A solution would seem to have several components:

1. Offer certain "specialists" a tenure status outside the usual "ladders."

2. Provide pay and status increments based on demonstrated skill maintenance (useful for active Steady Staters).

3. Involve the Steady Stater in the senior policy group, based on his time in the organization and maintenance of expertise as technician, expert, or middle manager—i.e., make the best

---

[23]Gordon, in *Synectics* (1961) describes very clearly how Spiral subunits can be set up within non-Spiral systems—so long as they are not seen as getting "special privileges."

Steady Staters part of the "in group"—or increase their centrality in Schein's (1971) sense.

4. For the more passive, provide fringe benefits and increasing time for family or hobbies. The time they do spend at work may thus be less in hours but higher in quality.

5. Some Steady Staters may be really quite Linear in some avocational area—i.e., electrical machinery. Better counseling and appropriate transfer of job might employ the Linear drive for the good of both the person and the organization.

C. *Linear Career Concept Individual* - Again, despite "fit," problems do occur. Often there is a lack of feedback, no clear timetable on movement, "plateauing," and, perhaps most problematical, the transition between Technical and Managerial or People Linear patterns.

Suggested general solutions include:

1. Effective career guidance—especially via a mentor of similar Career Concept.

2. A well-managed MBO program

3. Clear time frames for expectations of movement in the system

4. Frequent feedback

5. Use of sufficiently challenging initial job assignment

More particular problems include success forecasting, the "technical-people gap," and plateauing. Success forecasting has largely concentrated on managerial success. Two basic approaches seem to emerge (see Boulgarides and Driver, 1977):

1. A generalist view

2. A contingency view

The generalist view suggests that energy and intelligence generally predict managerial success (see Graves, 1977; Grimsley and Jarrett 1975; Ghiselli, 1966). McClelland (1961, 1969) asserts that high need for achievement is also a factor in general management success (a clear Linear component). McClelland's view is borne out by several other studies (Grant et al., 1967; Wainer and Rabin, 1969). Other generalist findings concern values and cognitive styles—see Hall, 1976.

The other point of view is that "success" is not unidimensional; that traits relating to success in one setting fail to relate to it in a different setting. An example of this approach is Fiedler's (1971) model of leadership effectiveness, which depends on situational factors. Another example is the Decision Style model mentioned above. In this view, Decisive managers will be most successful in stable, predictable settings (Boulgarides and Driver, 1977), whereas Integrative or Hierarchic managers will be more successful in more unstable, complex environments (Alawi, 1973).

My present view is that there are probably certain general traits, such as intelligence, that cut across all management jobs and can thus be used to effectively counsel Linear people regardless of their area. However, I feel that other critical aspects of managerial positions (for instance, people intensiveness, time pressure, data complexity) are variable. Therefore, a Linear person must be given adequate assessment on present traits and how well they fit a series or chain of positions in an ascending career path.

This kind of counseling can have several outcomes:

1. For a person low in general traits, a shift in Career Concept may be highly useful.
2. For a person with good general traits, there may be indicated places in a career path where situationally sensitive traits need to shift—e.g., from a technical to a people emphasis (see Thompson and Dalton, 1976) or from a Decisive to a Flexible style. Where such changes are needed, the Linear system should attempt to provide its Linear people with appropriate training prior to upward moves requiring changes (e.g., sensitivity training, Integrative style training).

At some point, even with the best counseling and training, the Linear person may "peak out"—either he cannot adapt or the pyramid gets so narrow that progress slows to a dead halt. What then? Some organizations might consider broadening the pyramid or setting up quasi-independent "profit centers" where the blocked Linear can get going again. Then again, the person might be "outplaced" into a new organization needing growth (possibly less demanding, if one suspects ability limits). Also, one might reassess the person for latent skills (artistic? technical?) to launch a new Linear path. Finally, one might try to shift the Linear focus from self to others—to foster a generativity or mentor type of achievement, where one's protégés carry on the upward movement.

D. *Spiral Career Concept Individual* - In a Linear system, the Spiral is often misread as a failure, or at best is seen as "weird." Contrary to this image, however, very many Spirals are highly successful. Tarnowiewski (1973) reports that even among top executives in his American Management Association study, 42 percent had changed fields or were thinking of doing so. Among professional/ technical people, the figure was 61 percent.

The answer to the Spiral's sense of entrapment in a Linear system is very similar to the one for his dilemma in a Steady State system. Setting up special Spiral units (see Gordon, 1961), creating sabbaticals, counseling, reentry procedures are familiar. Xerox, HEW, and some other organizations are beginning to experiment with moving people temporarily out into other organizations. Leaves for non-job-relevant "reeducation" would also be essential. Quasi-Linear schemes for rewarding quality of output, creativity level, or contributions to the total system might somehow be worked out.

The issue of encapsulating Spiral persons or units in non-Spiral systems and of changing whole organizations into Spiral systems is clearly beyond the scope of this chapter. It will be dealt with, however, in a subsequent paper.

IV. *Spiral Organizations* - Since the shift from Linear to Spiral systems is seen as a crucial "career revolution" which requires a separate analysis, this type of organization's problems will be dealt with only very briefly here.

A. *Transitory Career Concept Individual* - Although there is some compatibility, certain problems can be expected. The intense focus on inner development may be regarded as an invasion of privacy or a violation of freedom. Commitment may be lacking. Solutions would need to include making counseling or similar inner-growth activity purely voluntary. Movement into and out of the Spiral organization (with or without outplacement) should be made quite easy.[24]

B. *Steady State Career Concept Individual* - Persons with this view should feel very threatened by the potential loss of their current identity, as well as by the relatively low structure. Possible solutions might be to provide "insulated" Steady State units in Spiral organizations. Tenure and title might also be retained for those desiring them. Again, protection of privacy can be given by making growth options voluntary.

---

[24]As has been done in one Procter & Gamble plant operating in a Spiral "open-systems" mode—see McWhinney, 1973.

C. *Linear Career Concept Individual* - The obvious problem here will be the lack of a permanent ladder to climb. However, the achievement motive seems closely linked to the transition from Linear to Spiral concepts. Perhaps when this transition is better understood, the Linear aspiration can be rechanneled into striving for ever-greater self-awareness, breadth of job knowledge, and contributions to the welfare of the whole organization or society.[25] Other measures might include insulated Linear subsystems (potentially dangerous, since they will seek to dominate); shifting technical Linear people from quantity to quality of achievement; and moving "people Linears" toward achievement via teaching and aiding others.

D. *Spiral Career Concept Individual* - Despite the obvious fit, there may remain problems. For instance, one's family may be out of phase with the Spiral pattern. Van Maanen and Schein (1977) have very neatly described how a male may be entering a Spiral phase after a successful Linear career, just as his spouse is departing the Steady State "housewife" role for a Linear career. Their mutual clash of directions can be fatal to the marriage unless understood and dealt with. Perhaps one solution is to involve the whole family in the same organization. (See McWhinney, 1973.)

To sum up this section, I have tried in a necessarily abstract and preliminary fashion to indicate how organizations of each type might try to accommodate nonfitting and fitting Career concepts in employees. I look forward to considerable amplification and concretization of these ideas from researchers, managers, and all of us concerned with careers.

RELATED CAREER TYPOLOGIES

The Career Concept model presented here does not stand alone. Although originating in my work on Decision Style and motivation, the relatedness of Career Concept theory to other models is interesting both for their mutual supportiveness at times and at times for the areas they point out where the Career Concept model is deficient.

---

[25] Meade (1937) describes the fascinating system of the Maori, where competition is used to see who can give most to the tribe.

I. *Models Dealing with Direction of Career Change*

A. *Pellegrin and Coates* (1956) describe two patterns: an upward moving and a steady career. These seem in part forerunners to our Linear and Steady State Career Concepts. They suggest that the upward concept is most found at the top of organizations. Does this suggest that organizations may divide vertically into a Linear culture on top and a Steady State culture in the middle? If so, movement of Linear people through the Steady State layer must pose a problem very worthy of research and practical problem solving. Again, is the steady career they discuss an adaptation of blocked Linears to being plateaued? If so, does this adaptation lead to a true career concept change and satisfied middle managers, or is it a problem needing solution as described in the preceding section? I find this model particularly challenging for its notion of a possible organizational cycle of Career Concept change, which I will develop in the next section.

B. *Miller and Form* (1956) also presented a relatively early model with three direction patterns:

1. Stable

2. Trial period leading to stable

3. Unstable (which was largely seen as unsuccessful)

Clearly, the first two patterns foreshadow variants on Steady State. The final pattern seems a mix of Transitory and Spiral. What I find intriguing here is the hint that in the 1950s, non-Steady State careers were viewed somewhat negatively, at least in this approach. The absence of even a mention of Spiral or Transitory patterns in Pelligrin and Coates further reinforces my view that, sociologically, these were not favored concepts in the 1950s. These issues of sociological change will recur in the final section of this chapter.

C. *Nosow and Form* (1962) distinguish four patterns:

1. Upward

2. Random

3. Coherent (but not necessarily upward)

4. Change due to occupational shifts in society

These patterns seem to be clear precursors of the Linear and Transitory (which is not really "random" in a pure sense in my view), and possibly even of the Spiral career pattern—which in the early 1960s was perhaps gaining recognition if not acceptance. Does the apparent absence of the Steady State reflect its declining value in the 1960s?

D. *Ginzberg and Yohalem* (1966) developed the following patterns (for women only):

1. Planner
2. Recaster
3. Adapter
4. Unsettled

The Planner is in my terms like the Linear, who stays on one track. The Recaster is a Linear who meets a block by moving to a new setting. The Adapter, who has plans but always keeps them open, is in many ways getting very close to my Integrative-Spiral pattern, at least in directional and cognitive dimensions. The Unsettled is a less negatively value-laden version of Transitory than had emerged in the 1950s.

Of particular interest to me in this model is its cognitive flavor, the positive flavor of the possibly "Spiral" Adapter and, again, the absence altogether of the Steady State. Perhaps the 1960s can be seen as the point where the Spiral concept really began to gain some recognition in our society. Concern for the impact of failure found here will also be pursued in the next section.

E. *Tavsky* (1970) sees two patterns:

1. For executives—an upward view (Linear)
2. For blue-collar workers—a peer-group comparison model that rationalizes a Steady State view in this group

Note the disappearance of a Spiral and a Transitory type. Note also the repetition of Pellegrin and Coates's results: The top layer is Linear. Tavsky says the bottom level may be Steady State. Are we returning in the 1970s to a two-tiered model (Linear at the top, Steady State elsewhere) reminiscent of the 1950s? I will attempt an answer in the final section.

II. *Models Dealing with "Time of Career Choice and Direction."* Hall (1976) has developed two possibilities here:

A. *Occupational choice*—where careers are selected prior to job entry and are quite static in direction (clearly very close to my Steady State).

B. *Career development*—where choices are made repeatedly prior to entering work and afterwards, and the direction is "dynamic." Again, either a Linear or a Spiral pattern resembles this option:[26]

The absence of the Transitory concept in this mid-70s model may signify a real loss of acceptance for this concept since the 1960s.

III. *Models Concerned with Time Horizon of Planning."*
Roth (1968) specifically focused on a person's career plan timetable, delineating three types:

A. Clear

B. Stable

C. Vague

The Clear path looks very much like the elaborate planning horizon of my Linear. The Stable plan is clearly Steady State. The Vague timetable is closer to the Transitory but could in ways include the Spiral. It is interesting to me to see the reemergence of a Steady State view in 1968 and the somewhat more negative terminology for Transitory/Spiral views as opposed to the 1962–1966 models.

IV. *Models Concerned with People versus Technical Orientations*[27]

A. *McLaughlin and Tiedeman* (1974) found that, using career content (interests, values) models developed by Flanagan (Flanagan et al., 1973), Holland (1959), or Roe (1956) there was a distinct transition from technical (i.e., investigator, science) to people management (and artistic—Roe only) as people got older. They also found that stability increases with age in terms of content.

B. *Kornhauser* (1968) distinguishes between professional and bureaucratic career patterns. Both would seem to be Linear and lend support to my subtypes of Linear concepts as technical and people-oriented. (See section above, "Four Basic Career Concepts.")

These two studies do underline the crucial shift toward a people focus in a Technical Linear career, which may need to occur if it is

---

[26]At a later point, Hall distinguishes Protean and Traditional Careers in ways very like my distinction between Linear and Spiral.
[27]I deliberately do not review interest-oriented models such as Holland, Super, or Roe's except as they bear on the Technical-People distinctions I find useful in subgrouping Linear concepts.

to continue to advance. McLaughlin and Tiedeman's data suggest this shift may be relatively pervasive and easy. Yet many Technical Linear people in my acquaintance simply balk at making this shift or lack effective people skills. These issues will be dealt with at greater length in the next section.

V. *Integrated Models - Van Maanen* (1975) has developed a concept of career "themes" that appear to integrate time frame, direction (upward or limited) and anchors (e.g., security). The theme approach agrees with the Career Concept notion that coherent patterns of both structure and content may characterize career thought. It simply takes a somewhat different route in organizing these issues.

Two themes emerge from this review of career models:

1. Do Career Concepts change over time? How does job failure or occupational obsolescence affect concepts? How does class structure or education affect concepts? Is there some innate pattern or developmental cycle that overrides or competes with socialized or externally forced Career Concept patterns? I shall attempt to deal with these issues in the next two sections.

2. Is American society changing its valuations of Career Concepts? Public opinion can play a crucial role in affecting government policies on career issues, transcending the efforts any single organization can make (e.g., see Wirtz 1975; Van Maanen, Schein, and Bailyn, 1977). These issues will be examined in the final section.

CAREER CONCEPT DEVELOPMENT

This section will deal with three related questions:

1. Can Career Concepts change at all?
2. Can a person be trained for or socialized into a particular Career Concept?
3. Is there some innate human development pattern that affects Career Concepts?

The answer to question 1 seems to be a clear yes. I have already discussed several models showing "stabilization" of a career choice after a period of trial and apprenticeship (Miller and Form, 1956). This phenomenon clearly shows a transition from Transitory to Steady State or Linear.

Several models and sections have dealt with "plateauing" as a transition from Linear to Steady State (for instance, Pellegrin and Coates, 1956). I have alluded to another result of career blockage— the loss of direction that may occur in a Linear person who moves to a Transitory concept after a failure experience. This may be a peculiarly strong pattern during retirement also.

Finally, it is clear that "midlife crises" can signal shifts from all other concepts to a Spiral pattern (see, for one example, Gould, 1972). My conclusion, then, is that Career Concepts can become stable for many people, particularly after adolescence (see Mc-Laughlin and Tiedeman, 1974), but that changes do occur for others owing to organizational or occupational factors, as well as inner dynamics. Data on the proportion of consistency to change in Career Concepts would be most useful.

As to the possibility of training for certain Career Concepts, I must take a very cautious position at present. No direct studies bear on this issue, to my knowledge. Vocational training might seem to instill a Steady State or Linear concept in Transitory people. But the failure of such training, especially in Piore's "secondary" labor market (1970), or hard-core unemployed, may owe a lot to the program's changing only skills, not Career Concepts.

Developing a Transitory concept person into a Steady State or Linear pattern seems to require development of an identity (see Erikson, 1968), a sense of self-esteem, a sense of general competence (see Hall, 1976). This in turn requires very expert assessment and counseling, as well as carefully developed success experiencing. Only further research can lead to a clearer idea of this issue.

Somewhat more data exist on developing a Linear concept. In a sense, McClelland (McClelland and Winter, 1969) has developed a program for instilling high need for achievement, a sense of autonomy, and a liking for risk.[28] He presents some evidence that such training can be successful even for adults. In addition, another aspect of the Linear view—the Hierarchic planning mode—might be taught via techniques similar to those developed by Kepner and Tregoe (1965). Finally, and prior to training, a very careful assessment of "success potential" and career path analysis—with possible points of retraining—should be developed (see Hager, 1977). With some adaptation of the somewhat controversial McClelland approach

---

[28]It is a moot point whether a person must already be in a Steady State concept for Linear training to succeed.

plus particularized cognitive training, I believe Linear training to be close to a reality.

The Spiral route still remains much of a mystery. From some research still under way, I think three routes of access exist:

1. Extreme success in a Linear mode, leading to an emptiness—a sense of "is that all there is?"

2. A physical/marital crisis, such as a heart attack or divorce, may open the road for Linear and possibly Steady State or Transitory types.

3. Failure or blocking under the right circumstances can lead to a Spiral approach—although it can easily lead to a tailspin or downward Spiral (with a Linear view still desperately held) or to Steady State "adaptation" or to a Transitory mode.

Whatever the route of access, the stages of Spiral change now seem to me to require:

1. A period of withdrawal—either physical or mental, and perhaps lasting for days or years—coupled sometimes with a search for meaning

2. A rediscovery of a new identity, a new creative role to play—a process Gardner (1965) labels "self-renewal"

3. A reentry to the organization or social world, playing this new role

These phases may be collapsed on one another in a matter of days or may take extended periods.

Training for a Spiral pattern may become a distinct possibility, especially if timed in relation to one of the routes of access mentioned above. Combinations of creativity training, identity search methods, and self-analysis, plus expert counseling on reentry may form the basis of such training.

In conclusion, training for Career Concepts does seem to be possible with further testing and development of procedures. Events in a person's life can serve as effective triggers to enhance such training. For instance, illness might spur on a Steady State or Spiral move. Skill obsolescence in a Steady Stater might encourage a Transitory mode. Family enlargement might support a transition to a Linear mode. Sudden success can be a route of access to the Spiral Concept.

The third question concerned innate or socially learned development patterns in Career Concepts. There are indeed a wide variety of life stage or career stage theorists whose work is very suggestive of possible Career Concept developmental sequences.

I. *Theories Suggesting a Transitory-Steady State Transition*

   A. *Super* (1957) has developed a model that encompasses three innate life stages:

   1. Growth and Exploration (which seems Transitory to me)

   2. Establishment and Maintenance (which seem largely Steady State, with a possibility of Linear)

   3. Decline (possibly a return to Transitory)

   B. *Miller and Form* (1956), working more from a social learning viewpoint, suggest three similar stages:

   1. Preparation, initial work, trial work (which seem quite Transitory)

   2. Stable work (which appears Steady State)

   3. Retirement (Transitory again, or possibly a new Steady State?)

   Again it is interesting to note the overlap of psychological and sociological models. It is also interesting to note the virtual absence of Spiral and even Linear concepts in these models of the 1950s.

II. *Theories Suggesting a Transitory Concept Leading to a Steady State or Linear Concept Branch*

   A. *Hall and Nougaim* (1968) have developed a subtle model that begins with a Pre-work trial period, which allows a person to discover successful self aspects. Although this has a Transitory flavor, it almost seems to suggest the possibility of a youthful Spiral pattern.

   Following this Pre-work trial and error, a period of *Establishment* occurs, where repeated success builds a career identity. This period could be Steady State or initial Linear, as I see it. Then comes a period of *Advancement* based on success, which is apparently Linear. Next, there appears a *Maintenance* phase, which is probably a Steady State. Finally comes *Retirement* and the enigmatic question usually not dealt with: What Career Concept fits retirement?

   B. *Thompson and Dalton* (1976; see also Dalton, Thompson, and Price, 1977) have developed a very clearly organizational career stage model as follows:

   1. *Apprentice*—Seems largely Transitory (although an early Spiral is not ruled out).

   2. *Professional*—Seems largely a technical Linear phase where a person seeks to become an expert. This could involve, how-

ever, a People Linear emphasis on being a managerial problem solver. It could even suggest a Steady State phase—especially and obviously for those who do not move on.

3. *Manager or "Idea Man"*—In this stage, concern shifts from purely self-orientation to developing products, services, or ideas via a limited set of other people. This phase seems ideally suited to favor the People Linear type's advancement, although as an "idea man," a Technical Linear who acquires some people skills might continue to advance.

4. *Policy Maker or Idea Innovator*—In this phase, the People Linear advances to director of large enterprises and deals with external strategies. The Technical Linear Innovator creatively develops new concepts via total systems. Here again, one senses the trouble brewing for a Technical Linear who has not shifted interest (a la McLaughlin and Tiedeman) and skill to more of a people focus. An interesting component of this fourth stage is that a certain opening for creative ideas or generative mentoring of others comes into play. Thus, a possible option for a Spiral Concept emerges in this late phase, as I view this model.

Thompson and Dalton present clear evidence that in the R&D organizations studied (Linear?) the person staying at Stage 2 (Steady State expert) is in trouble in terms of ratings and salary. He may be very effective (see Graves, 1977) but is not rewarded— illustrating the dilemma of person-organization mismatch in a Career Concept sense.

This model also poses another intriguing issue: If Spiral concept people can emerge in Stage 4 (which is my view of their model), how do they survive Stages 2 and 3? Can we assume that either (1) organizations permit "closet Spirals" to move up, perhaps role playing a Linear mode, or (2) the success of reaching Stage 4 permits some Linears to embark naturally on a Spiral path?

It is evident that these models open up fascinating research and organizational problem-solving vistas.

III. *Theories Explicitly Including a Spiral Stage*

A. *Van Maanen and Schein* (1977) build a four-stage model, as follows:

1. *Exploration*—Can consist of merely a series of tentative choices (rather Transitory) or the development of a self-image (neo-Spiral?).

2. *Establishment*—A career "theme" (somewhat akin to my Career Concept, see above) emerges. This theme can be either

Steady State or Linear (as I understand their model). They hint that failure is the predecessor of a Steady State mode in this phase. I agree but suggest that this concept may be the result of positive choice as well.

3. *Maintenance*—A period that could be purely Steady State. However, the "mid-life crisis" common in this stage could generate a Spiral concept at this time.

4. *Decline*—Again it is not clear what happens to Career Concepts here.

An important point is that this is the first (to my knowledge) organizationally focused career stage model that opens the door to a Spiral path clearly at such an early stage (although one might see this in Hall and Nougaim or Thompson and Dalton).

B. *Erikson* (1963, 1968) has developed one of the earliest and most clearly psychological (as opposed to organizational) adult life stage models. I shall pass over his preadolescent stages, since in this chapter I do not desire to address these critical years at all. So the first phase in this model for my purposes is the "Identity Crisis" phase. Erikson sees this as a period emerging in adolescence in which childhood adaptations are all reexamined. The adolescent searches now for a new creative, autonomous role in which he or she can contribute to society and derive a sense of meaning and faith.

To the extent that a truly "democratic identity" emerges, I think we are close to the emergence of a Spiral Career Concept; for this type of identity is creative and autonomous as well as achievement-oriented. However, some "solve" the identity crisis by adopting a more "totalitarian" identity—retaining faith and achievement, and perhaps even autonomy to a degree, but abandoning creativity. This would parallel in some ways the emergence of a Linear concept. A Steady State concept might stress autonomy more than achievement. But in Erikson's view, some Steady State people would be seen as "mere conformists" with no real identity, who are simply killing time.

In his view, the Transitory concept might well represent "identity confusion," in which a great loss of concentration ability as well as other "symptoms" occur—for example; faddism. Erikson clearly places strong value on achieving identity—especially a "democratic identity."

He then goes on to postulate three more stages:

1. *An Intimacy crisis*—In which one develops an open, honest, non–"mirror image" relationship with one or more other people.

2. *A Generativity crisis*—In which one comes to grips with mentoring or developing others—especially the new generation

3. *An Integrity crisis*—In which one comes to an acceptance of the inevitable "rightness" of one's life, and all reality.

In my view, both intimacy and generativity can become crucial aspects of a Spiral Career Concept. I take issue with Erikson's idea that there is one identity crisis that, when solved (or not), leads on to other crises at given successive age periods. As I see it, one may go through repeated identity crises (self-renewal, in Gardner's term), each with a slightly different identity outcome— perhaps one "identity" stresses intimacy, another creative contributions to society, still another a generative concern for developing others. (See below.)

I am not sure, but I feel that the "integrity" resignation of Erikson is not the only alternative to despair in the twilight of life. I believe that the truly Spiral person (and perhaps Linear or Steady State as well) can continue to develop new roles, to achieve more, or to retain his expertise right to the end of physical existence. To me, Erikson's "finale" is that of a Steady State adaptation.

C. *Gould* (1972) has also contributed an interesting life stage model with powerful Career Concept implications. Somewhat recast for my purposes, it looks like this:

1. *Apprentice/Autonomy Phase (16-22 years old).* In this phase, there is a crucial separation from parental dominance, testing for an identity, openness, variety seeking. To the extent that no self is found, the pattern remains Transitory for me. To the extent that an identity is given by the environment, either a Steady State or a Linear concept emerges. (There is even a possibility of a Spiral concept emerging, and creative self- definition—but Gould seems to feel that this is of low probability at this age.) What is very important to me here is the idea that ultimately Linear or Steady State concepts are derived from social models, whereas Spiral concepts represent a unique self-created pattern.

2. *Adult Mastery (ages 23-28)*—Proving oneself as an adult. I would interpret this to mean either in a Linear mode, testing one's ability to achieve, or in a Steady State mode, forging one's niche (possibly via an apprentice route). An active Transitory might establish his capacity to successfully take repeated risks, whereas the passive Transitory might prove his ability to keep on moving—he owes no one anything.

3. *"30s Crisis" (28-33)*—A major dissatisfaction with any of the modes above may set in. Requestioning of externally imposed Linear or Steady State concepts can lead to the emergence of a relatively early Spiral concept (a la Erikson). The crisis may, however, lead only to a new direction in a Linear route or a reaffirmation of prior modes. For a Transitory, it can signal a move toward settling down into an identity.

4. *Continued Mastery (33-43)*—Usually a period of intense effort to "make it" by Linears, to end apprenticeship by Steady Staters (my interpretations).

5. *Settled Down (43-50)*—This can often signal a "resignation to reality"—a feeling that the die is cast. Linears may slack off; perhaps a strong Steady State resurgence occurs, often to refocus energy on family. I suspect that for some in this stage, a Spiral concept may emerge—but around intimacy, not work.

6. *Late Renewal (50+)*—Gould is quite optimistic about the possibility of an autumnal renewal at this point. Strong seeking for self-defined Spiral concept occurs. This may lead to a new intimacy, a new creative contribution, or possibly a Spiral Generative shift to mentoring others (see Thompson and Dalton, 1976).

What I find particularly interesting in this model is that Spiral patterns can emerge at different life stages—including the pre- and post-retirement period.

D. *Levinson* (Levinson, et al., 1976; Levinson, 1977) has developed an equally intriguing life stage model, as follows:

1. *Leaving Family and Getting into Adult World* (16-29)—At this point, there is a focus on autonomy, exploration, and provisional commitments. It is a primarily Transitory period (with some possible identity, but Levinson sees this coming later than Gould does).

2. *30s Transition*—Here, Levinson sees acceptance of an identity (externally given?), which he calls "settling in," as a path many take. For me, this signifies acceptance of Steady State or Linear concepts. Levinson does see a possibility of continuance of an unsettled life—which is clearly Transitory. One has a less clear sighting of the Spiral possibility here than with Gould.

3. *Settling Down (30-35)*—A period for some of order and stability (Steady State) or long-range upward striving (Linear). There may be an autonomy reassertion that could signal a Sprial pattern—but this is not clear to me.

4. *Becoming One's Own Man*—Strong autonomy push; this seems to me most characteristic of the Linear, but certain Steady Staters may "set up for themselves" at this point. Of course, for the Transitory this is the real issue all along.

5. *Mid-Life Transition (38 to mid-40s)*—Levinson and his associates find that nearly 80% of the people they surveyed underwent a rethinking at this stage—a soul-searching. At this point, Levinson clearly sees a Spiral option opening—he terms it "breaking out." In men, it often involves an opening up to more feminine, artistic, creative activities; in women, it leads to assertion of analytic, managerial, "masculine" traits (see Jung below).

   However, not all break out. Some, because of illness, failure, etc., shift to a rather sad "weighted-down" Steady State.

6. *Middle Adult (45–?)*—The Spiral concept person goes on to new creativity (e.g., Frank Lloyd Wright), new social contribution (Gandhi), new mentoring (Jung). The Steady Stater, though, is seen by Levinson as a kind of "has-been," lingering along (e.g., Dylan Thomas or F. Scott Fitzgerald).

My reaction to this powerful model is to suggest that the Spiral path may emerge earlier than mid-life and that some people continue in Linear or Steady State or Transitory paths with apparently no feeling of malaise.

E. *Jung* (1934) is in some sense the earliest to formulate a clear life stage model. He saw the first half of life as looking outward to the world, and the second half focused more on developing one's self, the integration of all aspects of one's personality. The first phase could be seen as Linear, but in his discussion of "personality" (1934), he describes the possibility of a person's developing "fully" early in life. What this early development meant was a tuning in to an inner voice, a message about one's possible role or destiny coming from within one's own unconscious mind. A conscious choice to accept this inner awareness constitutes a developed personality. A person who is overwhelmed by his/her unconscious is on the road to madness, but a person who never tunes in is, in Jung's terms, a mere conformist with no real purpose.[29]

This inner voice "is a voice of a fuller life, of a wider, more comprehensive consciousness . . . an increase of self consciousness" (Jung, 1954, p. 184). Jung identifies this phase in early life

[29]He felt that man's lack of developed personality can lead to mass unconscious movements to find purpose, often very violent—e.g., Nazi Germany.

with the archetype or unconscious motif of the *hero*.[30] He sees human development as a widening incorporation of unconscious elements, including archetypes, into our conscious self. It seems clear to me that the "developed personality" in Jung's sense may well be on the Spiral path to self-awareness well before mid-life.

Jung himself, as far as I know, never laid out an elaborate "archetypal stage" model of life; however, I shall try to do so, since I believe it sheds much light on my own unfolding concept of Career Concept development.

Perhaps an obvious beginning is with the "Youth" (or *Puer Aeternus*) archetype (see Jung, 1940). This unconscious factor signifies potential. It is characterized by wandering and focuses heavily on development of emotion. I would see a link in the emergence of this archetype into adolescent consciousness as possibly underlying the Transitory Career Concept phase of early youth.

Somewhat later (in my view) might emerge the "Trickster" archetype (Jung, 1954). This archetype stresses a wily, elusive role in which intuition is used heavily and autonomy is very important. It may in my judgment remain the prevailing archetype in persons retaining a Transitory Career Concept for life.

Then comes the emergence of the Hero (or Heroine) archetype (see Campbell, 1956). The "inner voice" mentioned above activates a strong, active, intellect-dominated role where achievement becomes very crucial. Although this may lead in a Spiral direction, I'd see this stage as largely similar to the Linear Career Concept.

About the same time, or perhaps later, the Father/Mother archetypes (see Whitmont, 1969; Chetwynd, 1972) may emerge, where the emphasis is on establishment of order and authority. Practicality and convention are critical. I would strongly associate this with the Steady State concept.

Finally emerges the Wise Man or Great Mother archetypes[31] (see Jung, 1945), which are nurturing (intimacy?) and generative. They clearly signify a type of Spiral Career Concept. If the Hero/Heroine persists along with the two archetypes mentioned

---

[30]Archetypes are extremely hard to define. Jung believed that deep within our unconscious mind, there lie objective patterns that are basic to all human life. These patterns can project into our conscious minds as people in myths and dreams or symbols. They can signify a particular role or purpose to the conscious mind that is in tune with unconscious and deeper reality. (See Jung, (1959.)

[31]In Jung's thought, female and male archetypes tend to become more balanced—equalized in mid-life. (See Levinson, 1977.)

above, a kind of Messiah pattern may emerge, where the inner wisdom and nurturing of this phase are not passive and inward but continue to act on the world indefinitely (e.g., Gandhi).

The five models of development described here clearly do not agree on the timing or even credibility of certain Career Concepts. In the absence of careful empirical data, I find it difficult to devise anything more than a very preliminary sketch of Career Concept development as I see it, by drawing on these Models.

1. *The "Apprentice-Youth" or Transitory Phase*—Most models agree that we begin in a Transitory, tentative, noncommitting mode. Common to this phase may be a desire to assert autonomy (especially from parents) and to find and test a "self."

   Some people seem never to end this phase. They never find a stable self-identity. Whether this is due to a fear of commitment or a basic lack of trust (in Erikson's sense, 1965) is not clear, although the possible role of the "Trickster" archetype suggests a deep lack of trust.

2. *The Heroic or Linear Achieving Stage* (probable emergence 18-32)—At this point, an identity (externally imposed) is found and the person strives to achieve success, to act out his identity and receive recognition from others. Advice from a mentor (a Wise Old Man or Great Mother?) may be crucial. The Hero may at times go through periods of adversity (death and rebirth being an extreme symbol of this). A new identity may emerge (self-renewal) that is more internally defined (as Jung suggests). At this point, a more creative, less achievement-oriented synthesis of Linear and Spiral patterns may develop.

   The Heroic pattern may persist on its own throughout life—the eternal Linear path—particularly if one is always only *partially* successful. It may merge with other patterns as just described above (i.e., a Linear/Spiral mix), or it may give way entirely—e.g., failure may move it to Steady State. Extreme success may move it toward a more generative or intimacy-oriented Spiral path.

3. *The Steady State Stage* (possible emergence 32-42)—As already noted, this stage may emerge right after Stage 1. It may then persist for life. One suspects here a strong role of parental values being played out and training in a very authoritarian, strict mode.

   Another kind of Steady State may be simply a pre-stage for a Linear take-off—i.e., developing "expertise" in Thompson and Dalton's phrase. Still again, and perhaps most commonly (how badly data are needed), the Steady State may simply be a natural outcome of a prior Linear phase that has been severely blocked or where family or hobby increasingly take one's interest. The first type of accommodative Steady State may harbor the bitterness mentioned by Levinson. The second may really be simply a refocusing of energy from work to nonwork and perhaps signal a nonwork Spiral or Linear career getting under way.

4. *The Wise Old Man/Great Mother Spiral Phase* (possible emergence 40-?)—Jung and many others see this more passive Spiral path as coming later in life. It could be preceded by any of the paths outlined above: The pure Transitory may finally "find himself." The Steady State person may discover some "inner voice" and get moving in a developmental sense, particularly in relation to intimacy and generativity. The Linear may turn inward for self-definition and either continue to merge a creative achievement modality with the nurturing, generative modality of this later Spiral path or move off in an active creative mode. In any event, the essential quality of this phase is maximum self-awareness combined with a desire to develop others.

It should be clear that I am not restricting the Spiral Career Concept to this phase. It may occur early in life as a Heroic Spiral phase in which creative achievement is central (a Linear/Spiral), which may emerge in the 20s or 30s.

The later Spiral pattern could take three distinct forms:

a. A Nurturant/Intimacy (Great Mother; Anima) Spiral phase, which may emerge in the 40s and 50s. Concerned with building deep relationships or developing other individuals.

b. A Mentoring/Generative Spiral (Wise Old Man plus Hero) phase, which may occur in the 50s and 60s and be concerned with developing whole systems, organizations, societies.

c. A very personal, self-absorbed Spiral phase (pure Wise Old Man), which may characterize the final phase of life, a phase of getting into contact with greatest awareness of the ultimate meanings, with possible apparent overt passivity. One might see this phase turning into a very special mentoring, brought to mind by the concept of the "Sage."

I do not see at this point any necessity for age typing[32] or even a particular order (for instance, I see John Lilly, 1972, as already in a rather Sage-like posture at a fairly young age). It is my

---

[32]Therefore, at this point, I do not recommend use of chronological age as a guide to Career Concepts in people.

hope that research and sharing of experiences will ultimately broaden the awareness of these phenomena.

APPLICATIONS OF CAREER CONCEPT THEORY—THE DYNAMIC VIEW

It will be clear from the foregoing that only the most tentative statements about applications can be made at this point. The basic directional shift seen in the preceding section seems to be Transitory, Linear, Steady State, Spiral. The Linear and Steady State seem interchangeable and can be dropped altogether for some people.

If this model proves valid, it does suggest that different types of organizations (in terms of Career Concept Culture) can anticipate different planning problems.

Given its ephemeral nature, the Transitory organization probably would need no long-range developmental plans at all. The Steady State organization, though, can anticipate several problems:

1. Providing challenge to young Linear "Heroes"
2. Providing looseness for permanent Transitories
3. Providing outplacing for later Linear and Spiral products of varied crises from ages 30 to 50

However, it is quite conceivable that the Steady State organization might very well wish to shelter Linear or Spiral people as a hedge against environmental or sociological changes. One thinks of the utility companies faced with energy shortages, or the oil and automobile companies faced with changing public opinion and worker attitudes.

The basic planning need in a Steady State organization is good initial assessment and placement for Steady State employees. A secondary need is to aid the transition of young Transitories into Steady State concepts via effective assessment, carefully planned early success experiences (esteem building), and initial tolerance for Transitory patterns.

For Linear organizations, the major anticipation based on career development is what to do with the Spirals developing via crises, the ex-Linear Steady States bitterly adapting to a plateau, and the chronic Transitories. Given the developmental trends discussed in the preceding section, it may be quite possible to:

1. Train young Transitories as described for Steady State organizations but then move them on to Linear training
2. Develop young Steady State people over time via achievement training, cognitive training, advancing challenge
3. "Retread" blocked Linears by assessing and developing new skills or outplacing
4. "Shelter" Spirals in special groups (a) because their creativity is needed (see Driver, 1976a), and (b) as a hedge against societal or environmental trends requiring a more Spiral orientation
5. Be prepared for crises, mid-life or otherwise, with effective courses, counseling, etc.

For Spiral organizations, if the model is right, time will increasingly aid the development of Spiral Career Concepts. However, the organization may wish to more directly:

1. Develop young Transitories into early Heroic (democratic identity) Spirals.
2. Encourage the Steady Staters to find a creative zone and generate a "Heroic creative" Spiral pattern or encourage an interpersonal (intimacy) or generative Spiral pattern.
3. Merge the Linear achievement patterns with the Spiral—a combination of Hero and Wise Old Man/Great Mother. But what do we do with Messiahs?

One last developmental point is that organizations themselves may be going through developmental states, related to Career Concept states. One can envisage a "start-up" entrepreneurial phase that is primarily Transitory; a shift to either a period of consolidation (Steady State) or planned "big company" growth (Linear); a possible retrenchment of the Linear to Steady State, given government blocking or saturation of market; and finally, a phase emphasizing creative new products or services and moving to employee development for its own sake. This last phase may be heavily influenced by increasing lack of growth and/or changing societal values.

If organizations do develop in this fashion and individuals develop in a similar way, very interesting policy solutions emerge that would be quite beyond the scope of this chapter to develop.

What all of this does suggest is that Van Maanen and Schein (1977) and Hall (1976) are on target center when they claim that managers in and out of personnel departments must become experts on career management. I hope that the maps outlined in this chapter will be an aid in this direction.

SOCIETAL TRENDS IN CAREER CONCEPTS

Previously (Driver, 1977c) I noted a possible trend in human history from fairly simple hunter-gatherers societies (largely Transitory) to more settled agricultural villages (Steady State) to Linear imperialistic and intellectually expansive cities (Athens, Greece) to the possible emergence of Spiral patterns in the European Renaissance (such as Da Vinci).

It is clear that many societies today remain heavily Steady State or Linear. Transitory patterns may remain endemic in certain social strata (Piore, 1970). The issue at hand is whether American society at some or all levels is exhibiting a trend in its prevailing career concept.

The issue is very complex, and I propose only a sketch of an approach in this chapter. An obvious start is the "frontier" concept. It has dominated general American thought, and some believe it still does. In my view, the frontiersman is the quintessential Transitory— one thinks of "Jeremiah Johnson" or the real-life mountain men, of Natty Bumpo in the *Last of the Mohicans,* of Captain John Smith—the first to propose the New England colony—who always kept "moving on."

Probably the earliest English settlers in Jamestown were largely Elizabethan Transitories. Much of the population of early New England also had a Transitory component, which was in sharp conflict with the Pilgrim and Puritan groups with whom they mingled and fought (see in particular Caffrey, 1975). The early Puritan farmers and artisans were largely Steady State types who gradually pushed the Transitory frontiersmen further and further West.

However, as the seventeenth century progressed, a new Linear element entered New England. The English mercantilists were nothing if not embodiments of the Linear concept. As they flooded New England towns during the late seventeenth and the eighteenth century, their drive for achievement gradually gave them control in their towns over the Steady State people scattered over villages and farms[33] (see Bailyn, 1955).

In the South, the plantation system seemed to be a bastion of the Steady State concept. But in the North, mercantilism gave way to the even more energetic and Linear industrial system (see Cochran and Miller, 1961). In the Civil War, the Southern Steady State can be said to have lost to a very Linear North. The high peak of need for achievement (a very Linear motive) is found in the period 1870-1910 (McClelland, 1961). While I believe the power groups increasingly became Linear, small business and agriculture may have stayed largely Steady State, with the cowboy West being the last frontier of the Transitory.

In the early part of the present century, the frontier closed. One view is that the Transitory concept then shifted to entrepreneurial, financial speculation (which may have been a factor in the 1929 crash). While the Linear mind continued to dominate, in the early 20th century, some elements of a more people-centered, creative, Spiral pattern did seem to emerge in several places. Weinstein (1968) cites a big-business-dominated National Civic Federation as a major source of the reforms in pure Linear business introduced under Teddy Roosevelt, Wilson, and even FDR. John Dewey's new views on education, emerging during the 1920s, seem to have a certain Spiral quality that has deeply penetrated American education.

Obviously, the Great Depression led to a new wave of Transitory wanderers. Fear of anarchy and socialism seems to be behind the relatively strong Spiral-type changes introduced into government by FDR. But Linear thought remained most potent and was, I believe, strongly reinforced by the Second World War.

The 1950s represent a rather complex pattern, and here I can begin to connect with some theory cited previously. It seems that models reviewed in earlier sections (for example, Super, 1957; Miller and Form, 1956) both stress a "settling down", a Steady State pattern. I believe that, possibly in reaction to the war, America did move strongly to a Steady State ideology for a period in the early 1950s. However, a strongly Linear elite still persisted in power, as

---

[33]The connection of this rivalry with the Salem witch trials is fascinatingly discussed in Boyer and Nissenbaum, 1974.

Galbraith (1967) has described and Pellegrin and Coates (1956) confirm.

The Soviet launch of Sputnik seems to have set back the Steady State personified by Eisenhower. The Linear concept seems to have emerged as at least as strong. I believe that both institutional changes and survey data (as in Yankelovitch, 1972) point to a peak interest in both achievement (Linear) and security needs (Steady State) in 1960. The Linear ideal of achievement was personified in John Kennedy's determination to land an American safely on the moon.

However, during the 1940s and 1950s, a curious countercurrent seems to have occurred. Stemming from the liberal Dewey philosophy, a more person-centered, creativity-oriented education was spreading. The first wave of people brought up entirely in this fashion probably hit America in the early 1960s—and "hit" is a painfully apt word, since the impact of the youth on a largely Linear and secondarily Steady State society has been explosive.

This education seems to favor either a Transitory or a Spiral pattern. Its youthful products stress freedom and important, meaningful work (see Yankelovitch data on 1970 youth). Hall (1971) finds a strong stress on openness, personal fulfillment, the ultimate value of work, and shared authority. O'Toole et al. (1973) reach similar conclusions, based on a wide variety of sources. Career models of the early and mid-1960s now began to focus on Spiral concepts and to accord the Transitory concept a less negative tone (see Nosow and Form, 1962; Ginzberg and Yohalem, 1966; Erikson, 1968).

Can self-employment absorb this horde of Transitory or Spiral youth? Evidence is that self-employment is declining in all fields (see O'Toole et al., 1973; Wirtz, 1975). Therefore, unless government intervenes to refurbish self-employment, the problems of today's new Career Concepts must largely be solved within public and private organizations (which in my view are largely Linear or Steady State in culture.)

Is there evidence that organizations can "train" out the Spiral patterns? Most data agree that the change is here to stay. Transitories can be trained into Steady States or Linears, but Spiral Career Concept people probably cannot. After Spiral changes are made to work, it seems very hard to return to Linear or Steady State conditions.

Is it possible that the massacre at Kent State, the view of corruption epitomized by Watergate, and the recent recession with unemployment have shifted youth back to Linear or Steady State views? It is true that career theorists from 1968 to 1970 (such as Tavsky, Roth, Hall, and Nougaim) seem to downgrade Transitory and even Spiral concepts and that they restress the Steady State concept.[34] However, theorists from 1972 on (for instance, Gould, Levinson, Hall, Thompson and Dalton, Van Maanen and Schein) have reemphasized the growth of the Spiral concept and the necessity of the Transitory concept. We are just completing a study of educational impact conducted in 1976 in Southern California. We can find no evidence of a "return" to Linear/Steady State concepts of any sort. The college graduate still seems Transitory or Spiral in orientation.

The difference now, I believe, is that young people are coming into organizations not to destroy but to try to either:

1. Make enough money to have a Transitory/Spiral life on the side or "after I'm 30," or

2. Work with the organization to make the career management changes I believe most non-Spiral organizations will want to make in order to retain their "best" people and produce optimal output for all concerned.

The challenge these trends raise for managers can, I hope, be better met by the use and amplification of career theories by organizations and all concerned. It is my hope that the Career Concept model developed here will encourage or provoke an increasing consciousness of the critical necessity for better methods, concepts, and data in this crucial area.

REFERENCES

Alawi, H., "Cognitive, Task, and Organizational Complexities in Relation to Information Processing Behavior of Business Managers," D.B.A. dissertation, GSBA, USC, 1973.

Bailyn, B., *The New England Merchants in the Seventeenth Century*. New York: Harper & Row, 1955.

[34]Just why this temporary regression in 1968-1970 occurred is unclear. It could be mere coincidence, or it could suggest that a return to non-Spiral or anti-Transitory or even anti-Linear concepts is quite possible.

Bailyn, L., "Career and Family Orientation of Husbands and Wives in Relation to Marital Happiness," *Human Relations,* 23 (1970), 97-113.

Barton, I., R.B. Cattell, and G. Vaughn, "Changes in Personality as a Function of College Attendance or Work Experience," *Journal of Counseling Psychology,* 20 (1973), 162-65.

Bolles, R., *What Color Is Your Parachute?* Berkeley, Calif: Ten Speed Press, 1977.

Boulgarides, J., "Decision Style, Values, and Biographical Factors in Relation to Satisfaction and Performance of Supervisors in a Government Agency," D.B.A. dissertation, GSBA, USC, 1973.

Boulgarides, J., and M. Driver, "A Decision Style Contingency Model of Managerial Satisfaction and Productivity: I. First Line Supervisors in a Government Bureaucracy," unpublished manuscript, Dept. of Management, USC, 1977.

Boyer, P., and S. Nissenbaum, *Salem Possessed.* Cambridge, Mass.: Harvard University Press, 1974.

Brousseau, K., "Effects of Job Experience on Personality," Technical Report No. 14, School of Organization and Management, Yale University, 1977.

Bryson, J., and M. Driver, "Cognitive Complexity, Introversion, and Preference for Complexity," *Journal of Personality and Social Psychology,* 23 (1972), 320-27.

Byham, N.C., "Assessment Centers for Spotting Future Managers," *Harvard Business Review,* 48 (1970), 150-67.

Caffrey, K., *The Mayflower.* New York: Stein & Day, 1975.

Campbell, D., "The 1966 Revision of the Strong Vocational Interest Blank," *Personnel and Guidance Journal,* 44 (1966a), 744-49.

————,"The Stability of Vocational Interests within Occupations over Long Time Spans," *Personnel and Guidance Journal,* 44 (1966b), 1012-1019.

Campbell, J., *The Hero with the Thousand Faces.* New York: Meridian, 1956.

Campbell, J., M. Dunnette, E. Lawler, and K. Weick, *Managerial Behavior, Performance and Effectiveness.* New York: McGraw-Hill, 1970.

Carson, J., and G. Steiner, *Measuring Business's Social Performance: The Corporate Social Audit.* New York: Committee for Economic Development, 1974.

Census of Population, 1970, Volume PC2IE, "Occupation and Residence in 1965."

Chetwynd, T., *How to Interpret Your Own Dreams,* New York: Dell, 1972.

Cochran, T., and W. Miller, *The Age of Enterprise.* New York: Harper & Row, 1961.

Dessler, G., *Organization and Management.* Englewood Cliffs, N.J.: Prentice-Hall, 1976.

Donahue, R.J., "Flexible Time Systems: Flex Time Systems in New York," *Public Personnel Management,* 4 (1975), 212-15.

Dressel, P., and L. Lehman, "The Impact of Higher Education on Student Attitudes, Values, and Critical Thinking Abilities," in O. Milton and E. Shoben, Jr., eds., *Learning and the Professions,* pp. 105-14. Athens: Ohio University Press, 1968.

Driver, M., "The Relationship between Abstractness of Conceptual Functioning and Group Performance in a Complex Decision Making Environment," M.S. thesis, Dept. of Psychology, Princeton University, 1960.

————, "Conceptual Structure and Group Processes in an Inter-Nation Simulation: Part One: The Perception of Simulated Nations," Educational Testing Service Research Bulletin RB 62-75, 1962.

————, "The Career Revolution in Aerospace Engineers," paper given at Annual Meeting, Society of Allied Weight Engineers, Philadelphia, May 1976a.

————, *Self Renewal Questionnaire,* Dept. of Management, USC, 1976b.

————, "Individual Differences as Determinants of Aggression in the Inter-Nation Simulation" (1965), in M. Hermann, ed., *A Psychological Examination of Political Leaders.* New York: Free Press, 1977a.

————, "The Loss of Expertise in the Personnel Field—and a Possible Corrective," paper given at meeting of Federal Personnel Council, 1977b.

————, "Career Concepts—A New Approach to Career Research," in J. Paap, ed., *New Dimensions in Human Resource Management.* London: Prentice-Hall International, in press, 1977c.

————, *The Multiple Achievement Pattern Inventory, Dept. of Management,* USC, 1977d.

————, "A Study of Education and Work." Technical Report, Dept. of Management, USC, 1977e.

Driver, M., and T. Mock, "Information Processing, Decision Style Theory and Accounting Information Systems," *Accounting Review,* 50 (1975a), 490-508.

————, "Some Experimental Results in MIS, Human Information Processing and Tailored Information Systems," paper given at Annual Meeting of ORSA/TIMS, Las Vegas, 1975b.

Driver, M., and S. Streufert, "Integrative Complexity: An Approach to Individuals and Groups as Information Processing Systems," *Administrative Science Quarterly,* 14 (1969), 272-85.

Dunnette, M., R. Arvey, and P. Banas, "Why Do They Leave?" *Personnel,* May-June 1973, 25-29.

Erikson, E., *Childhood and Society.* New York: Norton, 1963.

_____,*Identity, Youth and Crisis.* New York: Norton, 1968.

Feldman, K., and T. Newcomb, *The Impact of College on Students.* San Francisco: Jossey Bass, 1969.

Fiedler, F., *Leadership.* New York: General Learning Press, 1971.

Flanagan, J.C., D. Tiedeman, M. Willis, and D. McLaughlin, *The Career Data Book: Results from Project Talent: Five Year Follow-Up Study.* Palo Alto: Project TALENT Office, American Institute for Research, 1973.

Galbraith, J., *The New Industrial State.* New York: Signet, 1967.

Gallagher, J., "Productive Thinking," in M. Hoffman and L. Hoffman, eds., *Child Development Research,* Russell Sage Foundation, 1964.

Gardner, J., *Self Renewal: The Individual and the Innovative Society.* New York: Harper & Row, 1965.

Ghiselli, E., *The Validity of Occupational Ability Tests.* New York: Wiley, 1966.

Ginzberg, E., and A. Yohalem, *Educated American Women: Self Portraits.* New York: Columbia University Press, 1966.

Goldstein, H., and W. Delaney, *The Need for Job Related Training Throughout Adult Life.* Washington, D.C.: The National Manpower Institute, 1974.

Golembiewski, R., "Flexitime and Some of Its Consequences: Some Modest Structural Interventions," in *The New Technology in Organizational Development.* New Orleans: NIL Institute, 1974.

Gordon, W., *Synectics.* New York: Macmillan, 1961.

Gough, H., "Graduation from High School as Predicted from the California Psychological Inventory," *Psychology in the Schools,* 3 (1966), 208-16.

_____,"Personality and Personality Assessment," in M. Dunnette, ed., *Handbook of Industrial and Organizational Psychology.* Chicago: Rand McNally, 1976.

Gould, R., "The Phases of Adult Life: a Study in Developmental Psychology," *The American Journal of Psychiatry,* 129 (1972), No. 5.

Grant, D.L., W. Katkovsky, and D. Bray, "Contributions of Projective Techniques to Assessment of Management Potential," *Journal of Applied Psychology,* 51 (1967), 226-32.

Graves, P., "Successful Managers and Organizational Mugging," paper given at Western Academy of Management Meeting, Sun Valley, Idaho, 1977.

Greiner, L., "Patterns of Organizational Change," *Harvard Business Review,* May-June 1967.

Grimsley, G., and H. Jarrett, "The Relationship of Past Managerial Achievement to Test Measures Obtained in the Employment Situation: Methodology and Results II," *Personnel Psychology,* 28 (1975), 215-31.

Hackman, J., and J. Suttle, *Improving Life at Work.* Santa Monica, Calif.: Good-year, 1977.

Hall, D., *Careers in Organizations.* Pacific Palisades, Calif: Goodyear, 1976.

_____,"Potential for Career Growth," *Personnel Administration,* 34 (1971), 18-30.

Hall, D., and K. Nougaim, "An Examination of Maslow's Need Hierarchy in an Occupational Setting," *Organizational Behavior and Human Performance,* 3 (1968), 12-35.

Harmon, S., "Responsibility of Businessmen," paper commissioned by Special Task Force on Work in America, Washington, D.C., 1973.

Hogan, R., C. DeSoto, and C. Solano, "Traits, Tests, and Personality Research," *American Psychologist,* 32 (1977), 255-64.

Holland, J.L., *The Psychology of Vocational Choice.* Waltham, Mass.: Blaesdell, 1966.

_____,"A Theory of Vocational Choice," *Journal of Counseling Psychology,* 6 (1959), 35-45.

Jacobson, G., "An Examination of Possible Changes in Authoritarianism, Values, and Cognitive Complexity with Their Implications for Business," D.B.A. dissertation, GSBA, USC, 1974.

Jenkins, D., *Job Power.* Baltimore: Penguin, 1973.

Jung, C.G., *The Archetypes and the Collective Unconscious.* Princeton, N.J.: Princeton University Press, 1959.

_____,"The Development of the Personality" (1934), in *The Development of the Personality.* Princeton, N.J.: Princeton University Press, 1954.

_____,"On the Psychology of the Trickster Figure" (1954), in, *The Archetypes and the Collective Unconscious,* pp. 255-74. Princeton, N.J.: Princeton University Press, 1959.

_____,"The Phenomenology of the Spirit in Fairytales" (1945), in *The Archetypes and the Collective Unconscious,* pp. 207-54. Princeton, N.J.: Princeton University Press, 1959.

_____,"The Psychology of the Child Archetype" (1940), in *The Archetypes and the Collective Unconscious,* pp. 151-79. Princeton, N.J.: Princeton University Press, 1959.

Kagan, J., and M. Freeman, "Relations of Childhood Intelligence, Maternal Behaviors, and Social Class to Behavior during Adolescence," *Child Development,* 34 (1963), 899-911.

Kepner, C., and B. Tregoe, *The Rational Manager.* New York: McGraw-Hill, 1965.

Kornhauser, W., "Professional Incentives in Industry," in B. Glaser, ed., *Organizational Careers: A Sourcebook for Theory*, pp. 114-23. Chicago: Aldine, 1968.

Kotter, J., V. Faux, and C. McArthur, *Self Assessment and Career Development.* Englewood Cliffs, N.J.: Prentice-Hall, 1977.

Lawrence, P., and J. Lorsch, *Organization and Environment.* Homewood, Ill.: Irwin, 1969.

Leach, P., "A Critical Study of the Literature Concerning Rigidity," *British Journal of Social and Clinical Psychology,* 6 (1967), 11-22.

Levinson, D., "The Mid-Life Transition: A Period in Adult Psychosocial Development," *Psychiatry,* May 1977.

Levinson, D., C. Darrow, E. Klein, M. Levinson, and B. McKee, "Periods in Adult Development in Men: Age 18 to 45," *Counseling Psychologist,* 6 (1976), 21-25.

Lilly, J., *The Center of the Cyclone.* New York: Bantam, 1972

Likert, R., *The Human Organization.* New York: McGraw-Hill, 1961.

_____,*New Patterns of Management.* New York: McGraw-Hill, 1961.

McClelland, D., *The Achieving Society.* Princeton, N.J.: Van Nostrand, 1961.

McClelland, D., and D. Winter, *Motivating Economic Achievement.* New York: Free Press, 1969.

McLaughlin, D., and D. Tiedeman, "Eleven Year Career Stability and Change as Reflected in Project Talent Data through the Flanagan, Holland, and Roe Occupational Classification Systems," *Journal of Vocational Behavior,* 5 (1974), 177-96.

McWhinney, W., "Phenomenarchy: A Suggestion for Social Design," *The Journal of Applied Behavioral Science,* 9 (1973), 163-80.

Maslow, A., *Toward a Psychology of Being.* Princeton, N.J.: Van Nostrand, 1962.

Meade, M., *Cooperation and Competition among Primitive Peoples.* New York: McGraw-Hill, 1937.

Miller, D., and W. Form, *Industrial Sociology.* New York: Harper & Row, 1956.

Morse, J., "Organizational Characteristics and Individual Motivation," in J. Lorsch and P. Lawrence, eds., *Studies in Organizational Design.* Homewood, Ill.: Irwin, 1970.

Nosow, S., and W. Form, eds., *Work, Man, and Society.* New York: Basic Books, 1962.

O'Toole, J., E. Hansat, W. Herman, N. Herrick, E. Liebow, B. Lusignan, H. Richman, H. Sheppard, B. Stephansky, and J. Wright, *Work in America.* Cambridge, Mass.: M.I.T. Press, 1973.

Owens, W.A., "Age and Mental Abilities: A Second Adult Follow Up," *Journal of Educational Psychology,* 57 (1966), 311-25.

Pellegrin, R., and C. Coates, "Executives and Supervisors: Contrasts, Definitions of Career Success," *Administrative Science Quarterly,* 1 (1956), 506-17.

Piore, M., "Jobs and Training," in S. Beer and R. Barringer, eds., *The State and the Poor.* Cambridge, Mass.: Winthrop, 1970.

Porter, L., E. Lawler, and J. Hackman, *Behavior in Organizations.* New York: McGraw-Hill, 1975.

Prince, Bruce, "Adult Life States and the Dalton-Thompson Career Stages Model," unpublished manuscript, Department of Management, USC, 1977.

Rapoport, R., and R. Rapoport, *Dual Career Families.* Baltimore: Penguin, 1971.

Rapoport, R., *Mid-Career Development Research—Perspectives on a Developmental Community for Administrators.* New York: Tavistock Publications, 1970.

Raynolds, P., "Cognitive Style, Self Concept, and Effective Creativity Training," paper given at American Psychological Association Meeting, Honolulu, Hawaii, Sept. 7, 1972.

Reif, W., and F. Luthans, "Does Job Enrichment Really Pay Off?" *California Management Review,* Fall 1972, pp. 30-37.

Richards, J., J. Holland and S. Lutz, "Prediction of Student Accomplishment in College," *Journal of Educational Psychology,* 58 (1967), 343-55.

Roe, A., *The Psychology of Occupations.* New York: Wiley, 1956.

Roth, J., "The Study of Career Timetables," in B. Glaser, ed., *Organizational Careers: A Sourcebook for Theory,* pp. 35-49. Chicago: Aldine, 1968.

Schein, E., "Career Anchors and Career Paths: A Panel Study of Management School Graduates," in J. Van Maanen, ed., *Organizational Careers: Some New Perspectives.* London: Wiley-Inter-Science, 1977.

_____ ,"The General Manager: a Profile," lecture given to Eastern Academy of Management, May 5, 1972, Boston, Mass.

_____ ,*The Individual, the Organization and the Career.* Reading, Mass.: Addison-Wesley, 1968.

_____ ,"The Individual, the Organization and the Career: A Conceptual Scheme," *Journal of Applied Behavioral Science,* 7 (1971), 401-26.

Schroder, H., M. Driver, and S. Streufert, *Human Information Processing.* New York: Holt, Rinehart & Winston, 1967.

Seashore, S., and T. Taber, "Job Satisfaction Indicators and Their Correlates," in A. Biderman and T. Drury, eds., *Measuring Work Quality for Social Reporting.* New York: Wiley, 1976.

Sheppard, H., and N. Herrick, *Where Have All the Robots Gone?* New York: Free Press, 1972.

Streufert, S., "Increasing Failure and Response Rate in Complex Decision Making," *Journal of Experimental Social Psychology,* 5 (1969), 310-23.

Streufert, S., and S. Streufert, "Effects of Conceptual Structure, Failure and Success on Attribution of Causality and Interpersonal Attitude," *Journal of Personality and Social Psychology,* 11 (1969), 138-47.

Streufert, S., P. Suedfeld, and M. Driver, "Conceptual Structure, Information Search and Information Utilization," *Journal of Personality and Social Psychology,* 2 (1965), 736-40.

Strong, E., *Vocational Interests of Men and Women.* Stanford, Calif.: Stanford University Press, 1943.

Super, D., *The Psychology of Careers.* New York: Harper & Row, 1957.

Tarnowiewski, D., *The Changing Success Ethic.* New York: AMACON, 1973.

Tavsky, C., *Work Organizations—Major Theoretical Perspectives.* Itasca, Ill.: F.E. Peacock Publishing, 1970.

Thompson, P., and G. Dalton, "Are R&D Organizations Obsolete?" *Harvard Business Review,* Nov.-Dec. 1976, pp. 105-16.

Trent, J., and L. Medsker, *Beyond High School.* San Francisco: Jossey Bass, 1968.

Tseng, M., "Comparisons of Selected Familial Personality and Vocational Variables of High School Students and Dropouts," *Journal of Educational Research,* 65 (1972), 462-65.

Van Maanen, J., *Experiencing Organizations: Notes on the Structure and Meaning of Organizational Socialization.* Cambridge, Mass.: M.I.T. Press, 1975.

Van Maanen, J., and E. Schein, "Career Development", in J. Hackman and J. Suttle, eds., *Improving Life at Work,* pp. 30-95. Santa Monica, Calif.: Goodyear, 1977.

Van Maanen, J., E. Schein, and L. Bailyn, "The Shape of Things to Come: A New Look at Organizational Careers," in J. Hackman, E. Lawler, and L. Porter, *Perspectives on Behavior in Organizations.* New York: McGraw-Hill, 1977.

Vinacke, W.E., *The Psychology of Thinking.* New York: McGraw-Hill, 1974.

Wainer, H., and I. Rabin, "Motivation of Research and Development Entrepreneurs: Determinants of Company Success," *Journal of Applied Psychology,* 53 (1969), 178-84.

Walton, R., "The Diffusion of New Work Structures: Explaining Why Success Didn't Take," *Organizational Dynamics,* 1975, pp. 3-22.

_____,"Innovative Restructuring of Work," in J. Rosnow, ed., *The Worker and the Job: Coping with Change.* Englewood Cliffs, N.J.: Prentice-Hall, 1974.

_____,"Work Place Alienation and the Need for Major Innovation," paper commissioned by Special Task Force on Work in America, Harvard University, 1973.

Warr, P. (Ed.), *Thought and Personality.* Baltimore: Penguin, 1970.

Waters, L., D. Roach, and N. Batlis, "Organizational Climate Dimensions and Job Related Attitudes," *Personnel Psychology,* 27 (1974), 465-76.

Weinstein, J., *The Corporate Ideal in the Liberal State: 1900-1918.* Boston: Beacon, 1968.

Whitmont, E., *The Symbolic Quest.* New York: Putnam, 1969.

Wilensky, H., "Work as a Social Problem," in H. Bedser, ed., *Social Problems: A Modern Approach.* New York: Wiley, 1966.

Wirtz, W., *The Boundless Resource.* Washington, D.C.: New Republic Book Co., 1975.

Yankelovitch, D., *The Changing Values on Campus.* New York: Pocket, 1972.

CHAPTER 6

Decision-Making Styles: A New Approach to Management Decision Making

Michael J. Driver
Alan J. Rowe

INTRODUCTION

Decision making has been undoubtedly one of the most widely discussed topics in the field of management, primarily because it is one of the most crucial attributes of successful management. Decision making is even considered synonymous with management, as defined by experts such as Simon (1957). Thus, one definition of a management position is its unique capacity to make decisions. In this view, the more decision making one does, the more one is a manager. However, management is not universally effective, since not all decision making is equally effective. For purposes of this chapter, effectiveness is defined as matching the potential capacity of the organization to meet environmental demands. Potential capacity, in turn, refers to the optimal match of individual decision styles, task demands and organizational climate. This is in contrast to the use of short run "results" as a measure of effectiveness.

Our purpose is to demonstrate that a manager's decision style (i.e., information processing habits) by itself does not provide for effective performance, but that the complex interaction of decision style with social, task and environmental factors determines the outcome in any given situation. These relationships will be presented in the framework of situational forces and the decision process. Because of the sheer magnitude of the problem and the importance of achieving meaningful results, an understanding of the new concepts of decision style and the decision-making process can be construed as having a significant role in achieving organizational effectiveness.

APPROACHES THAT HAVE BEEN TAKEN TO DECISION MAKING

Although decision making is central to effective managerial performance, little is known about the actual process. Past approaches tended to focus on normative bases that defined what was considered the one best way in which to make decisions. These typified what has been termed the "principles" of management. Another approach was taken by Drucker, who examined the experiences of many companies and then reported them in an anecdotal fashion. However, the result was still "here is the way to do it." Although this approach has proved useful for the practicing manager because it provided guidelines, it nonetheless did not provide the fundamental basis for understanding real-life decision making.

Another approach widely considered has been the use of quantitative methods and computer applications. These have been applied to the development of optimal decision strategies. When examined closely, these approaches use mathematical models which are primarily applicable to structured situations.

We consider that decision problems can be looked at as:

1. Deterministic or structured
2. Stochastic or probabilistic
3. Complex systems or organizational
4. Ill-structured or behavioral

It is probable that quantitative approaches are most applicable to the first two categories and have limited value in the second two. Although there is increasing usage of quantitative methods, including simulation and heuristics, they have limited applicability in the decision-making process carried out by managers.

Normative or "how to do it" approaches, although well intentioned, often lead to less than optimal performance, because they tend to focus on a limited aspect of the decision-making process and ignore individual differences.

We will attempt, therefore, in contrast to the generally used "normative" to focus on a *Descriptive-Differential* approach which matches the individual decision style, task demands and social factors with the decision process employed and then determines the fit to environmental demands. The decision styles relate to the individual's cognitive-information processing and provide a differential basis for understanding managers. The decision phase model (shown in Figure 6-1) defines in a descriptive mode the process in which individuals

FIGURE 6-1   Decision Process

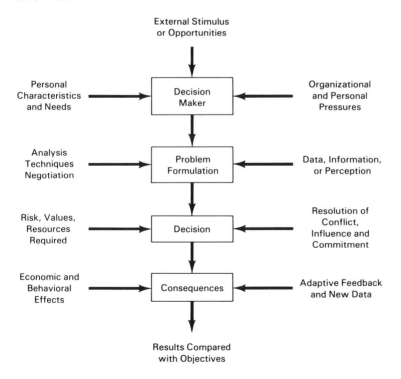

react to a stimulus and the steps taken to obtain results. Environmental demands refer to changing forces in one's socio-economic milieu as well as to organizational cultural factors. Using the *Descriptive-Differential* approach we propose to examine the following questions:

1. How does a manager know when a good decision has been made?
2. How are good decision makers selected?
3. What is the relation between the decision maker and the roles or jobs occupied?
4. How can really useful information systems, particularly computer applications, be developed?
5. How much sharing of decision making with others is appropriate?
6. How can effective organization design be utilized to facilitate decision making and achieve the results desired by management?

Answers to these questions will be based on:

1. A *Descriptive* "decision process" approach using general decision process models that represent the causal effects in a given situation. The predictive approach depends on an understanding of the decision process and the fundamental behavior, drives, and motives of the individual. Contingency theory provides the basis for identifying the factors in a given situation that contribute to the understanding of decision making.
2. A *Differential* approach to decision making that recognizes the differences that exist among individuals and groups. The latter approach will be most useful in the application of decision styles.

The Descriptive-Differential approach allows accurate classification of different types of decision processes, decision makers, tasks, information systems, organizations and environments. It is our basic premise that when these six factors are matched, effectiveness in organizations will be optimized.

THE DECISION PROCESS AND FOUR FORCE MODEL

To illustrate the Descriptive-Differential approach we will elaborate two models: a descriptive decision process model and a "four force" model postulating four factors which affect the decision process.

If one takes a systems view of the factors involved in a given problem, it becomes obvious that decision making is far more than simply making a choice from among alternatives. A number of models have been developed that describe the process by which decisions are, in fact, made and carried out. Perhaps the most elaborate was one developed by Gore (1964), in which he defined how decisions were carried out in the Kansas City fire department. Although a minute, detailed description of the process, such as developed by Gore, is useful for instructional purposes, it is cumbersome to use in carrying out decisions in practice. A simpler four-phase model developed by Rowe (1974) is shown in Figure 6-1.

It is important to recognize that a decision process starts with a stimulus or a need. This need, when analyzed and evaluated becomes the basis for response and the development of a strategy by which a decision is carried out. The decision choice then becomes a means by which the manager uses a political process or conflict resolution while taking into account risks and values in order to arrive at an "acceptable" alternative. Often, the decision has to be modified to match the goals and needs of the participants. Once a decision is made, the next phase is a plan of action and a control system that, in effect, assures the implementation of the decision. During this latter process, generally only direct consequences are considered in terms of impact. However, as is true with most decision processes, there are both indirect and interactive time effects that influence the final outcome of the decision. It is this complex interweaving of both the technical and behavioral considerations that leads to the final results desired by management.

As pointed out in Patz and Rowe (1977), a decision process also involves a political and exchange process. People are not generally aware of the conditions that determine their actions. A decision process involves skills of political activity and an exchange process that allows negotiation. Thus, if a person is not aware of the existence of a given political situation, he may find that his actions do not necessarily conform to what is acceptable, rational behavior.

Each phase of the decision process model represents an important managerial function. Starting with the initial sensing of the problem, the manager responds to some stimulus and starts gathering data in order to correctly formulate the problem. Often, this involves dealing with people, and includes technical analysis or application of optimization methods. The third phase, which is called the decision choice, represents that portion of the process dealing with finding acceptable alternatives that will, in fact, be carried out in an effective manner. Finally, there is implementation, which includes planning, organizing, controlling, and assuring that plans meet the desired results. It is obvious that in many respects when viewed as a process, decision making closely resembles the managerial function, which is why it is often considered synonymous with management.

The question that is sometimes raised, however, is, Why not separate out "choice" as truly representing decision making and have the remainder of the process concerned primarily with managerial functions? It is our contention that this is not feasible. For an individual to make a choice, there must be the need to analyze the alternatives as well as the convincing of and negotiating with constituents to gain acceptance of alternatives. Too often, so-called optimal decisions are not implemented simply because they do not take into account political and behavioral considerations that are required to make the decisions work.

The decision process outlined above is not uniformly the same across people, organizations or situations. A model describing four basic forces that influence the decision process, developed by Rowe (1974), is shown in Figure 6-2.

FIGURE 6-2   Four Force Diagram

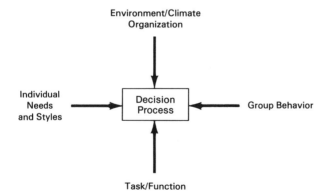

This model describes the four basic factors that influence the decision process in a given situation. By examining each of the four factors, the decisions that are made and resultant behavior can be better understood. It is from this perspective that we shall attempt to answer the questions previously posed.

Starting with the environmental factors at the top of the diagram, this represents the organizational forces which shape the decisions and affect the outcomes. This force involves both demands of the environment on the organization, e.g., time pressure exerted by competitors, as well as the decision climate of the organization—often set by the style of key leaders.

On the right hand side of the diagram is peer group pressure. All people interact with others in the organization and are thus subject to group pressure. This suggests that one of the roles of a group, whether it is a formal committee, informal unit, or any combination of individuals, is that it has a significant influence on the decision process. Here again, our concern is with trying to determine what kind of interpersonal interaction is important and how involving others in the sharing of decisions can improve the effectiveness of decision making.

The task or technical aspects of a situation are shown at the bottom of the diagram. This factor concerns the requirements of the task—knowing how they impinge on the decision maker and thus relate to the decision process. For example, when an individual is introduced into a new decision-making situation, can job analysis be used in conjunction with the decision style approach to shed new light on how to best match individuals to jobs? Or, if necessary, when should jobs be redesigned in order to improve decision making, given the style and characteristics of the people involved?

The fourth factor, shown on the left hand side of the diagram, is perhaps the one that is most relevant in terms of our concern with decision style. It is this factor that permits us to examine powerful developments in the understanding of individual behavior. Using decision style analysis as a new tool, we are in a better position to provide answers to such questions as: How do we find a good decision maker? How should the decision maker improve the manner in which decisions are made? and so one. It is by understanding the thinking habits, perceptions, needs, drives, motives, aspirations, and anxieties that influence the decision maker that we can better understand why decisions are made and carried out the way they are.

Each of the four forces leads to decision related skills or motives in the individual. For example, a skill related to the environmental force is considered situational sensitivity, or political astuteness. A skill relating to peer-group pressures is interpersonal competence. A skill relating to task requirements is the technical competence of the individual. And lastly, individual personality focuses on motives as well as decision styles as they tie to the decision process.

Thus, the combination of the Descriptive and the Differential approach appears to offer potentially powerful tools in approaching the problems confronting the decision makers who are attempting to achieve more effective organizational performance. The key questions on decision making presented on page 144, when linked to decision styles, can provide decision makers with an effective tool for dealing with key managerial issues.

DECISION STYLES

From the above four force discussions we see that individual differences can mediate the fit between decision process and major forces impacting decision quality. Perhaps the clearest illustration of this is seen in the individual factor. While a great array of personality variables affect decision making, decision style seems to emerge as a very central and inclusive model for relating personality to decision process. We believe that via decision style analysis a better understanding of all factors in the decision effectiveness equation can be obtained. Further we believe that decision style can act as an integrative surrogate for a wide range of complex human motives and skills; therefore we will concentrate on decision style as the integrative individual difference variable in our approach.

What is meant by decision style? It can be thought about from two perspectives: (1) the manner in which the decision maker reacts to a given situation, or (2) the manner of interaction with other people. The term *style,* as used here, has been derived from the cognitive portion of psychology. Following the groundbreaking work of Freud (1933, 1947, 1953) on instincts in man, interest began to develop in thinking processes both by followers of Freud (such as Hartmann, 1939) and by others—Lewin (1936), Piaget (1936), Goldstein and Scheerer (1941), and Klein (1949, 1951). A quiet revolution occurred in the early 1950s and 1960s among American psychologists (Adorno et al., 1950; Gardner, 1935; Kelley, 1955). They attacked Freud's overemphasis on the unconscious emotions and drives (such as sex). They developed an approach that dealt with cognitive or ego aspects of psychology. The concern of the cognitive psychologist has been mainly with conscious thought processes, including perception and memories. In each of these cognitive domains, investigators noticed consistent differences in ways of individual thinking, remembering, or perceiving. These learned cognitive habits gained the name "cognitive styles." Measures were developed to assess these styles based on considerable experimental research in laboratory settings (see Warr, 1970).

Among the many styles analyzed, one focus was on "information processing." This work grew out of research on authoritarianism (Adorno, et al., 1950) and dogmatism (Rokeach, 1960). In these early studies, it was found that certain people tended to think in a more simplistic or dogmatic, closed fashion than others. This work closely linked ideology and cognitive styles, which have subsequently been found to be mainly independent factors; that is, not all conservative thought is also simplistic.

Harvey, Hunt, and Schroder (1961) began to focus more on a "pure style," based on their idea of "conceptual systems" of increasing complexity and flexibility of organization. This model is still being fruitfully explored by Harvey (Harvey and Schroder, 1963; Harvey and Ware, 1967; Harvey, 1967).

A still more purely cognitive model was developed by Schroder, Driver, and Streufert (1967) and Driver and Streufert (1969). This model suggested that environmental pressures (or load) systematically affected the complexity of information processing in persons and groups in an inverted-U-shaped function (see Figure 6-3). Each individual or group can be considered to have a unique and consistent curvilinear information use pattern, such as those designated by curves A and B in Figure 6-3. It is significant to note that although A and B both show maximum information use at moderate

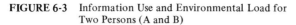

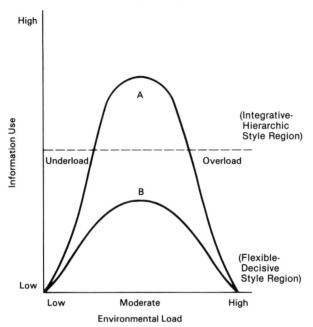

environmental load,[1] they both show decline in overload or under-load; yet A remains consistently the higher data user.

This model finds information use empirically unrelated to more conventional IQ or aptitude measures. Complexity of information use also differs logically from IQ. Whereas IQ refers to maximum capacity to handle information and is seen as largely innate information use, style is seen as one's normal operating pattern vis-à-vis information and is assumed to be largely a learned habit.

More recently, Driver and Streufert (1969) and Driver and Mock (1975, a and b) used this information processing model as the basis for developing "decision style" theory. The early form of this theory suggested the existence of two high information using

---

[1]Load is defined as the sum of effects of three environmental factors: information complexity, noxity (i.e., negative input level such as failure, threat), and eucity (i.e., positive input level such as reward, praise).

styles—one loose and fluid, the other quite structured. The present model was first articulated by Driver and Lintott (1972) and tested in laboratory and field settings (Alawi, 1973; Boulgarides, 1973; Testerman, 1976; Athey, 1976; Hager, 1977).

It states that decision making differs among people in two key dimensions: (1) complexity or amount of information used, and (2) focus or number of alternatives generated from the information. These two dimensions generate a fourfold table (Table 6-1) showing four basic decision styles. Each style will be described in rather succinct terms to highlight the differences.

TABLE 6-1   Four Basic Decision Styles

		Amount of Information Used	
		Moderately Low (Satisfice)	*High (Maximize)*
Focus / *Number of Alternatives*	*Uni*	Decisive	Hierarchic
	Multi	Flexible	Integrative

The *Decisive* style is one in which a small amount of information is used to generate a "good enough" decision. Once a decision is made, it is final. There is no going back and reanalyzing data. This style favors speed, efficiency, and achievement of results. Although some people consider this style too rigid and simplistic, it is dynamic, strong, and reliable. Harry Truman is a good example of this style.

The *Flexible* style also employs a minimal amount of data to reach a decision. However, this style continuously absorbs new data and generates new solutions as needed. Adaptability as well as speed and efficiency is prized in this style. It is a style that is strong in intuition, getting along well with others, and rolling with the punches;

yet critics find it shallow and "indecisive." Franklin D. Roosevelt seems an excellent example of this style.

The *Hierarchic* style presents a sharp contrast to the other two. This style shows a very high use of all available information to meticulously generate one "best solution." Then the solution is often implemented using an elaborate contingency plan. It is a style that utilizes rigor, precision, and long-range planning. Its critics find it dogmatic and overcontrolling. Richard Nixon and possibly Jimmy Carter exemplify this style.

The *Integrative* style also uses a large amount of information, but simultaneously generates a number of possible solutions for implementation. There is also a greater tendency to rely on creative synthesis rather than pure logic. This style is highly inventive, empathic, and cooperative, yet to critics, it seems too complicated and "wishy-washy." Adlai Stevenson was an outstanding example of this style.

In sum, the model proposes that there are four basic styles. Each person has acquired at least one basic or "dominant" style that normally shows up under moderate environmental load. For most people, a second or "backup" style shows up where there is under- or overload. For instance, a person might show a dominant Hierarchic style but shift to a backup Decisive style when there is overload,[2] as shown in Figure 6-3.

At this point, it appears appropriate to examine the applications for decision styles in the context of the four-force model frame of reference and the decision process in terms of how decisions are carried out. A set of basic questions were asked at the beginning of this chapter. Each of these can now be recast in terms of the two models above:

1. A "good" decision will be considered from the perspective of the fit between decision process and the factors in the four force model.

2. Selecting good decision makers will be related to the fit between the individual's decision style and task, peer and environmental factors.

3. Matching individuals to jobs is related to the fit between decision style and task demands.

4. The design of information systems will be related to the decision style of

---

[2]Overload is defined as the individual's response to information where maximal information use begins to decline.

the manager. Significant change is possible when MIS systems are matched to user styles and environmental demands.

5. The use of participation in decisions can be related to fit of organizational design to decision styles and environmental demands.

6. The relationship of organization design to facilitation of effective decision making is considered in the light of decision styles, decision processes, and the interactive four force model.

Each of these basic issues, which are concerned with achieving more effective organizational performance by improved decision making, will be treated in detail.

How Do We Know When a Good Decision Has Been Made?

We are confronted from the outset with the problem that the very nature of this question reveals a normative bias. For example, many quantitative approaches define *good* in terms of risk minimization or the applicability of utility functions. On the other hand, more qualitative approaches have stressed the maximum use of data or careful analysis as outlined in Kepner and Tregoe (1965). Rowe (1974) and others have developed a multidimensional measure for determining when a decision can be considered a good decision. Obviously, once we enter the multidimensional realm it becomes quite difficult to define a single estimate of good; rather, what can be defined is an "appropriate" strategy.

Viewed from this perspective, it is not whether a general definition of a "good" decision can be considered possible, but rather can we define the most appropriate match of situation and decision process. For instance, we often consider risk minimization as our objective in finding a good solution. Yet this has been recognized as an overconservative approach and is obviously not best under all circumstances. Rather, what should be considered is the "fit" between risk level and situational factors—e.g., high risk may be most appropriate when stakes are low or when the situation is desperate.

As another example, consider the rule that one should use all the information available in order to make a good decision. Here again, if time pressure is great, or if a problem can be solved with minimum data, a better decision, in fact, can be made using less data.

Even the widely held idea that decisions must be rational, in the sense of maximizing expected utility, was shown by Rowe (1974) not to describe actual decision-making behavior. Playing hunches, which seems to work toward consciously low-rated goals, may in fact turn out best in the sense that they satisfy some unarticulated, however vital, need in a person. Excessive rationality can in fact be dysfunctional.

Similar criticisms can be made of rules such as those concerning contingency planning, use of multiple alternatives, reliance on experience, and so on. The central thesis we are advancing is that the "goodness" of a decision process depends on its fit with situational factors. For instance, where time pressure is high, a quick decision fits and is, all else being equal, a good one. A number of codifications of types of environments and decision processes exist. We present a simple model here (Table 6-2) as an illustration. Two dimensions of environment will be related to four types of decision. We will assume that environments vary on two dimensions:

1. Amount of structure—i.e., clarity of situations, relevance
2. Amount of complexity—i.e., number of people involved, amount of data

TABLE 6-2   Environmental Dimensions and Optimal Types of Decisions

		Low *Structure*	*Hi*
Complexity	*Hi*	Hunches	Fast Satisficing Decisions
	Low	Creative Synthesis	Elaborate Analysis

Four types of decision processes can be fitted to these dimensions, as shown in Table 6-2. In complex, highly structured situations, we would agree with the normative approach in recommending the use of exhaustive data research, multiple alternatives, elaborate risk and utility analysis, as well as long-range contingency planning. However, when the situation is structured but less complex, then it would seem that rapid decisions using "enough" data to find a good satisficing conclusion are superior. Information use should parallel the needs of the situation. It is in situations of high structure and low complexity that experience may well be the best guide.

On the other hand, where situations are unclear or unstable, a heavy reliance on experience or logical process may not be best. In simple, unstable situations, one might be as well off, or better, relying on intuition and staying open to new hunches. Our unconscious perceptual system can often provide an excellent working synthesis of data at a speed roughly ten times that attainable by our conscious mind.

In more complex, unstable situations, one might do best to defer decisions, take in data, mull it over, and allow a slow-acting, creative synthesis to occur.[3] This process is especially useful in competitive situations where original solutions are valuable.

There are other crucial environmental dimensions that also affect the type of decision that is made. Clearly, as time pressure increases, the value of elaborate analysis or creative synthesis decreases.[4]

The type of decision styles and skills available will also affect "fit," as will peer and task factors. Ultimately the decision process will be *best* when it fits the situation in all its dimensions: task demands, individual styles, organizational culture and environmental pressures. In subsequent sections we will pursue this issue by looking at how decision styles, jobs, information systems, participation or power systems and organizational design issues more specifically are related.

How Does One Find Good Decision Makers?

This question reveals a normative bias. From a Descriptive-Differential approach, the question is translated as follows: What

---

[3]Similar in principle to hunches in its use of the creative process. Creative synthesis differs by consciously piling up relevant data in the unconscious, then permitting creative ideas to emerge over time.

[4]Except where anticipatory strategies can be used, such as rehearsing problems before they occur, or stocking the mind with useful data prior to the need for them.

are important differences among decision makers and how do these differneces relate to an optimal match of situation and decision maker?

In our view, past normative approaches have not been successful precisely because they ignore individual differences (which assumes that one type of decision maker is always best) or ignore situational variation. Consider several examples of normative solutions:

1. The best decision maker is one with the best track record of past results. Yet, as is abundantly clear from the Peter Principle, performance in one situation (e.g., engineer) may be a poor predictor of performance in other settings (e.g., manager).

2. The best decision maker is one with the highest intelligence. Yet empirical data do not consistently support I.Q. as a success predictor. In some settings (e.g., low level jobs) high I.Q. can actually predict failure; and in other settings (e.g., sales) social skills or creativity (not measured by I.Q.) may be crucial elements in successful decisions.

The central thesis of the Descriptive Differential approach is to:

1. Isolate crucial dimensions of persons which affect decision making.
2. Determine demands of situations.
3. Effect an optimal match of person dimensions and situational demands.

The four force model suggests at least three types of individual dimensions: social skills (relating to environmental and peer forces), task skills and motivational factors. While each of these can be measured separately, decision style offers a framework for integrating these factors into a single model. Decision style does not completely map all these personality dimensions, but as a relatively simple comprehensive model it can serve as a useful frame of reference.

Decision style can relate to personality dimensions, as follows:

A. Social skills
  1. Decisives will show forceful leadership, honesty and a strong dislike for committees and interaction.

2. Flexibles will show great concern for other's views, be excellent smoothers of difficulty, and often be quite popular.

3. Hierarchics will provide great skill in organizing others and establishing organizational control systems, but will like only limited participation by others.

4. Integratives will reveal great talent for team selection and team building as well as a strong bias toward participation.

B. Task skills

1. Decisives will excel where speed and quick results or resolute pursuit of goals is needed.

2. Flexibles will be best where fast, adaptive manuevering with considerable intuition is useful.

3. Hierarchics will be optimal where rigorous analysis and long range elaborate planning are essential.

4. Integratives will be most valuable where systemic, creative solutions are imperative.

C. Motivational factors

1. Decisives will respond to situations permitting achievement of action oriented results.

2. Flexibles will respond to situations containing great variation in task as well as when affiliation needs are central.

3. Hierarchics will react well to situations generating complex challenge, which permit the building of understanding and predictive control.

4. Integratives react best to situations fostering individual growth and development of complex systems.

Decision style can thus serve as a surrogate for total personality. The basic premise then is that the best decision maker is one whose style or combination of styles best matches situational demands (i.e., task, peer, organizational and environmental demands). Most research to date deals solely with fit between style and job or tasks.

It is apparent that there is no single "best" style that fits all jobs.[5] Rather, research has shown that any given style appears to perform better when there is an appropriate match between the job and the individual. This implies that for a job that requires moderate

[5]In contrast, McClelland (1976) has argued that a power-oriented manager, comparable to the Decisive style, is the most effective.

to low data, high time pressure, high structure, and clear-cut frequent decisions, the Decisive style fits best. This approach to finding a good decision maker has been demonstrated by the results of a study in a government bureaucracy of first-line supervisors, made by Boulgarides and Driver (1977). In this setting, the job characteristics matched the Decisive style, and the only style that predicted success in the situation was the Decisive.

Conversely, in a much more fluid, unstable job (claims underwriter) we have found that the Flexible style is more predictive of success (Driver, 1977). In certain high-complexity areas, such as aerospace research, we have found that Hierarchic and Integrative styles are more predictive of successful decision making (see Alawi, 1973; Hager, 1977). In research done by Rowe, Weingard, and Provenzano (1977) at the System Development Corporation on navy leadership patterns, the most effective navy leader was shown to be the creative or Integrative-style individual.

Considering the executive's information processing, the span of information as shown in Figure 6-4 increases rapidly with the level in the organization. Although upper level executives use summary information, nonetheless the time span of that information or complexity is far greater than at the operating level.

FIGURE 6-4   Time Span of Information vs.
Organizational Level

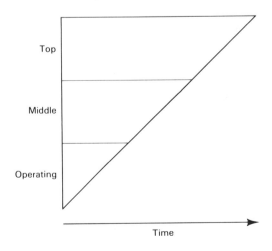

If we examine which style best matches jobs of increasing responsibilities (load), the Integrative and Hierarchic styles are increasingly appropriate up to a certain organizational level. Beyond that point, the Decisive, who has the capacity for fast reaction, becomes more appropriate (Hager, 1977). Thus, organizational level is related to decision complexity and the match of the individual's cognitive complexity to the job determines the effectiveness of decision making.

The important point is that in order to find good decision makers, one must not only consider the individuals, but also match the individuals to the situations. Can this be done? We believe so. At present, there are several measures of job demands that can provide dimensions relevant to this question. They will be described in the following section.

Decision styles can be measured with instruments that have had extensive testing and validation. Two current tests for measuring decision style are:

1. The Driver Decision Style Exercises[6]
2. The Driver-Streufert Complexity Inventory[7]

The first measures the actual decision style a person uses when making decisions in a non-self-conscious manner. The second measures both a person's self-concept of his style and his liking for complexity. The self-concept measure predicts actual decision making when a person is apparently consciously concerned with how he is making a decision ("This is an important decision, therefore I should consider all the facts. . .").

Both instruments offer good reliability (the Driver Decision Style Exercises and the Driver-Streufert Complexity Index have a reliability test-retest correlation index ranging from .62 to .86). The validity of the DDSE has been found to be high both in laboratory-type studies of decision making (see Driver and Mock, 1975, a and b) and in field studies of actual decision making (Boulgarides and Driver, 1977; Hager, 1977; Testerman, 1976; Alawi, 1973). The

[6]Also known as IST or APSE instruments.

[7]Also known as CXSD.

DSCI also has proved its validity over a long period of time (see Owens, 1969; D'Antoni, 1972, Hager, 1977; Driver, 1977).

Given these measures of jobs and cognitive styles of persons, we now suggest that matching, which considers these factors, will lead to more optimal decision making. This type of matching is now being validated and is being used in several major organizations.

When attempting to find a match between the decision maker and the job, an important consideration is the environmental impact. Referring to the four force model, the organization's external demands, which represent environmental forces, significantly impact the individual's ability to perform effectively. Thus, matching the individual to a job ideally requires more elaborate measures than decision style. For example, where organizational demands are excessive, as shown in Figure 6-5, this requires a committed individual who is willing to exchange personal needs for meeting the organization's needs. This is referred to as point A in the diagram and generally represents upper level managerial positions. Whereas, point B is characteristic of those persons whose primary concern is their own needs (in a win-lose sense). The match, therefore, is dependent on organizational demands as compared with individual willingness to meet those demands.

FIGURE 6-5   Matching Goal Congruence with
                 Organizational Demands

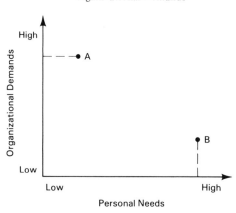

The interpersonal requirement shown in the four force diagram can be compared to a model developed by Moment and Zaleznick (1963) in which they consider the cathexis of the decision maker in relation to the position held. On the left hand axis, as shown in Figure 6-6, are the three different conditions: the people-oriented individual, the fusion or combination of ideas and people, and the idea-oriented person.

On the top axis are shown the three approaches—the homeostatic or reactive, mediative, and proactive. Each box indicates the possible way in which the manager can interact with the position as a function of this orientation. Here again, as with goal congruence or decision style, the idea is that decisions are "best" when personal characteristics are matched to comparable job or environmental dimensions.

The degree to which person-job matching should add other factors beyond decision style (or any one factor) would seem to depend on two issues—how relevant style is to success in the job and how important the job is (see Driver, 1977, on how well decision style alone predicts success).

The matching strategy is not, however, the only possible route. Another approach involves training people to fit their jobs better. Athey (1976) has found that an intensive training course can shift some Decisive-style people to a more Integrative style. Hager (1977) found that certain military training (flight school) is associated with a more Decisive style. It appears that style training may become a basis for grooming people for new jobs whose cognitive styles and information-demand characteristics are known. Such approaches are being tried in several firms.

FIGURE 6-6   Interaction of Predispositional Sets and Executive Functions

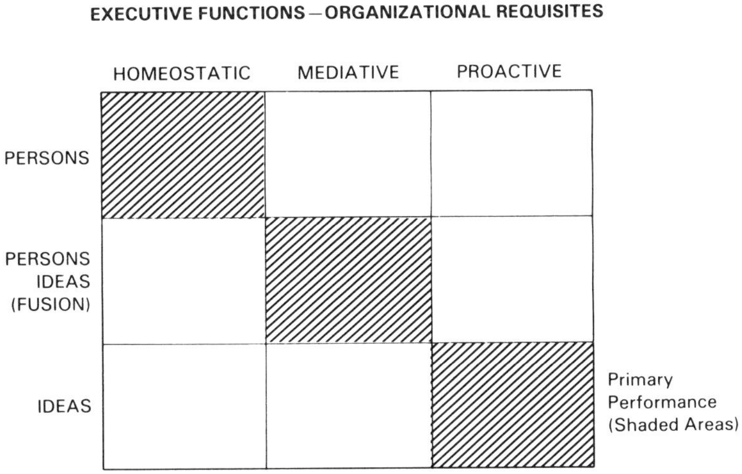

EXECUTIVE FUNCTIONS—ORGANIZATIONAL REQUISITES

Still another option is to redesign jobs to fit existing people. Some jobs may be informationally configured so that no style really fits them. For instance, jobs with long stretches of zero input and short bursts of extremely high data use, or jobs with long stretches of overload that cannot be relieved, may simply be impossible to fit.

Job redesign can involve both enrichment and simplification in order to fit new incumbents. Techniques of job redesign have been refined to a high level; however, too often, they are applied in a nonselective way (that is, by enriching all jobs) with unsuccessful results (see Reif and Luthans, 1972; Srivastra et al., 1977). Our suggestion is that job redesign should be preceded by both job and person measurement. Enrichment (or simplification) becomes useful when matched to the style desired or obtainable from job occupants.

Based on the research to date, it is obvious that finding a good decision maker depends on our ability to measure the individual's cognitive style, identifying the job characteristics as measured by various instruments and relating these to the four-force model. That is, an optimal fit is one where the style characteristics match the task demands, the peer pressures, and the organizational environmental pressure.

We have concentrated on job-person fit above; however, person-person and person-organization fit are equally important. Some of our earliest research suggests that style is a crucial factor in interpersonal attraction. Alawi (1973) has found that fit with organization culture is at least as important as fit with job requirements.

In the final analysis, selecting a *good* decision maker involves fitting the style of the person to task, peer and organizational factors. And in the long run, this matched pattern within the organization must fit the environment for optimal organizational effectiveness.

How Can Task Demands Be Measured to Achieve Optimal Decision Making?

From the above discussion it is evident that the fit between the style of a decision maker and the job is an essential ingredient in effective decision making. While not as advanced as style measurement, considerable progress has been made in job analysis in a decision style framework. There are job measures available which are based directly on the style model, as well as measures developed for other reasons which touch on other crucial dimensions.

Central to any job analysis, from a decision style view, would be the following job dimensions:

1. Complexity of input
2. Time pressure
3. Need for creativity
4. Structure, repetitiveness, uncertainty
5. Responsibility[8]
6. Planning demands
7. Social complexity (i.e., span of control, type of influence needed, type of people supervised.
8. Control process/autonomy
9. Motivation/reward system

Many current job measures involve some of these dimensions. For instance, the very elaborate job analysis of the Dictionary of Occupational Titles (Berwitz, 1975) provides elaborate ratings of jobs on complexity demands, uncertainty level and other relevant dimensions. Other approaches have mainly stressed the motivational properties relevant to style (e.g., Hackman and Oldham, 1975).

One of the earliest approaches to job analysis using a style approach involved a simple rating form on four crucial factors (information use in actions, creative planning, social complexity and responsibility) (Peters, 1965). It formed a useful basis for salary decisions in a major university.

More recently Alawi (1973) developed a very extensive measure of information complexity and time pressure which has proven useful in a variety of organizational settings. A group at the University of Southern California (e.g., Driver, Olson, Sundby and Testerman, 1976) has developed a multi-dimensional job analysis approach called the Position Description Questionnaire (PDQ).

---

[8]Responsibility often refers to the "noxity" and "eucity" of the environment. Noxity refers to the amount of negative input—i.e., risk to self and others. Eucity refers to the amount of positive input—i.e., rewards possible if correct decisions are made. Noxity and eucity are both high when responsibility is high. Noxity and eucity added to information complexity define environmental load.

The PDQ has been employed in one nation-wide job analysis program (Driver, 1977) and meets the requirements of being practicable in use and valid in results.[9] It tags almost all of the key dimensions mentioned above and is being refined for general use.

While matching persons to jobs is central to our approach, the match to peers, or organization culture are equally crucial. Copeman (1972) finds that the key factor in executive success was the ability to interact with people. For example, matching individuals on their decision styles appears to maximize the potential for successful interaction. In general, similar styles interact best. However, individuals with Hierarchic styles are not compatible with each other, but relate better with those who are Decisives. The use of Decision style measures in an organization to match people for various task groups has produced significant results.[10]

Measures of organizational culture are less clearly developed. Alawi used an adaptation of the Likert System Four questionnaire and the Laurence and Lorsch measures of integration and differentiation with good results.

Based on the results achieved to date, a suggested procedure would be to combine job measurement, organization culture measurement and individual style classification in order to obtain optimal matching.

Cognitive style thus is significant in determining whether a person can, in fact, match the position requirements or can carry the job out effectively. Using the decision style model, we have examined the requirement of matching the person and the organization to achieve more effective decision making. In the remaining sections we will examine these organizational issues in more detail. First, we will indicate how style relates to power sharing or participation in decision making. Then we will examine how style relates to design of information control and reward systems. In these discussions, it should be remembered that fit can occur either by selecting people whose style matches existing organizational patterns or by re-designing the organization to fit the people.

---

[9]E.g., it validly discriminates complexity level between clerical and white collar jobs.

[10]Recent use in a large utility firm confirms the advantage of matched vs. random groups, as does the design of a top management group in a small firm.

How Should Decision Making
Be Shared?

Traditional management theory has stressed unity of command as essential for managers who have final authority (e.g., Fayol, 1949). On the other hand, authors such as Likert (1961) propose participation as the most effective organizational mode. Proponents of both sides of this issue cite studies to show improved performance using their preferred approach to decision making. For example, Mark Mulder (1971) showed that workers, by and large, are indifferent to the sharing of power because they feel that they do not have the expertise or the information on which to base a decision. (But also see Jenkins, 1973).

Although in many instances improved performance results where there is sharing of decisions—such as at Texas Instruments, TRW, or American Airlines (see Jenkins, 1973)—results are contingent on the match of individual's social skills, technology, task demands, and organizational climate. Thus, participation is no panacea and it sometimes does not work well, as illustrated by Nonlinear Systems where the company almost went bankrupt because of their participative approach.

What is the basis on which to decide when participation is appropriate? Two factors appear relevant:

1. Situational pressures
2. Characteristics of the people involved

For example, Fiedler (1965) developed a contingency model which stressed task and situational pressures. He showed that sharing decisions depended on the leader's power position, task structure, and relations with the group. Tannenbaum and Schmidt (1973) have shown that managers vary from authoritarian approaches to democratic approaches and that they do share a considerable amount of power, depending on the situation. As shown in their original article, they suggested that the effective manager knows when to share authority and when not to. This work was expanded by Heller (1971), based on interviews of 250 managers in California. He determined the basis on which managers were willing to share power with subordinates. Table 6-3 is a representation of the data which Heller found in his studies.

Based on his research data, Heller showed that power is typically shared when the decision maker considers that the matter under concern is of more importance to the individual than it is to the organization. On the other hand, when the manager feels that he has better information or that the decisionis important to the organization, he tends not to share the power or the decision with subordinates.

A further extension of the conditions for power sharing is described by Vroom and Yetton (1973). They developed a detailed analysis of when power sharing is most effective—that is, the set of conditions that would lead to more effective performance. Heller, on the other hand, identified what managers do, rather than the prescriptive approach proposed by Vroom and Yetton.

TABLE 6-3   Criteria for Sharing Decisions

Power Sharing Style	Decision Important to the Company	Decision Important to the Individual	Manager has the Information	Experience or Age of the Subordinate
1. Makes decisions alone	V		V	
2. Informs others	V		V	
3. Consults others	V	V		
4. Makes decisions jointly		V		V
5. Delegates decisions		V		V

Note: A Check (V) indicates most likely style used in a given criterion situation.

In contrast to the models above, decision styles and the four force model include both the factors and the cognitive differences of the people involved.

The cognitive decision style model shows that each style has a preferred mode of participation. The Decisive style, for example, generally dislikes lengthy committee meetings and discussions, and the model suggests that if a Decisive person has a dominant position, all else being equal, there will be minimal participation. At most, where the opportunity to vote is provided, majority rule with minimal discussion would be the favored approach.

The Flexible style, however, enjoys talking far more—but again, after some discussion, a vote would probably be seen as most efficient. The Hierarchic style, on the other hand, takes a very different tack. Voting is seen as reducing quality to the least common denominator. Participation is seen as useful only to provide the most competent person with data on which he or she makes a decision. Likert would term the Hierarchic preference a "consultative" system.

The Integrative style would favor some participation all the time. Voting would be rejected in favor of discussion until a creative synthesis is arrived at by group consensus. The Integrative prefers to operate with a non-hierarchic team at all times.

Research on the group aspects of decision style is still being developed. However, pilot studies suggest that it may be valid to use decision style as a major variable in determining how much participation to use. These ideas are summariezed in Table 6-4.

TABLE 6-4   Decision Style and Decision Sharing

Style	Preferred Group Process
Decisive	Autocratic or Voting
Flexible	Voting
Hierarchic	Consultative Autocratic
Integrative	Consensus

The situation is the other half of this decision style approach. Factors such as autocratic cultural values cited by Tannenbaum and Schmidt (1973), time pressure, unequal information or skill distribution (as noted by Heller), and task clarity would operate to counter participation. For example, where task complexity is high, one could argue for participation as a means for improving decision making, unless time pressure was also high. Table 6-5 summarizes situational factors favoring varying degrees of participation.

TABLE 6-5 Factors Favoring or Opposing Participation in Decision Making

Pro	Con
Unclear problem	Time pressure
High personal stakes	Unequal information
Democratic values	High organizational
	importance
High risk	
Complex tasks	Autocratic values

A major issue concerns clashes between the style of people in a group and external demands. What does one do with an Integrative group under high time pressure? The answer may lie in the emergence of backup styles. For instance, if one knew a group had to move from complex decisions with no time pressure to decisions with high time pressure, one would select membership in the group having an Integrative dominant style and Decisive backup style.

Thus, a knowledge of decision styles and situational demands can provide useful information toward helping a manager decide how much participation is appropriate in a given environment. Because of the increasing emphasis on participation, knowing when and how to apply it can make the difference between success and failure. The significant aspect of the decision-style approach is that it helps explain why participation does not always work. Even where research has shown the value of participation, a decision-style analysis would help validate the approach.

On the other hand, even using a decision-style approach, we find that other aspects enter into the degree of sharing needed, such as those mentioned above. There are other factors, such as empathy for people, persuasiveness, support, being concerned, having respect, liking to engage in meetings, and so on, that involve not only the processing of information or cognitive style but also the people orientation or concern for the individual. This latter aspect, people concern, represents still another dimension of the manager, which, although directly related to the cognitive style, is often a separate and distinct category. Research is continuing on the development of a cognitive-contingency model (Rowe et al., 1977), and its applicability to the organizational problem appears to be emerging. The people concerns of the decision maker are reflected in his interaction with subordinates, in participation, in power sharing, in control, through to career planning and organization design.

The Relation of Information System Design to Decision Style

We have examined the environmental and task factors in the four force model. Another aspect of both the task and organization environment is the information that is used by managers to make decisions to take appropriate action. This will become increasingly important as more information systems are computerized. For example, managers are often inundated with information that is seldom related to their cognitive capability. It is this latter concern which has given rise to the examination of decision maker's preferences in use of computer reports and how information system design can more closely match the decision style of the manager or of a group of managers in an organization.

From the perspective of perceptual processes, it is obvious that there are different styles that managers employ in utilizing information. According to Lindblom (1959), most managers "muddle through" when solving problems. Or, if we look at Miller's research (1956), in which he decribes the mind's ability to process information, we quickly recognize that it is difficult to design an information system that will broadly meet all requirements. Decision style data suggest that managers range from being Decisive to Integrative in various organizations (Alawi, 1973; Driver and Boulgarides, 1977). In addition, environmental pressure or load varies in the same job, often over extreme ranges. How, then, can one develop a major effective information system given varied manager styles and situational pressures?

The problem is further confounded when one recognizes that the predominant style of information system designers is Integrative (see Testerman, 1976). A combination of increasing technical capacity and a stylistic bias toward high data levels among MIS designers has led to a strong tendency for chronic data overload. In this setting, only the Integrative manager (and perhaps the Hierarchic manager) is well served. A study by Driver and Mock (1975b) showed that the Flexible manager does not need costly extra data and the Decisive manager is actually better off (in terms of profit) with less data.

An approach coming into vogue is to design systems that allow the manager to select his own optimal level of information. Unfortunately, research data on information search and purchase

(Streufert, Suedfeld and Driver, 1965; Suedfeld and Streufert, 1966; Driver and Streufert, 1969; Driver and Mock, 1975a) suggest that decision makers do not select optimal amounts of data. In underload conditions where the environment is generally low in information, most people select too much data. (As seen in Figures 6-7 and 6-8 purchase of information greatly exceeds use of data, thus generating unnecessary cost and possible confusion.) In overload conditions, people still slightly overselect or tend to select or buy too little data compared to the amount needed for optimal decisions.[11]

FIGURE 6-7   Information Search and Use for More
                 Decisive/Flexible Style

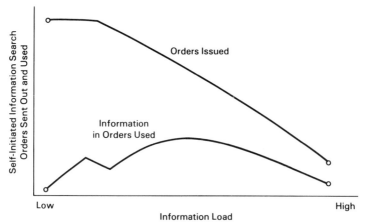

Adapted from S. Streufert, P. Suedfeld, and M. Driver, "Conceptual Structure, Information Search and Information Utilization," *Journal of Personality and Social Psychology,* 2 (1965).

What this suggests is that a management information system should be "tailored" to fit the style of the key decision maker or a representative group of decision makers, or be based on the domi-

---

[11]The excess of use over search for Integrative/Hierarchic people in Figure 6-8 reflects the capacity of Integrative/Hierarchic style people to add on to the external data and internal integration (i.e., from memory or creative synthesis). See also Bryson and Driver, 1972.

FIGURE 6-8 Information Search and Use for More Integrative and Hierarchic Style

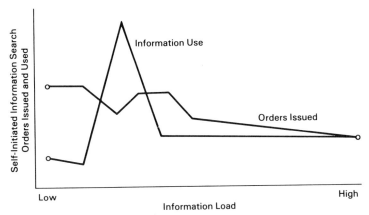

Adapted from S. Streufert, P. Suedfeld, and M. Driver, "Conceptual Structure, Information Search and Information Utilization," *Journal of Personality and Social Psychology*, 2 (1965).

nant style of a group. Use of style measures, along with standard questionnaires, could enable data to be summarized for more Decisive people while retaining the capability of elaborate MIS for the more Integrative people. Such a design effort is currently under experimentation in a scientific government agency.

As has been noted, an important issue concerning the application of management information systems, particularly computer-based systems, is the concern with environmental load. Obviously, where there are intense time pressures or very complex task structures, this has a direct effect on the application of a management information system. However, if the fit between manager decision style and job load factors is widespread, as shown by Alawi, then matching the personal style with job demands facilitates the information system design. Environment load and incumbent style will both favor the same MIS design. Where person-job fit is poor, then either better selection or job redesign can improve fit. But if there still is a conflict between the job demands and the cognitive style of the individual, then we can examine the backup style to determine whether a certain pattern of dominant and backup styles would fit. For example, where a complex job situation constantly shifts from a clear to a fuzzy condition, a Hierarchic style with an Integrative backup would be most appropriate. This style mix might then require an MIS design with fixed solutions alternating with interactive variable solutions as the situation changes. Table 6-6 summarizes style-situation matches in one possible format.

In Table 6-6, six possible job environments are first presented. For instance, a job may vary from low to high complexity but remain relatively stable all the time. After each job type, an optimal decision style match is given for the job incumbent. Finally, we present an optimal MIS for the job-decision style pair. Thus, in a job of high stability that shifts at times back and forth from low to high complexity, we suggest that incumbents with a Decisive/Hierarchic dominant and backup style mix (or the reverse)[1 2] would fit best. We also suggest that the appropriate MIS would shift from summary data and fixed solutions (in low-complexity situations) to elaborate data and fixed solutions when the job situation shifts to high complexity. Environmental shifting of MIS could either be preprogrammed (based on prior job analysis), or be based on some sort of ongoing environmental load sensing system.[1 3]

It is obvious that the design of a management information system is an extremely complex task and very difficult to change in terms of meeting the requirements of all types of managers, especially because managers change positions, have career life cycles, and have changing responsibilities. As new managers enter positions, their demands, requirements, and cognitive styles may not fit the system design. Is it feasible, therefore, to precisely relate the design of an information system to the cognitive style of an incumbent group? What, then, is the best course of action? Should one design systems in such a way as to provide flexibility, or to provide a number of options so that as groups change, the design of reports can be modified to one that is more useful? It is suggested, therefore, that systems in an organization would not be the same, but would have the ability to accommodate or adapt to the cognitive style of meaningful subdivisions or groups.

[1 2]The dominant style would obviously be the one most suitable to the most frequent state of the job environment.

[1 3]Good executive secretaries provide this sort of environmental load scanning in a rough manner for their bosses.

TABLE 6-6 Optimal Matches of Decision Styles (Dominant/Backup) and MIS Designs for Certain Information Environment Patterns Found in Jobs

Information Environment Patterns	Optimal Decision Style Pairs	Optimal MIS Design
Low Complexity ←→ High Complexity (low uncertainty)	Decisive/Hierarchic	Fixed solution, summary data ←→ Fixed solution, elaborate data
Low Uncertainty ←→ High Uncertainty (low complexity)	Decisive/Flexible	Fixed solution, summary data ←→ Alternate solutions, summary data
Low Uncertainty ←→ High Complexity (high uncertainty & complexity)	Decisive/Integrative	Fixed solution, summary data ←→ Interactive system, varied solutions, complex data
Low Complexity ←→ High Complexity (high uncertainty)	Flexible/Integrative	Alternate solutions, summary data ←→ Interactive system, varied solutions, complex data
Low Complexity ←→ High Uncertainty (high complexity, low uncertainty)	Flexible/Hierarchic	Alternate solutions, summary data ←→ Fixed solution, elaborate data
Low Uncertainty ←→ High Uncertainty (high complexity)	Hierarchic/Integrative	Fixed solutions, elaborate data ←→ Interactive system, varied solutions, complex data

Can Organization Design Facilitate Effective Decision Making?

The structure and operation of organizations is directly dependent on decision style. The exercise of power, political maneuvering, interaction with subordinates and type of control employed are manifestations of the manager's decision style. The Decisive manager who insists on tight control obviously functions differently from the Integrative manager who is comfortable with loose control. The ability to influence subordinates and the ability to convince others in the organization is a function of the manager's decision style. If we examine the decision process, it is obvious that carrying out decisions involves style. Thus, the match of the manager's style with the organizational requirements determines the potential outcome of decisions.

A key issue in organization design—participation vs. centralization—has already been discussed. However, other issues still remain:

1. How much control should be used?
2. How much feedback should be given?
3. What motivational schemes are most useful?

Obviously, it would be difficult to deal with each of these issues in any depth without a fairly lengthy discussion. However, because of the importance of these issues, it appears appropriate to at least provide an overview of their relevance and concern for decision making and the appropriateness of decision styles as a crucial factor in organizational design.

Possibly the most important concern is with managerial control. In order to achieve effective results, managers do exercise control; however, the type of control employed varies, depending on the manager's decision style. For instance, a Decisive-style manager likes immediate or frequent feedback, while the Flexible and Hierarchic managers dislike control or a power-oriented approach from superiors. But both types of managers also want feedback from above, although perhaps at a slower rate than the Decisive manager. The Integrative style, on the other hand, is neutral in terms of both control and feedback.

174

If the basic cognitive styles are extended to incorporate the factors in a cognitive-contingency model, additional dimensions can be added. These would show that for some purposes, control interacts with the achievement, affiliation, and power needs of the managers, and thus not only must satisfy the organizational requirements but also must meet the motivational needs of the individuals, which are reflected in their styles.

One approach to this problem is to view it in terms of a motivation control model developed by Rowe (1977), as shown in Figure 6-9. Classic management using a normative approach establishes the objectives and goals of the organization, which are given to the manager who in turn communicates them to the subordinate who is expected to carry out performance as specified. By inserting feedback and computers, we have achieved more direct measurements of performance, but we hardly can use this as the basis for improving performance. What is missing is goal congruence or recognition of individual needs and using negotiation to help achieve commitment. Without these behavioral concerns, the effectiveness or the level of performance is often minimal.

FIGURE 6-9   Motivation and Control Model

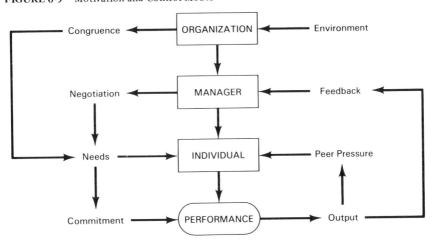

Managers have attempted participation and negotiation in a number of ways. For example, Management by Objectives has attempted to achieve more direct involvement concerning goals and thus have some degree of participation in order to gain goal congruence. However, as is obvious from Figure 6-9, MBO does not directly deal with behavioral considerations. Thus, it is difficult to assure either effective control or effective performance if the decision style or motivational needs of the individual are not directly taken into account. For example, classical MBO might work very well for a Decisive person, but fail miserably for an Integrative manager.

There are other aspects of control that relate directly to the issue of cognitive style. For example, organization structure influences the span of control and determines the number of people reporting to a single manager. Obviously, the more Decisive the manager, the fewer people he would want reporting directly to him. Or, to put it differently, Decisive people prefer less interaction with the subordinates who report to them. Partly, this reflects the desire to achieve high levels of control and power, and thus a lack of concern for sharing of decisions or participation. On the other hand, it partly reflects a bias toward simple, efficient procedure. However, as the span of control broadens, more information, more variables, more individual needs have to be taken into account. This would shift the style demands to the more Flexible or Hierarchic type, in contrast to the more Decisive orientation. The Flexible orientation would be toward a broad, loosely structured, and often overlapping set or subordinates (such as in FDR's New Deal), whereas the Hierarchic mode would be a broad cut, tightly controlled span of control. The Integrative tends to think in terms of teams using consensus rather than control of any type.

As concerns reward systems, decision style can be linked to individual motivation. For example, the Decisive generally responds best to a situation providing clear, frequent external rewards based on immediate results. Absence of "red tape" and endless committees would also be reinforcing as is the power to get things done. The Flexible is reinforced by autonomy, positive social climate and variety of assignments. The Hierarchic would seem to be reinforced by capacity to achieve ever more complex control over environments, as well as by recognition and status based on prior accomplishment. The Integrative would be most attracted to those situations where there is opportunity for active developments within their own personality as well as within the organization. They also respond well to team oriented activity.

In looking at the motivational relationship to decision styles, it becomes obvious that there is a need to extend the domain to more extensively incorporate the motivational, along with the cognitive, concerns of the decision maker (as has been done by Boulgarides and Driver, 1977).

A cognitive-contingency model, which is under development, attempts to move in this direction. In initial studies that have been done with this model by Rowe (1977), it demonstrates that one is able to predict organizational effectiveness of decision making as a function of the manager's decision style. For example, if we relate the cognitive-contingency model to the basic motivators defined by McClelland (power motivation, achievement motivation, and affiliation motivation), we see that the Decisive manager is the one who is primarily power-oriented, who focuses on results and satisfices, and who uses speed to accomplish tasks under his control. As research continues with the cognitive-contingency model, its applicability to the organizational problem appears to be emerging. Style and concerns of the decision maker reflect in his interaction with subordinates, in participation, in power sharing, and in control, including career planning and organization design.

CONCLUSION

With the number of changes taking place in the organizational environment, and the rising need for a better basis for understanding how decisions influence performance and for finding ways to achieve more effective decisions, it is obvious that a new approach is needed to provide more definitive answers than have been available in the past. The normative approach that has been utilized by managers for many years provides a point of departure, but as indicated by Lindblom, this approach still represents a muddling-through, because there are no predictive ways of determining the suitability of the norm to other individual or situational idiosyncrasies. Furthermore, in terms of rapid change and contingency, a more adaptive, flexible approach appears to be important. Finally, as organizations grow in power to affect the fates of people around the world, a more profound, analytic approach to decision making seems justified.

The need for a person centered model of decision making is well attested in the literature. Zaleznik (1970) indicates that the important concern in an organization is not the rationalistic basis for decisions, but the fact that personality and politics play a significant, if not overriding, role in terms of what really happens. Added to this is the consideration of heuristics and intuitive approaches for more effective problem solving, and the application of computers for more effective information processing systems. In Gore's study of the Kansas City Fire Department (1964), he concluded that every decision involved persuasion as well as negotiation and concessions. There was not a single instance of an executive making a decision through a formal mechanism. It is clear that a personality oriented model such as Decision style theory is deeply needed to better cope with today's problems.

What is required to implement the decision style approach? This kind of question is one that must be dealt with in order to have a sound basis for ascertaining whether the manager's cognitive style, including his backup styles, will facilitate decision making that deals with the range of complexities confronting today's managers. Further search and current initial uses of the model will help clarify how the decision style approach can best be implemeented.

The descriptive-differential approach appears to provide a significant basis for dealing with many aspects of decision making in organizations. The four force model provides a framework for examining situational factors that affect the decision process. Matching the individual's decision style to the organizational demands, peer pressures, task requirements and self definition provides a basis for dealing more effectively with organizational problems. Information systems design, organizational design, job placement and decision effectiveness can all be related to the manager's decision style. The combined approach portends a major shift in the way organizations are viewed, in achieving optimal fit of individuals in the organization and in achieving effective decision making.

REFERENCES

Adorno, T., et al., *The Authoritarian Personality,* New York: Free Press, 1950.

Alawi, H., "Cognitive, Task and Organizational Complexities in Relation to Information Processing Behavior in Business Managers," D.B.A. dissertation, USC, 1973.

Athey, T., "The Development and Testing of a Seminar for Increasing the Cognitive Complexity of Individuals," D.B.A. dissertation, USC, 1976.

Berwitz, C., *The Job Analysis Approach to Affirmative Action,* New York: Wiley-Interscience, 1975.

Boulgarides, J., "Decision Style, Values, and Biographical Factors in Relation to Satisfaction and Performance," D.B.A. dissertation, USC, 1973.

Boulgarides, J., and M. Driver, "A Decision Style Contingency Model of Managerial Satisfaction and Productivity," unpublished manuscript, Management Dept., USC, 1977.

Copeman, G., *The Chief Executive and Business Growth,* New York: Leviathan House, 1972.

D'Antoni, J., "Content-Oriented and Process-Oriented Value Systems," D.B.A. dissertation, USC, 1972.

Driver, M., "A Study of Education and Work," Management Dept., USC, 1977.

Driver, M., T. Olson, D. Sundby, and W. Testerman, "The Position Description Questionnaire," Dept. of Management, USC, 1976.

Driver, M., and J. Lintott, "Managerial Decision Diagnostics," unpublished manuscript, Dept. of Management, USC, 1972.

Driver, M., and T. Mock, "Information Processing, Decision Style Theory and Accounting Information Systems," *Accounting Review,* 50 (1975a), 490-508.

_____,"Some Experimental Results in MIS, Human Information Processing and Tailored Information Systems," paper presented at annual meeting of ORSA/TIMS, Las Vegas, 1975(b).

Driver, M., and S. Streufert, "Integrative Complexity," *Administrative Science Quarterly,* 14 (1969), 272-85.

Fayol, H., *General and Industrial Management,* London: Putnam, 1949.

Fiedler, F.E., "Engineer the Job to Fit the Manager," *Harvard Business Review,* 1965.

Freud, S., *The Ego and the Id,* London: Hogarth Press, 1947.

_____,*The Interpretation of Dreams,* London: Hogarth Press, 1953.

_____,*New Introductory Lectures on Psychoanalysis,* New York: Norton Press, 1933.

Gardner, R., "Cognitive Styles in Categorizing Behavior," *Journal of Personality,* 1953.

Goldstein, K., and M. Scheerer, *Abstract and Concrete Behavior,* Psychological Monographs, 1941.

Gore, W.J., *Administrative Decision Making,* New York: Wiley, 1964.

Grimsley, G., and H.F. Jarrett, The Relationship of Past Managerial Achievement to Test Measures Obtained in the Employment Situation, *Personnel Psychology,* 26 (1973), 31-48.

_____ ,The Relationship of Past Managerial Achievement to Test Measures Obtained in the Employment Situation, II *Personnel Psychology,* 28 (1975), 215-31.

Hackman, J., and G. Oldham, "Development of the Job Diagnostic Survey," *Journal of Applied Psychology,* 1975.

Hager, J., "The Feasibility of Using Decision Making Style as a Criterion for Career Assignments in the U.S. Air Force," D.B.A. dissertation, USC, 1977.

Hartman, H., *Ego Psychology and the Problem of Adaptation,* New York: International Universities Press, 1934.

Harvey, O.J., "Conceptual Systems and Attitude Change," in C. Sherif and M. Sherif, eds., *Attitude, Ego Involvement and Change,* New York: Wiley, 1967.

Harvey, O.J., D. Hunt, and H. Schroder, *Conceptual Systems and Personality Organization,* New York: Wiley, 1961.

Harvey, O.J., and H. Schroder, "Cognitive Aspects of Self and Motivation," in O. Harvey, *Motivation and Social Interaction,* New York: Ronald Press, 1963.

Harvey, O.J., and R. Ware, "Personality Differences in Dissonance Reduction," *Journal of Personality and Social Psychology,* 1967.

Heider, F., "Attitude and Cognitive Organization," *Journal of Psychology,* 1946.

Heller, F.A., *Managerial Decision Making,* London: Tavistock Institute, 1971.

Hill, P., *Towards a New Philosophy of Management,* Epping, England: Cower Press Ltd., 1971.

Jenkins, D., *Job Power,* Baltimore: Penguin, 1973.

Kelly, G.A., *A Psychology of Personal Constructs,* New York: Norton, 1955.

Kepner, C.H., and B.B. Tregoe, *The Rational Manager,* New York: McGraw-Hill, 1965.

Klein, G., "Adaptive Properties of Sensory Functioning," *Bulletin of the Menninger Clinic,* 1949.

_____ ,"The Personal World through Perception," in R. Blake and G. Ramsey, eds., *Perception: An Approach to Personality,* New York: Ronald Press, 1951.

Lewin, K., *Principles of Topographical Psychology,* New York: McGraw-Hill, 1936.

Likert, R., *New Patterns of Management,* New York: McGraw-Hill, 1961.

Lindblom, C.E., "The Science of Muddling Through," *Public Administration Review,* 1959.

McClelland, D.C., and D.H. Burnham, "Power is the Greater Motivator," *Harvard Business Review,* 1976.

Miller, G.A., "The Magical Number Seven, Plus or Minus Two," *Psychological Review,* 1956.

Moment, D., and A. Zaleznick, *Role Development and Interpersonal Competence,* Cambridge, Mass.: Harvard Graduate School of Business Administration, 1963.

Mulder, M., "Power Equalization through Participation," *Administrative Science Quarterly,* 1971.

Owens, W.A., "Progress Report: A Developmental Investigation," University of Georgia, 1969.

Patz, A.L., and A.J. Rowe, *Management Control and Decision Systems,* Santa Barbara, Calif.: Wiley/Hamilton, 1977.

Peters, D., *Position Evaluation Form,* Purdue University, 1965.

Piaget, J., *The Origins of Intelligence in Children,* New York: International Universities Press, 1936.

Reif, W., and F. Luthans, "Does Job Enrichment Really Pay Off?" *California Management Review,* Fall 1972, pp. 30-37.

Rokeach, M., *The Open and Closed Mind,* New York: Basic Books, 1960.

Rowe, A.J., "Effective Decision Making," unpublished manuscript, USC, 1977.

————,"Making Effective Decisions," *Chemical Engineering,* 1974.

————,"The Myth of the Rational Decision Maker," *International Management,* 1974.

Rowe, A.J., S.R. Weingart, and R.J. Provenzano, Navy Leadership Management Analysis Study, System Development Corporation, TM5835, 1977.

Simon, H., *Administrative Behavior,* New York: Macmillan, 1957.

Soelberg, Peer, "Unprogrammed Decision Making: Job Choice," *Industrial Management Review,* 1967.

Srivastra, S., P. Salipante, T. Cummings, W. Notz, J. Bigelow, and J. Waters, *Job Satisfaction and Productivity,* Kent, O.: Kent State University Press, 1977.

Streufert, S., P. Suedfeld, and M. Driver, "Conceptual Structure, Information Search and Information Utilization," *Journal of Personality and Social Psychology,* 2 (1965), 736-40.

Suedfeld, P., and S. Streufert, "Information Search as a Function of Conceptual and Environmental Complexity," *Psychonomic Science,* 1966.

Tannenbaum, R., and W.H. Schmidt, "How to Choose a Leadership Pattern," *Harvard Business Review,* 1973.

Testerman, W., "Decision Style and Job Selection in the Computer Industry," D.B.A. dissertation, USC, 1976.

Vroom, V., and P. Yetton, *Leadership and Decision Making,* Pittsburgh, Pa.: University of Pittsburgh Press, 1973.

Zaleznick, A., "Power and Politics in Organizational Life," *Harvard Business Review,* 1970.

CHAPTER 7

Identifying and Coping with Stress in Organizations: The Personnel Perspective

Cary L. Cooper
Derek Torrington

The extent to which stress at work produces a degree of psychological impairment has become a central issue in the current debate on the quality of working life. Various analyses of alienation as a result of paced assembly lines and other forms of mass production have spawned a range of possible initiatives to mitigate that condition; job enrichment, autonomous work groups, and versions of industrial democracy are some of the best known.

More recently, considerations of managerial or executive stress, such as those of Carson (1972), Gowler and Legge (1975), and Cooper and Marshall (1978), have sought to identify the nature and causes of the psychological impairment that can affect the quality of managerial life. Both authors of this chapter have already considered either the analysis of executive stress or particular initiatives that could lead to its modification (Cooper and Marshall, 1975a, 1975b;

This is a slightly modified version of a paper that appeared in *Personnel Review*. We would like to thank the journal and its publisher, Gower Press, for permission to use this material.

Torrington, 1972; Naylor and Torrington, 1974.) The purpose of this chapter is to discuss certain initiatives for the management of stress that might be attempted by the personnel function within an organization, in the hope of moving the debate forward from analysis to action.

CAUSES AND SOURCES OF STRESS

Researchers so far have identified a long list of causal factors in stress, which can be conveniently grouped under seven headings (see Figure 7-1). This should not be taken as a simple list of factors to be

FIGURE 7-1   Sources of Work Stress

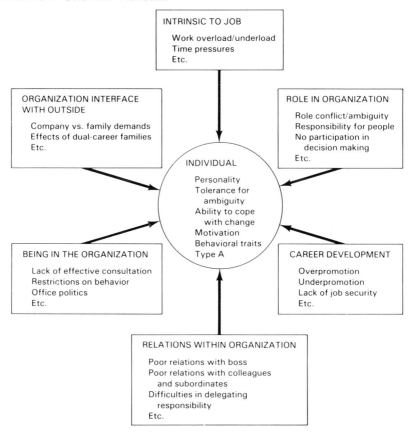

eliminated, because the grouping includes factors that are essential for any sort of achievement, and the removal of one—like too much work—can result in simply producing the opposite, which is equally stressful—too little work. Furthermore, there is the inescapable paradox that stress to one man is satisfaction to another. For some, the lack of job security is a stimulus to the satisfaction of living dangerously; for others, the existence of tight deadlines is the challenge in their job that provides the greatest satisfaction. Lazarus (1967) has demonstrated that a stressful situation cannot be defined by reference to objective criteria. Only the individual can define his own stressors as a result of his own experience and apprehensions, and for each person there will be a range of potential factors that will put him under stress. "Stimulating pressure" will change to "debilitating stress" when the person feels unable to cope, becomes anxious about that "feeling of inability," and begins to adopt defensive behaviors.

COPING WITH STRESS

Once the individual experiences his stress, he will adopt a series of behaviors reacting to it. In most cases, these will be adaptive behaviors dealing directly with the stressful situation by producing solutions to it. Typical stressors and adaptive behaviors might be:

Stressor	Adaptive Behavior
Overworked	Some work delegated
Not aware of company policy on a particular matter	Finds out what policy is
Poor working relationship with colleague	Confronts issue with colleague and negotiates better relationship
Underpromotion	Leaves organization for another
Company vs. family demands	Takes a holiday
Role ambiguity	Seeks clarification with colleagues or superior

Each of these tackles the basic cause of the stress and solves it, at least temporarily and perhaps permanently.

An alternative set of behaviors contains those that are maladaptive, in that they do not deal with the problem; they avoid it and probably aggravate it. Typical of these might be:

Stressor	Adaptive Behavior
Overworked	Accepts work overload, with result that general performance deteriorates
Not aware of company policy on a particular matter	Guesses incorrectly and performs inappropriately
Poor working relationship with colleague	Attacks colleague indirectly through third party
Underpromotion	Loses confidence and becomes convinced of own inadequacy
Company v. family demands	Blames company for family discontent
Role ambiguity	Withdraws from some aspects of work role

In all these situations, the initiator is always the person under stress, and it is reasonable to suggest that an external intervention is only going to become potentially useful as a way of altering maladaptive behaviors, which harm both the individual and his organization, into adaptive behaviors.

THE PROBLEM OF THE EXTERNAL INITIATIVE

External initiatives to assist a stressed individual may come from a number of sources, and an agent of the employing organization, such as a personnel officer, may be the least likely to succeed. Partly this is because the person may not realize that the organization is the source of his problem, or because it actually derives from a combination of causes (perhaps an overbearing boss *and* a disgruntled wife). Partly it is because of the widespread reluctance of people to acknowledge that they are under stress at all. The reasons for this can be attributed to a variety of cultural factors, such as conventional assumptions about "proper behavior." Many of the middle-class British, for example, like to ascribe to themselves such attributes as "stiff upper lip," sangfroid, imperturbability, unflappability and self-reliance. All have the self-illusion or self-assurance of being able to cope with stressful situations and a feeling of disapproval or condescension about those who are not able to cope and are, by extension, "dependent, weak, and lacking in moral fibre." Acknowledging a difficulty in coping with stress is likely to be seen as a severe loss of face.

The situation in the United States appears, at least superficially, different, with a larger proportion of the population utilizing psychoanalysis and other forms of psychotherapy and counseling. Nevertheless, there is still a reluctance in business to accept stress as an inevitable consequence of organizational life. This degree of inhibition in owning up to being under stress is the main problem of the external intervention and means that a range of interventions from outside the organization may be more likely to succeed. An individual may seek or accept intervention from a spouse, family doctor, priest, parent, marriage guidance counselor, friend, or lawyer more readily than from his employing organization.

THE SCOPE FOR PERSONNEL INTERVENTION

Within the framework so far presented, and with the reservations that have been mentioned, we now move to consider a range of interventions that could come from the personnel specialists within an organization. They are grouped under two headings:

> *Operational*—These strategies modify existing personnel operations to take account of their potential for stress mitigation.
>
> *Influential*—These refer to the potential for stress mitigation secondhand, through the influence of personnel specialists on overall management philosophy and policy.

Operational 1: Performance Review

The current trend in performance appraisal is to move away from the *judgment* of a superior on the performance of a subordinate, toward a *discussion* between colleagues about the progress of a job in which they both have an interest, one as the jobholder and the other as being responsible for the performance of the jobholder. Among others, Beveridge (1974) and Randell et al. (1972) have identified this trend and expounded its method. Personnel officers monitoring "performance review programs" and coaching managers in interview method could incorporate an element of stress identification in the procedures they advocate. Beveridge's approach is particularly susceptible to this type of development, as the jobholder is encouraged to identify and comment upon the problems blocking effective performance. An interviewer with the requisite skill and sensitivity may enable the interviewee at least to engage in catharsis, with the possibility of going further by helping to work out adaptive behaviors for the jobholder to initiate or to encourage stress-relieving initiatives within the organizational context in which the job is done.

The potential dangers of this approach are the temptation of the interviewer to play God—"Come unto me, all ye who are heavy laden and I will give you rest"—or to seek out personal problems of the interviewee as a convenient reason for unsatisfactory performance, neatly absolving the interviewer from taking any action or bearing any responsibility. Notwithstanding this hazard, the performance review still provides an opportunity for stress identification, as it is an occasion when matters are being discussed in a manner more detached and reflective than in most interactive encounters at work.

Operational 2: The Professional Counselor

An alternative may lie in the work of the small number of people employed in organizations in a quasi-professional counseling capacity. Occasionally an organization will have in its rank a professional psychologist, whose job is to be available to discuss personal problems with employees. His service could be extremely helpful in providing a means toward stress mitigation. The problem lies in the reluctance of the employee *to be seen* seeking such assistance, and it may be more effective if the expert masquerades under a title like Welfare Officer, or even Management Development Officer; then his advice could be sought without one's necessarily being seen as acknowledging a personal psychological impairment. A similar type of function could, however, be exercised by at least two other professionals who feature in some organizations: the doctor and the industrial chaplain, both of whom have the great advantage of being perceived as independent of the organization and its decision-making processes and thus as people not likely to weaken an employee's career prospects. Both are seen as appropriate repositories of confidences and as sources of two kinds of solace—medication or spiritual guidance—beyond the capacity of the organization.

A British Institute of Management survey (1971) indicated that only 5 percent of companies that have health-care schemes included psychiatric counseling as part of the scheme, but this referred only to organizations actually employing a psychiatrist specifically for this purpose. The survey included the comment:

> ... if one believes that managers need health care primarily because of the stress of their work, then this would be a useful adjunct to a normal checkup, and many doctors do include this as part of the regular medical check-up.

If counseling on stress is available from the doctor on demand, then it may well produce the type of inhibition already described for other possible initiatives, but an established practice of regular health checks on executives sets up a cycle of encounters in which there is the possibility that stress will be discussed. There are additional obvious advantages—that the doctor will be able to diagnose a wider range of stress symptoms than would other potential interveners, as well as being able to infer stress-proneness from a medical history. It is beyond our competence to consider the place of medication in mitigating stress, but if it is appropriate, only the doctor, within the organization, can provide it. There is however, an encouraging pharmacological advance in beta-adrenergic blockers, which may help to prevent or delay stress manifestations, especially ischemic heart disease and, possibly, hypertension.

The BIM survey showed there to be 600 full-time company doctors and 1,000 part-time in the U.K. in 1971. Prentice (1976) calculated that there were 150 full-time industrial chaplains and 450 part-time in 1976, so that they are numerically fewer than others. This is because there has been no ecclesiastical equivalent of the U.K. Health and Safety at Work Act to boost the number of chaplains, and their services are not as universally acceptable as those of the doctors. It also appears that their activities are mainly directed toward the needs of shop-floor workers rather than managers. Nevertheless, they are perceived as being neutral, and they carry out their duties principally by walking around and talking to people without arousing too much suspicion about their motives. Like doctors, their training and vocation has familiarized them with the counseling role and the revelation of people's deep fears and anxieties. Here, potentially, is another source of external intervention.

Operational 3: Training

A third area of operations, usually under the control of the personnel specialists, is training and, again, there are stress-relieving possibilities. The purpose of training courses is to aid the operational performance of course attenders when they return to their normal role and, if the course succeeds in this, it is likely to reduce stress-proneness by increasing the feeling of competence and confidence that the trainee has in relation to his work. Also, the course extracts a person from his normal work environment for a period during which he is relieved of the normal pressures of his duties, with the opportunity to reflect upon them, discuss them with others, and, potentially, set them in a more healthy perspective. Both of these are "built in" to almost any course.

Certain features of training could be considered to deal with stress symptoms more directly. The first is sensitivity training, which is a method of enabling people to see themselves as others see them, by stripping away cultural inhibitions about self-presentation and self-awareness (Cooper, 1976). This can help a person to a more realistic perception of himself and, possibly, help him to cope better with some of his stresses. This is a method of training that has been criticized because of its potential *stressfulness* for some people (Cooper, 1975a), and it may seem strange that it is advocated as a means of stress mitigation, but it is another feature of the overall dilemma already mentioned: What may be stressful for one person may be stress-relieving for another. Second, the course could include training in methods of slowing down the physiological processes, such as yoga or transcendental meditation. No doubt this will be regarded as an absurd suggestion by many management trainers, who would envisage the incredulity and resentment of some course attenders to the suggestion that such techniques could have an appropriate place in management training. Nevertheless, it has been demonstrated that these are methods that succeed in enabling people to relax. For that reason, they have a potential place in management training. The third possibility is probably the easiest, and that is to include in a course some focus on, or discussion of, stress at work. This would at least succeed in bringing the issue out into the open and moderating the degree of shame that course members may feel in acknowledging their own stress-proneness.

Operational 4: Lessening Organizational Dependency

If an individual employee is overdependent on his employing organization, there are a number of disadvantages: He is likely to become overcautious, anxious, and reluctant, and generally to view his compliance to the employment contract as being obligatory rather than volitional. Coincidentally, it may make him more susceptible to stress, as the anticipated whims and vagaries of superiors assume alarming significance. U.K. readers will remember the success of the ASTMS press advertisements of the late 1960s, when the membership of the union rose dramatically as a result of focus on that particular anxiety.

In the middle 1970s, we have a situation of many managers feeling very dependent on their current employer because of the sluggishness of the managerial job market. Other jobs are hard to find, and the numbers of the "executive jobless" continue to rise. Although personnel specialists may not be able to influence the external job market, there are other opportunities to heighten job security by reducing organizational dependence.

One strategy, in which the authors may be seen to have a vested interest, is to give better opportunities for improving professional qualifications. Studies like that of Page (1976) show the relative difficulty of obtaining reemployment among those in executive positions whose skills and experience have been specific to one organization. When they are no longer required in that context, a period of retraining is necessary to find employment elsewhere. Allied to this is the more general problem of skill obsolescence, as some specializations become less important in organizational life. Enabling employees to enhance their general employability can increase their sense of job security by increasing the range of options they see before them. It has already been suggested in this chapter that the purpose of training is to aid the operational performance of those attending courses. If this is achieved by the in-company course, the range of skills and knowledge will be oriented toward those requisite within the organization. Provision of day-and block-release for externally moderated qualifications, life professional-body diplomas, and university masters and diploma programs can provide people with a wider range of enhanced capacities as well as "a piece of paper" with wider currency, avoiding the claustrophobia felt by many executives who see their skills as irrelevant outside their own bailiwick. It is presumably a narrow and outdated view to criticize such opportunities on the grounds that a prized member of the organization is more likely to leave.

A further possibility is to review personnel policy on fringe benefits. It seems particularly pertinent to mention this at a time when there are many rumors, and some evidence, that companies are seeking to extend fringe benefits for executives (as compensation, in the U.K. for example, by being constrained by an incomes policy) in adjusting salaries. Common executive benefits, like the company car, "assisted house purchase," and subsidized lunches, can make people organizationally dependent by reducing the freedom of movement of those enjoying the benefits. It would be unrealistic to suggest that such benefits should be removed, but their extension needs very careful consideration.

One of the main determinants of organizational dependency is, of course, the pension arrangement. Until now, most private-sector pension schemes have provided relatively attractive pensions to the managerial elite, but with the penalty of nontransferability or limited transferability. The new state pension scheme which came into effect in April 1978 in the U.K., for example, provides stronger competition for the private pensions industry, but there remain a range of options to employers within the state framework. Existing private pension schemes can be wound up, employees can be contracted out of the additional pension element of the state scheme, or state and private arrangements can be integrated. Many of these decisions have still to be taken, and we suggest that one question for personnel practitioners to ask is, Which arrangement will lessen organizational dependency?

Operational 5: Clarifying the Criteria
for Advancement

The personnel literature is replete with advice on career development and complaints about its scarcity. Glueck (1974) echoes the common cry:

> Unfortunately, most organizations are not at present concerned with career development. They would not think of ignoring financial

planning or materials replacement planning, but the human resource is likely to deteriorate or fail to be used well without career development plans.

The considerable, if short-lived, popularity of MBO was based on the simple proposition that performance was improved if people knew what they had to do and how they were getting on. We suggest here that this same simple proposition may be a way of reducing individual stress. It is axiomatic that the majority of people in executive positions are seeking advancement to a post of greater authority, scope, or financial remuneration; if this were not so, they would not put their foot on the first rung of the ladder. Yet how often do they know the performance criteria for advancement? Career development programs that we have seen are usually highly specific for junior positions, with a progressive decline in clarity as the program moves up the hierarchy. The problem is a dual one. First, a program of career development implies that the person who achieves the declared objectives will reap the benefit; if, for instance, five people meet the outline requirements to be the next marketing manager, only one of them will be successful, and even that depends on the present incumbent's deciding to leave or retire. Second, the career development program may be suspect in the face of change. Criteria set out in 1979 may have become irrelevant in 1980.

Despite the difficulties, there are usually ways in which the future can be made clearer and more comprehensible for people; and a realistic increase in clarity can help to moderate individual stress.

Operational 6: Self-Analysis Drills

The last of our operational suggestions is quite an original one. Whereas we have so far been considering possible developments in operations already existing in most organizations, this potential initiative is the provision of a self-analysis aid, whereby a person can carry out his own diagnosis of his own behavior in order to determine whether he is under stress or not. Symptom awareness training is one example of this, and many occupational health medics argue that this is the first step in stress prevention. Some company doctors would go further and suggest that this is all that is needed, since the successful management of stress must ultimately rely on the individual's own initiative, once he has been made aware of his own stress-related behavior. Not much has been done to implement this type of training in industry, but "model programs" are available from the mental health field (Noland, 1973).

Influential 1: Industrial Democracy and the Managerial Role

Moving now to our second category, we begin to consider those initiatives related to personnel influence in organizations rather than personnel operations, and the first suggestion is concerned with industrial democracy and the role of managers within that type of structure.

Weir (1976) has recently given sharp focus to the widely held belief that managers are apprehensive about the development of union involvement in the management of companies, even when the managers are union members themselves. He surveyed the attitudes of 1,147 managers in a large, profitable U.K. organization in the food and drink industry that had a good reputation for employee relations and is regarded as having an overt commitment to progressive personnel policies. Forty-five percent of them felt that they, as a category of employee, were "looked after" worse than in the past and that manual workers had more direct and comprehensive access to top management than they had themselves. Later he demonstrates that there is a feeling among his respondents that employees should have a greater say in running the company, but this does not necessarily mean *union* involvement. Forty-seven percent of the union members (14 percent of the sample), but only 17 percent of non-unionists, were prepared to advocate more involvement by unions in management.

The general trend toward industrial democracy (particularly in Europe) is a source of anxiety to managers, producing problems about self-esteem and considerable role ambiguity. Strategies to deal with this are easy to see, but less easy to implement. The obvious initiative is to involve managers in consultation and decision making to the extent they regard as desirable—76 percent of Weir's respondents felt that they were not sufficiently consulted about matters that directly affected them. The obstacles are considerable. First, they are likely to lack the machinery and the will to find and accept a common representative figure, because of the diversity of their interests and their concomitant uninterest in unionism. Second, other employees may regard consultation by management with managers as the opposing high command consulting with the supplies officers before launching the attack. Third, what managers seek from consultation may frequently be the maintenance of extension of a series of differential gaps between themselves and other employes.

The strategy that we hope personnel specialists may be able to adopt in this connection is to whittle down the traditional managerial view of status and self-esteem, of being seen in terms of hierarchical position and the number of subordinates. If managers can gradually adjust their sights to see their status in terms of contribution to the organization, instead of place in the organization's hierarchical structure, then the stressful potential of industrial democracy and its evolution will be reduced, and the potential value of such evolution will itself be enhanced. To achieve such a change will depend on some of the strategies already discussed, such as performance appraisal and training, and will inevitably be influenced by remuneration policy. But the general contribution of personnel specialists to the development of thinking and employment *policy,* within their companies, is another potential influence.

Influential 2: The Nature of Managerial Jobs

There is a tendency to believe that manual and some clerical employees have jobs that are routine and lacking in intrinsic motivations. We need to realize that some managerial jobs are also of this type. Campbell et al. (1970) surveyed 39 organizations with a high reputation for the development of managerial talent and concluded:

> Management was characterized by having rather narrow jobs and very tightly written job descriptions that almost seemed designed to take the newness, conflict and challenge out of the job.

The current interest in the quality of working life generally appears to assume that managerial life already has quality and that it is only the non-manager's working life that needs moderation. The irony is that so many studies and other indicators, like managerial membership of trade unions, reveal a growing disenchantment, with many managers failing to find in their work those intrinsic motivations that we are so busily trying to inject into the lives of those engaged in demonstrably prosaic work. The reasons for this are well documented, with specialization, technology, organization size, and degree of bureaucratization being the most common, together with the resentment of apparent union influence that we have already considered. We should add to this a particular version of the problem of specialization, and that is the growth in the number of specialists, each of whom reduce the wholeness of the job done by someone else. For years this has been seen as the particular problem of the foreman, who has seen his autonomy gradually reduced by the arrival of the work study specialist, the production controller, the industrial relations officer, and so on. More senior managers have not perhaps acknowledged and come to terms with the extent to which the specialists are reducing the wholeness of their jobs, too.

Out of the immense and ever-expanding literature on motivation and job satisfaction, Hackman and Lawler (1971) demonstrated the crucial importance of the scope for making a significant contribution to the total task in considering the sources of "achievement feelings" in people at work. Personnel officers should ask themselves to what extent they are now reducing the contribution of other managers, and so removing a key element from the jobs of their managerial colleagues. Personnel specialists have long cast themselves in the role of John the Baptist, crying aloud in a wilderness of managerial indifference. Influential and well-informed figures in the personnel management world (Swannack, 1975; Rogers, 1976) now aver that those days are past, and the reasons are evident; legislation, income policy, the need for collective bargaining, the growth of union membership, and the decline of employee deference are at the top of the list. The personnel specialist moves to the center of the stage, acquiring the status, power, money, and limelight he has always craved; but his gain is another's loss, because the advisory role becomes a control function to achieve consistency, and changes to increase consistency involve reducing the discretion and flexibility available to managers. The difficult question here for personnel specialists, in their influencing, is, How can managerial jobs gain features to replace the discretion that the specialists remove?

Influential 3: Selection and Promotion Criteria

Change of function within the organization, as well as joining a new one, is a time of stress for the individual. Conventionally, such changes of function are promotions or carry some other benefit to make the change attractive, so there is useful enthusiasm and commitment to counter the stress hazard. But apart from the normal "settling-in" problems of a new job, there is the question of whether the selection/promotion decision has been soundly based, so that the promotee is being drawn into a new role with which he can cope. The danger is that the Peter Principle will operate and the promotee will find that he has reached the level of his own incompetence, resulting in his remaining in that stressful situation because he is not able to display efficient competence to be promoted out of it. The conventional method of avoiding such an error is to exhort the decision makers to pay close attention to the fullness of the job description and to their selection criteria. Equally conventional, however, are the detailed job description and personnel specification that focus on the specialist aspects of the job, and guesses about the personal attributes of candidates that will equip them for those specialized tasks. Seldom is this approach effective in telling us what *skills* are called for.

A recent advance, achieved through the work of Rosemary Stewart (1976), may help in improving the effectiveness of job analysis for selection and placement and in attempting to provide generic classifications of management jobs. After analyzing some 450 managerial jobs, Stewart produced a typology based mainly on the nature of the contacts that the job required, since this was regarded as the main differentiation between them. A total of twelve jobs are in four groups: *Hub, Peer Dependent, Man Management*, and *Solo*. These terms partly explain themselves, but it is necessary to read the text to see the extent to which this typology succeeds in extending simple, commonsense ideas about the demands of jobs by drawing in the degree of contacts that jobholders have to make inside and outside the organization. The level at which they make internal contacts, the nature of their relationship with the people they contact, the importance of cooperation, the time spent in contact, the significance of bargaining and of risk-taking, and other factors give credence to the typology and thus make it possible to construct job profiles, providing a visual means of comparing the demands of the job a person is in with the demands of a job he might move into.

This provides the opportunity to draw up job descriptions and specifications with an additional dimension relating to the demands of a job, and then shows how the job profile could be used to describe the demands, constraints, and choices in a job in such a way that requisite skills can also be described. It would be naive of us to suggest that this would prevent the promotion of people who are not appropriately qualified. People's aspirations are seldom sufficiently rational for them to accept that a particular promotion would not suit them, in spite of the fact that it pays X dollars a year more than their present post; and those making appointments may not have a field from which to choose. Despite this, the Stewart job profile method might prevent some stressful promotions and would, at least, succeed in describing the demands, constraints, and choices of a new job in enough detail for a promotee to go into a new situation with his eyes open.

Influential 4: Grievance Procedure

There is little evidence recently available on the issues now being processed through grievance channels in organizations, but what is clear is that every employee of an organization, including managers, must be advised of the grievance-resolution channel personally available to him. Although this is traditionally the domain of the shop steward taking up the case of an aggrieved manual employee, there is now the possibility of more people using this procedure as a way of seeking satisfaction of complaints. We have earlier argued that the main problem of the stressed manager is the difficulty he has in acknowledging that he is under stress in the first place. Therefore, it is not likely that he will make a complaint that he is being stressed, but it may still be useful for the personnel specialist to monitor grievances in procedure as a possible stress indicator. Roethlisberger and Dickson (1939) made the simple and profound observation forty years ago that complaints involving the hopes and fears of employees had both a *manifest* and a *latent* content, saying one thing and meaning much more. If an organization has managers personally using grievance procedures—which seems unlikely—a pull on that particular communication cord can be a cue to the personnel specialist of a stressful situation. More likely is that grievances coming from other people in the area for which the manager is responsible may have a latent content indicating that the manager is showing stress symptoms in his dealings with subordinates.

Influential 5: Managerial Mobility

One very specific source of stress is the need for managers to move to other regions of the country. In certain large companies and public-sector organizations, this is a well-established aspect of personnel policy. Promotion accompanies movement. In this situation, the translated manager has the usual problems of a new job plus the domestic and family problems that relocating brings. We suggest that relocation problems are increasing rather than lessening. The direct and indirect financial commitment in buying and selling houses is generally regarded as getting greater, and parents frequently feel that the standard of education in schools varies so considerably that a geographical move could disadvantage their children. Most significantly of all, new factors in the mobility argument are the attitude and earning potential of the wife. We do not suggest that all managers are men, but the very great majority of executives are married men. If the wife is content to be a housewife, she has to cope with the loneliness of settling in a new town while her husband "escapes" to work with its built-in social contacts. If she is not content with being a housewife, there are a variety of developments that influence her mobility. Twenty percent of households now have the wife as the principal earner. Presumably, few of these are at the earnings level of the conventional mobile manager, but at a time of income policy and inflation, the significance of the wife's income is considerable and not to be jeopardized. Also, some of the jobs popular among the wives of mobile managers are less readily transferable than they were. The prime example is schoolteaching, where the numbers of unemployed schoolteachers make it unlikely that a woman can uproot from one part of the country and readily find a teaching post in another even though this was commonplace until the 1970s.

The research of Birch and Macmillan (1971) gives some indication of the scale of managerial mobility. Examining the period up to 1970 in the U.K., they found that the average number of regional moves per manager of 0.7 in 1940 had more than doubled to an average of 1.6 in 1970, with 15 percent of managers moving four or more times in their careers, and university-qualified managers moving more frequently than the average. Furthermore, in an in-depth study of mobile managers and their wives, Marshall and Cooper (1976) found that the stresses on the managers and their families during and after a relocation were greater and more complex than anticipated. They concluded that much of the stress and of the managers' ability to cope depended on the stage of their life cycle (single or married;—married with no children; married with young children; married with older children and an empty nest). Unfortunately, many managers are relocated at the most inappropriate life stage for the family—when the manager has young, school-aged children and a "captive wife."

The question we raise here is, How necessary is the policy of some organizations in explicitly or implicitly making willingness to move a condition of promotion? Many people will seek geographical relocation at some time in their careers, but if people are not able to determine when and where they move, but instead have to accept the move when it is offered or slip several prospective rungs on the promotion ladder, then they become candidates for stress because of family—company interface conflict. We believe that the widespread convention of linking promotion with geographical relocation could benefit from reappraisal.

FURTHER CONSIDERATIONS

Having presented our eleven possible initiatives, we mention some of the long-range features to working organizations that are stressful but whose solutions are hard to see. If they can be discussed, solutions may emerge, even though they seem intractable at the moment.

First we ask the question about movement in the hierarchy. Moving up the hierarchy is generally attractive; moving down is unthinkable. How can we learn to find a move down the hierarchy as attractive as a move up? Perhaps this is beyond the capacity of those of us who spend our working lives in organizations, but if such moves ever become attractive, we can see solutions to some of the stressful predicaments of those managers who have outlived their usefulness in a particular position, yet hang on grimly to avoid the nightmarish situation of losing face. Closely linked with this is our second question: Does the organization always have to be a hierarchy with the greatest rewards and prerequisites automatically going to the top? Is there any possiblity of an organization's succeeding in which the position of managing director or chief executive is just a job like any other? One of the inferences of Cooper's (1979) recent work is that many hierarchically middle- and junior-range positions are more stressful than those of more senior officeholders, even though the reward system does not usually acknowledge this. Third, will we ever reach a situation where the age of retirement is not the immovable watershed of the 65th birthday?

REFERENCES

Beveridge, W.E., *The Interview in Staff Appraisal* London: Allen & Unwin, 1974.

Birch, S., and B. Macmillan, *Managers on the Move: A Study of British Managerial Mobility,* London: British Institute of Management, 1971.

British Institute of Management, *Executive Health Care,* London: BIM, 1971.

Campbell, J., E.E. Lawler, M. Dunnette, and K.E. Weick, *Managerial Behavior, Performance and Effectiveness,* New York: McGraw-Hill, 1970.

Carson, I., "What Are the Causes of Executive Stress?" *International Management Review,* Vol. 27 (1972), 16-23.

Cooper, C.L., *Developing Social Skills in Managers,* New York: Halsted Press, 1976.

_____,"How Psychologically Dangerous Are T-Groups and Encounter Groups?" *Human Relations,* Vol. 28, No. 3 (1975a), 248-161.

_____, *The Executive Gypsy.* London: Macmillan, 1979.

Cooper, C.L., and J. Marshall, "The Management of Stress," *Personnel Review,* Vol. 4, No. 4 (1975c).

_____."Stress and Pressure within Organizations," *Management Decision,* Vol. 13, No. 2, (1975b), 292-303.

_____,*Understanding Executive Stress,* New York: McGraw Hill, 1978.

Glueck, W.F., *Personnel: A Diagnostic Approach,* Homewood, Ill.: Irwin-Dorsey, 1974.

Gowler, D., and K. Legge, eds., *Managerial Stress,* Epping, England: Gower Press, 1975.

Hackman, J.R., and E.E. Lawler, "Employee Reactions to Job Characteristics," *Journal of Applied Psychology,* Vol. 55 (1971).

Lazarus, R.S., *Psychological Stress and the Coping Process,* New York: McGraw-Hill 1967.

Maclean, A., "Emerging Trends in Industrial Mental Health Programs," in R.L. Noland, ed., *Industrial Mental Health and Employee Counseling,* New York: Behavioral Publications, 1971.

Marshall, J., and C.L. Cooper, *Mobile Manager and His Wife,* Bradford: MCB Publications, 1976.

Naylor, R., and D.P. Torrington, eds., *Administration of Personnel Policies,* Epping, England: Gower Press, 1974, pp. 483-97.

Noland, R.L., *Industrial Mental Health and Employee Counseling,* New York: Behavioral Publications, 1973.

Page, N., "Executive Unemployment and Personal Redundancy," *Personnel Review,* Vol. 5, No. 2 (1976).

Prentice, G., "Faith at Work: The Message Is the Mission," *Personnel Management,* Vol. 8, No. 3 (1976).

Randell, G.A., et al., *Staff Appraisal,* London: Institute of Personnel Management, 1972.

Roethlisberger, F.J., and W.J. Dickson, *Management and the Worker,* Cambridge, Mass: Harvard University Press, 1939.

Rogers, T.G.P., "Personnel Moves Centre Stage," *Personnel Management,* Vol. 8, No. 10 (1976).

Stewart, R., *Contrasts in Management,* London: McGraw-Hill, 1976.

Swannack, A.R., "Laying a Ghost to Rest," *Personnel Management,* Vol. 7, No. 12 (1975).

Torrington, D.P., *Face to Face,* Epping, England: Gower Press, 1972, pp. 53-70.

Weir, D., "Radical Managerialism: Middle Managers' Perceptions of Collective Bargaining," *British Journal of Industrial Relations,* Vol. XIV, No. 3 (1976).

CHAPTER 8

Action Research:
The Solution
or the Problem?

Milton G. Holmen

The manager of computer operations came to the personnel director with a problem. "I just published a new shift schedule, and the whole graveyard shift and at least half of the other two shifts say they won't come to work. On the old schedule, I could never keep the right mix of talent on the three shifts. What's the matter with those people? Don't they know that computer operators are easy to get these days?"

In a factory making tennis shoes, rubber gloves, and related rubber and fabric products, the personnel director has a problem. His training staff has until recently provided training only for new employees. The company has now begun a supervisory training program. In keeping with good practice, each trainee fills out an evaluation questionnaire on each training session. The ratings given are almost universally bad, even though the instructors have received very good ratings on the same material in other factories. The trainers are obviously well prepared, but the trainees are not satisfied.

The manager of administration of a large insurance company has just published plans for moving a large regional office of about 500 employees from an old, inefficient building to a new one with more light, more space per employee, and new furniture. The move has been publicized for many months in the company monthly magazine. There has been little response from supervisors and workers. Now, almost every supervisor is objecting to all or some aspects of the move. Some complain about having to move during their busiest month. Others insist they will have too little space, even though it is more than they now occupy. The plant engineering and maintenance staff, which expects to do most of the work during the move, is unhappy.

What do these cases have in common? First, the decisions have been made centrally, with little input from most of the people affected by them. Second, supervisors and workers in each unit agree about the nature of the problem, but there is little agreement *between* units about the problem or an acceptable solution. These are the kinds of problems that are amenable to an action research approach—using research methods for bringing about a change.

WHAT IS ACTION RESEARCH?

The simplest definition of action research is the use of research methods to bring about change or action. To avoid misunderstandings, we must recognize four different definitions of kinds of action research, identified as early as 30 years ago by Chein, Cook, and Harding (1948). They first discussed *diagnostic research* (today, generally referred to as applied research), intended to provide information for taking action; *empirical action research* (this would probably be called evaluation research today), in which the experimenter closely observes the effects of a program or a series of them; and *experimental action research* (which would now be called change research), controlled research on the relative effectiveness of various action techniques.

What Chein, Cook, and Harding called *participative action research* is the kind that will be most discussed in this chapter. As the name implies, it is characterized by involving in the research process the people most affected by the resulting decisions and most involved in their implementation. An equally important criterion of action research, as used in this chapter, is that its purpose must be to bring about action or change, not merely to help decide whether action or change is desirable.

When these two necessary criteria have been met, there are still four varieties of action research being practiced and written about in the late 1970s. First is "pure" action research—initiated to solve a problem or bring about an organizational change—in which responsibility for the research and action are delegated to the action research group by whatever person or persons have the authority to make such a delegation or decision. As with any "pure" phenomenon, it is rarely found. Few managers will delegate decisions and actions to a new, temporary group.

Second is "action training and research." This, as the title suggests, adds training or development of people and groups as a major goal of the process. It might better be called "action research and development" or "action training and development," since its goal is more often to strengthen a group (or interaction between groups) than to develop unconnected individuals. This form will be discussed in detail later.

Third, and most frequently found, is participative study leading to recommendations for action. It is done, not by the people who are to take the action, but by those expected to be most affected by it. Feedback is ordinarily provided to the reference or organizational groups to which the action researchers belong and also to those with authority to make decisions on the subject under study. The responsibility for studying the problem and making recommendations is given to representatives of affected groups, both to use their firsthand knowledge and to reduce their resistance to the pending changes. Such lowered resistance can come from the increased knowledge resulting from the research process and from their involvement in developing the recommendations.

Fourth, some people refer to data collection and feedback to members of an organization as action research. If no action is contemplated, it is more properly called "organizational sensing." Managements should be warned, however, that almost any topic on which people get feedback for a period of time will result in changes in that area. It seems that repeatedly calling people's attention to almost any aspect of their behavior will lead to change in that behavior. The summary cliche is, "You don't get what you *expect,* you get what you *inspect.*" Thus, the collection and feedback of information should be provided only in areas where management is willing for change to occur.

People engaged in research whose goal is to advance knowledge may object to applying the term *research* to an activity not yielding such knowledge. Applying it to this kind of change activity seems to them to overglorify this method of problem solving. However, the term is generally understood not to require an output of new knowledge.

WHAT KINDS OF PROBLEMS DOES ACTION RESEARCH ADDRESS?

Before we explore the ways to conduct action research, let us consider what kinds of problems action research is appropriate for and what kinds it is *not* appropriate for. First, action research is best used on problems not central to the functions of the organization doing it. A department store, for example, would not use it to make decisions on what lines of merchandise to carry. These are the responsibility of top management. An architectural firm would not use it to develop design concepts, as these are professional staff functions.

Second, it is used for problems more important to those affected by the impending action or change than to those with authority to make decisions about it. For example, whereas management might be more concerned than workers about whether to redesign a product line, workers will usually be more concerned than management about shift-rotation schedules of production workers.

Third, it is appropriate for nonrepetitive problems. Action research is not used to decide whom to hire in a large organization, because hiring decisions are being made daily, and staff composition is usually a management responsibility. This does not preclude consulting present staff about potential co-workers, of course. The problem of whether to provide an on-site snack bar or cafeteria service is not made routinely, and many nonmanagement people will be affected by it. Their involvement in the decision, especially if it is widely known in the organization, will probably improve both the quality and the acceptability of the final decision.

Fourth, it is appropriate for problems where there is likely to be resistance among those affected to making the expected change, or disagreement about which change is most desirable. In this sense, it is a way of reducing the strength of resisting vectors in a force-field analysis. This is generally preferable to management's increasing the strength of vectors for change, as the increased push by management for change is likely to result in a corresponding increase in the strength of the resisting vectors. This can lead to an escalating stalemate or to some kind of "blowup." A useful example might be development of an affirmative action program for increasing opportunities of women and minority-group members. This should be a one-time problem, but it is one on which there may be resistance and probably also a disagreement about the program desired; hence, it should be amenable to an action research approach.

Finally, an apparent or "phony" action research project to reduce resistance to a decision already made by management is likely to cause serious problems. The forces released in the action research process are genuine, and unless management is willing to commit itself to serious consideration of the output of an advisory action research project or to accept the changes of a delegated project, it may find itself losing strength and credibility with its people.

Some examples of problems that meet these criteria would be decisions about allocation of parking-lot space, redesign of internal procedures for processing some kinds of documents, whether to establish an employee credit union, and how to reduce tardiness of workers. In all these examples, the problems are not directly related to the central function of the organization, they are more important to those affected by the decisions than to those with authority to make them, they are not repetitive, and there may be resistance to change or to some kinds of change to correct an undesirable situation.

Lawler (1977) describes several instances in which workers participated, using action research methods, in decisions affecting their pay. In one organization, the mixture of salary and fringe benefits is now determined by employees; in another, the way pay increases are made is decided by employees; and in another, employees recommended a bonus system for reducing absenteeism. In one small appliance sales firm, the employees set their own wages, hours, and vacations. Lawler does not recommend these processes for all companies but points out that employees, the best source of information about how different pay systems and rates affect employees, are rarely consulted by management. Their participation can lead to designing more effective and equitable policies for both employees and employers.

IN WHAT KINDS OF ORGANIZATIONS MIGHT ACTION RESEARCH WORK BEST?

Action research works better in organizations that are more organic than mechanistic. The completely mechanistic organization does not provide a sufficiently flexible organizational environment for action research processes to function effectively. People in its hierarchy would be threatened or confused by the process, since it would be a discontinuity from their regular ways of making and carrying out decisions.

A fully organic organization, like Likert's system 4 (1967), operates in something resembling an action research mode all the time. Individuals and groups are united by goals more than by procedural rules. Decisions are made by people most interested in the outcomes, after they examine the data relevant to making the decision. There is open communication and sharing of information, both of which are characteristic of action research processes. A truly organic organization would be less likely than a moderately organic one to have the need for formally chartering action research projects, since interested individuals and groups would undertake such activities without a formal charter.

Action research probably works best and is best accepted in an organization that is "loosening up" its structure and procedures. It is a way to involve in decision making people who have not previously been involved in it, without the organization's committing itself to their continued decision making. It is a way of testing and signaling movement toward more organic processes. It is, however, relatively irreversible. Once people become involved in a certain class of activities and decisions, these become their "right," and can be taken away only with considerable difficulty, if at all.

WHAT PEOPLE SHOULD BE INVOLVED IN AN ACTION RESEARCH PROJECT?

Four categories of people are typically involved in an action research project:

1. *The person or persons with authority over the area in which a problem develops.* They can make or delegate decisions in this area. If an action research project is to be initiated, they must initiate it, or at least legitimize it, indicating who is to be involved in the final decisions.

2. *People affected by the decision*—They are likely to be either resistant to impending changes or protesting about something that needs changing. Not all the people affected are likely to be in agreement about the change needed. For example, nurses in a hospital may feel shift bonuses are unfair to some shifts and want a change. Management may be equally concerned because most of the best nurses, owing to the present bonus system, want to be on a shift where their skill and experience are least needed. Nurses on some of the shifts may defend the present system while others oppose it.

3. *People who will have to carry out the decisions*—For example, if the problem is one of improving lounge or recreational facilities in a plant, the building engineer should be represented on any action research team, because his expertise on structures, costs, materials, and schedules is a necessary input to the decision process.

4. *An action research consultant, usually from outside the affected organization*—This person may bring charismatic skills in getting groups to work together, or group process skills to keep the group moving toward its goal. The consultant or someone else on the team should have data collection and analysis skills, or the "research" aspect of the project will suffer from amateur design of data collection procedures and forms, and from inadequate or inappropriate analyses and interpretation.

WHAT STEPS ARE INVOLVED IN ACTION RESEARCH PROJECTS?

It is difficult to make a concise statement about the number of steps in a typical action research project, for two reasons: First, it is hard to find a typical project—there are many kinds of projects. Second, the last step in most people's list is "recycle." Gardner's Action Training and Research Model (1974) lists 12 steps, with "recycle" as the last one, implying that a full program may contain 20 or more steps. French (1969) lists 14 steps, the last three of which are "rediagnosis of the situation, etc., etc."

The following elements in approximately this order are found in most action research projects:

1. *Problem Identification*—A strong person or group identifies a problem for which ordinary decision processes in the organization seem inappropriate or ineffective, usually where change is needed and resisted, or where there is no agreement on the specific kind of change needed.

2. *Consultations with a Change Consultant*—Usually there will be several discussions between the consultant and key individuals and groups, and there may be some preliminary reconnaissance of the problem area and the organization by the consultant as a basis for developing an action research plan or proposal.

3. *Chartering and Contracting*—An agreement is made by all people and groups involved that an action research project will be initiated, on what its goals and limits are, and on the roles of its members, but time arrangements need to be specified.

4. *Data Gathering and Analysis*—This step may be conducted by the consultant, as in a typical organization development project. Or the consultant may assist the rest of the team by helping in the design of the research—data collection forms, sampling, interview schedules, and data analysis—but doing little or none of the actual data gathering himself, and only checking on the data analysis. If team development or training is a goal of the action research project, the consultant should work at passing on his skills to the team rather than doing jobs for them.

5. *Feedback, Joint Diagnosis, and Action Planning*—These steps may be taken separately but are often taken together. Feedback of analyzed data is to persons or groups chartering the action research team, to those affected by expected actions, and to those who will be needed to implement them.

6. *Action Taken.*

7. *Evaluation and Feedback*—The action research team is responsible for studying the effects of actions taken and for reporting back to those previously involved in the action research and its implementation. The consultant again should be a technical resource in the evaluation research design, data collection, analysis, and interpretation. If the action solved the problem that started the project, the team is publicly thanked and discharged. If not, there may be a new problem identification and a recycle of all major elements except Step 2, since the consultant is involved in the problem identification process.

CAN AN ACTION RESEARCH PROJECT BE DESIGNED, OR MUST IT BE DEVELOPED?

Most action research projects are more developed than designed, for at least five reasons: First, the interest and motivation of the action research team depend upon their fairly complete freedom to take their investigation wherever the problem leads them. Second, the action research team (and those to whom it later gives information) will be *better informed* about the problem, need for change, limits on some apparently feasible alternatives, and so on, than if they had not been involved in the research activity.

Third, it is not known at the start how much research is needed either to select a satisfactory plan for change or to overcome resistance to the proposed change. Fourth, designing the evaluation of the action taken, one of the last steps in the typical action research project, must follow action decisions. Finally, due to the cyclical nature of the process, evaluation of the effects of one change may lead to problem identification for one or more subsequent cycles or projects.

Some aspects of the action research process can be designed or specified in advance. People from whom data will be collected can often be identified—either by inclusion or by exclusion, or both. A decision may be made to send a questionnaire to all members of a university faculty in order to assure them all that "someone is looking at the faculty salary problem *now,* and this is the time to get involved if you want to make something happen." A decision could also be made in advance *not* to involve some group of employees, either because they have no interest in the problem or because they might be unduly "stirred up" by the involvement. A decision can also be made about whether data collection will be by interview, by questionnaire, or both, and whether to collect the data during working hours or to send materials to participants' homes.

Known limits on the change possibilities may also limit the research. For example, in an action research approach to improving in-plant food services, the team had to reach a change decision in less than 90 days, because the current food services contract had to be renewed or canceled by then. In the same project, the team was told that the estimated cost of a new solution could not exceed that of the present arrangement. Possible changes included hours of operation, items carried, and location of facilities. With these change limits, it would be foolhardy to ask affected employees if they wanted the facilities expanded or wanted the company to subsidize the food vendor in order to lower prices or improve quality.

HOW CAN ACTION RESEARCH BE EVALUATED?

Most people who design and conduct evaluation research consider it the most difficult of all kinds of research, for reasons that will be listed later. Evaluating an action research program may place evaluation research in its most difficult context. Nevertheless, plans for evaluation should be included when an action research project is being considered, and the evaluation process should be developed along with other aspects of the project. It is desirable to evaluate not only the outcomes of the change(s) resulting from the process, but also the effects of the action research process itself.

A publication by the U.S. Department of Health, Education and Welfare (1955) identified six steps essential to evaluation research. These are:

1. *Identification of the goals to be achieved*—The more complete and specific the goals statement is, the more likely the project is to achieve measurable success. The goal statement should include any requirements or limitations on method and outcomes so the evaluation can take these into account.

2. *Analysis of problems with which the activity must cope*—These will indicate why there is a problem. They may include legal, contractual, or environmental limitations on methods or actions.

3. *Description and standardization of the activity*—A description of the activity should certainly be included in an evaluation of an action research project. Too often, an evaluation report tells "how it worked out," but does not adequately describe what was actually done in a way that others can learn from. An organization wishing to build on its successes and avoid repetition of failures will want an adequate description of the actual processes, many of which will be known to only a few people on the project. *Standardization* refers to developing standard ways of carrying out each part of the project. Most action research projects, being one of a kind, are not subject to standardization, although it is possible in such areas as repetitive administration of survey research instruments, their analysis, and their use for feedback.

4. *Measurement of the degree of change occurring*—The difficulties of measurement will depend on the nature of the action research project. For some changes, it is easy to use regularly kept records to measure change. Examples are changes in absenteeism, tardiness, illness on workdays, numbers of minority-group job applicants, and new hires. Where the goal of the action research is organizational or group development, the changes may take place over a long period of time and may be quite subtle. Changes in attitudes can be measured by interviews, questionnaires, and many unobtrusive measures—that is, observations that the person being observed is not aware of (Webb, 1966).

5. *Determining the cause(s) of change*—This is often very difficult, but it is usually less difficult in action research projects than in most program evaluations. At least the action research project is started consciously to solve a problem or bring about a change, and can be evaluated on whether it accomplishes its mission. Since most action research projects are fairly short, the effects of the *process* can also be ascertained, although usually with less precision than the degree of change occurring.

6. *Determining durability of effects*—Most difficult, of course, in the short run is determining or estimating the durability of effects. Sometimes, in the glow of a good process that "made a problem go away," the effects may seem permanent. After the pleasures of the process have been forgotten, however, the quality of the change itself may seem to decline. An action research project on allocation of office space in a new building may lead to a highly desirable solution for the first year's occupancy but not provide flexibility needed for later additions of staff, which had been anticipated but not adequately dealt with before the solution was "set in concrete."

Four special problems of evaluation research have been identified (USHEW, 1955) in addition to those implied in the discussion above of the six steps in the process. These are:

1. Dealing with multiple organizations and objectives
2. Interference with objectives and processes
3. Difficulties in observing relevant activities
4. Disagreement on assumptions underlying the program

Fortunately, in these four areas, action research may be easier to evaluate than most programs attempting change. Action research usually involves only one organization and seldom more than one location. There may be multiple objectives for the action research, but these are usually consciously developed in the early part of the process, and the evaluation plan takes them into account. Interference with objectives and processes is unlikely when the evaluation is planned as part of the total program. In fact, the evaluation of the amount and effect of change may help to stimulate the change and to stabilize it, as it often does in evaluating the results of a training program.

The activities of an action research project are, by their very nature, open and easy to observe. They are intended to be visible, and most include plans to enhance their visibility. Disagreements about assumptions underlying the program are also less likely than in a regular program evaluation, because the assumptions are discussed and specified as part of the chartering and contracting procedure. This does not preclude the existence of other assumptions not openly stated, but the generally open process minimizes this problem.

WHAT FACTORS ACCOUNT FOR ACTION RESEARCH PROGRAM EFFECTIVENESS?

Seashore and Likert (1953) indicated six factors that accounted for action research program effectiveness in the community context. These seem equally applicable in the corporate context, as indicated by the parentheses below. The six factors are:

1. *Leadership*—How important is the program to its leaders? How well do they follow and represent the objectives of the other participants? What positions do they hold in the community (company)? To what extent do they reflect the varous community (company) interests?

2. *Organization Structure*—Can the action research organization (team) draw on the strength of a larger organization or organizations? What is its internal structure? Is it tightly enough organized to assure application of resources to its goals, and loosely enough to keep the commitment of the participants?

3. *The Community (Company) and its Groups*—How does the organization involve economic, ethnic, social, and professional groups in the community (company)? Does it work through groups, or only through individuals? How is it tied to local government, school, health, and other (corporate environment) groups?

4. *Breadth of Participation*—Does it involve all its own members actively in decisions as well as in work? Does it get the participation of other community (company) groups sympathetic to its purposes?

5. *Types of Appeals*—How do community (company) people find out about the program? To which of their needs or interests does it appeal? Are there different appeals for different groups or persons?

6. *Emphasis on Action*—Does the project get away from talking and into trying to do something? Does it set goals and consider alternative ways of achieving them? Does it make and implement plans for evaluating the success of different action approaches?

These six factors provide a guide for designing and planning the evaluation of action research in any context. Being forewarned about the important factors can help avoid program difficulties and failures.

WHAT ARE THE POTENTIAL DANGERS OF ACTION RESEARCH?

There are two kinds of dangers—those inherent in the action research process and those resulting from faulty application of it. Inherent in the process of action research is management's surrendering some of its prerogatives to investigate, to recommend or decide, and to inform people about matters related to management of the organization. It may find it difficult to get them back at the end of the project, especially in the project area. People involved in the process may find it "habit-forming." They may be unwilling to reassume their previous, less influential and less interesting roles in the organization.

Another possibility is that the process may create a pocket of openness or "organic style" that is out of context with the rest of the organization. Worse, the pocket may be closed and the open participants hurt. Finally, even a well-conceived and well-run action research project may fail to bring about satisfactory change or acceptance of it. The failure may discourage both management and participants from future attempts with the same processes.

The potential dangers from doing it wrong are greater, however. Perhaps the most frequent fault is lack of adequate problem definition, including roles, requirements, and limits. The process needs to include preliminary discussion, drafting of a problem or charter statement, and further discussion until there is agreement on all significant aspects of the problem and possible approaches for dealing with it. The roles and time commitments of participants are dependent on content aspects of the project, and need to be reviewed before a project is formally chartered. Related is the fact that the looseness and vagueness of the concept often lead people to run around not really knowing what they are supposed to be doing.

Another common fault is inadequate preparation for the process and for legitimization as an early part of it. A management that is accustomed to delegating by writing a memo or holding a single meeting may try to move too fast in starting an action research project. Organic organizations tend to make decisions rather slowly and with several iterations of data gathering and tentative planning. The process of creating an action research project will come naturally in such an organization.

A third common fault is inadequate commitment of resources, including sufficient time for the percolating processes of action research to have their effect. Failure to involve outsiders frequently defeats the project. If those intimately involved in the problem had been unable to solve it before, regrouping them without adding any resources may be fruitless. The "outsiders" need not be from outside the organization itself, but should be from outside the immediate problem area group. He, she, or they can help the group see itself in a new role and can provide experience in the process and expertise in the research and other technical aspects of the project. And when the outsiders go away, the insiders know the project has ended.

Finally, management must be honestly committed to support the project and to accept its outcomes. If some potential outcomes would be unacceptable, that should be indicated in advance. Fortunately, the most likely failure is a project that "fizzles" or "dies with a whimper," rather than one that makes a dramatic mistake or causes serious problems. The dangers, then, are relatively minor compared to the benefits obtained from a successful project or series of them.

WHAT PROFESSIONAL PROBLEMS FACE
ACTION RESEARCH CONSULTANTS?

Professional consultants, whether from outside or inside the organization, face problems of ethics, goals, and initiatives in connection with their work. These problems are increased when they undertake action research consulting. Robert N. Rapoport (1970), drawing upon the Tavistock action research experience, described the dilemmas in these three areas as they affect those of us who are research consultants.

The first of the ethical dilemmas he described was concerned with what clients to accept. Should we work only with clients whose purposes we support, or only on projects supporting our value systems? Or should we work where there is a need for intervention or new knowledge, even if we do not agree with all of the clients' values? Some middle road must be taken, or we will either be doing no relevant research or be prostituting ourselves.

After we have solved the client problem, we still have to face the problem of confidentiality of personal information and protection of respondents. Who should get access to the information accumulated on an action research project? For example, if workers' attitudes are surveyed, does the labor union as well as management have a right to the information?

Many consultants face the question of whether they can work for clients who are in competition, directly or indirectly, with each other. If we do not work for similar (therefore, often competing) organizations, we are always amateurs in the organization we are working in. If we move from one organization to one or more of its competitors, are the later ones paying us for information from the earlier ones? Both the potential client and the action researcher should be aware of the problems in this area and should agree on how they will be dealt with.

Personal involvement in the client organization—especially if one is offered a job there—presents another dilemma, usually resolved by keeping some distance from most of the organization. Finally, how do we deal with competing action researchers, or with potential clients who want us to help them discredit the work of another researcher? Not all research consultants and not all clients will agree on the answers to these ethical dilemmas, but agreement between client and consultant on them is essential from the start.

Goal dilemmas are the second kind identified by Rapoport. The problem was the extent to which the action research person or group should satisfy the client's needs versus the needs of science for new knowledge. A very high proportion of action research is client-initiated and paid for, just as it is for other kinds of change assistance or applied research. It seems evident that the client's needs must be served if the client is paying for the effort. It is certainly desirable to use action research opportunities to add to new knowledge. Since the client is benefiting from knowledge developed at others' expense, it is not unreasonable to expect him to contribute to the cost of further knowledge, although it is also appropriate for the researcher to do this with his own time and funds. Again, any agreement between a research consultant and a client must consider this dilemma.

The third dilemma is that of initiatives. In a university, the research initiative is taken by the scientist and maintained by him. In the action research environment, the initiative is usually taken by the client, although, as the problem changes, initiatives to change the course of the research and action may be taken by the scientist. There is also the difficult question of what the research consultant should do if members of the client organization reject his interventions. Among other things, he should obviously reconsider his methods, review progress and problems with his client, and invite discussion with those rejecting his help. Finally, what is to be done in the event of discovery of a problem for which there is no responsible profession or group? Uncovering a really new problem is the least structured of all the problems raised by Rapoport; fortunately, it is one not often faced.

CAN ACTION RESEARCH BE USED AS AN EVALUATION RESEARCH METHOD?

Perhaps the boldest suggestion for the use of action research is as a means for members of an organization to evaluate their (or their organization's) performance on a project or program (Kirkhart, 1974). Just as there is resistance to change in an organization, resistance to evaluation is endemic in project groups. Everybody agrees that evaluation is necessary, but it is difficult to get agreement on what should be evaluated and by whom. Action research may be considered for overcoming this resistance. It presents problems, however, in that the same people who are conducting the project are conducting the evaluation. They may have a conflict of interest, and they do not get the benefit of an outsider's perspective on what they are doing. Evaluating your own project is a little like measuring your own height. If you don't have very good measuring instruments, your answers will lack precision.

One way to get the benefits of action research for evaluation without suffering its disadvantages is to use action research to design and to review periodically the evaluation research that is conducted by people outside the project staff. As the total project is being designed, someone (or a small group) takes responsibility for assuring that competent evaluation of the project is included in the plans. The total group planning the project then participates in planning the evaluation research and its role in providing feedback to project participants periodically as a basis for review of the adequacy of various parts of the project. Outside evaluators conduct their presumably objective evaluation following the agreed-upon plan and provide feedback both to project managers and participants and to the people and/or agency to which they are responsible.

WHAT IS THE RELATION OF ACTION
RESEARCH TO TRAINING?

Over the past two decades, action research has been increasingly merged with training, using a single process—action research and training to achieve the objectives of organizational change (or development) and increasing the capability of its members.

Neely Gardner has been both an instigator and chronicler of this process. In 1957, writing *Training as a Framework for Action,* he laid the groundwork for looking at training as organizational development. In 1960, he formally brought training into the action research picture in a widely read and reprinted article in the *Journal of the American Society of Training Directors.* He listed ten propositions or assumptions about the training director's job, including the following:

> The chief function of training is to effect change, and the role of the training director should be that of change agent. Training efforts should influence and assist in the understanding and implementation of organization, philosophy, and policy. Training should create in management an understanding of organization as a social system. We should aim for "organization development" as well as for "management and employee development."

Gardner can take some satisfaction from the fact that the organization has renamed itself the American Society for Training *and Development.*

In 1957, Gardner described the use of action training and research for such diverse projects as reducing infant mortality in Brazil, changing the structure and operations of the California State Compensation Insurance Fund, and developing and institutionalizing a state training department. He lists six assumptions that apply to action training and research philosophy: The first is that it should help officials, administrators, and employees to help themselves. Second, key people in the organization need to understand the objectives and must have an awareness of the potential risks and benefits of such a program.

The third assumption is that each manager and supervisor must "see himself" and possess the skills of an action trainer and researcher; that is, he must have congruence or self-awareness and must be trained as an action trainer. Thus, he learns to participate with his employees in problem solving. Fourth, action training and research belong where the problems are, rather than at a remote institution. People are not trained away from the job; groups of people are trained on the job. Fifth, leadership and experimentation may be the most important function of central training units. Finally, the best strategy is to "lead from strength"—to use action research and training in organizations that are ready to expand talent and effort to make good operations even better.

The unique approach of action training and research as described by Gardner is that the training department, instead of providing skill training that employees are expected to use in their work groups, trains managers and supervisors on the action training and research process and then assists them in conducting such projects with their own employees. Thus, the managers become equipped to understand, acquire the skills for, and receive active organizational support for executing the processes and duties required to solve their problems and contribute to the evaluation of the action taken. The action training and research process is not fast, but it does tend to produce fairly immediate results in areas where the training group wants to solve a problem or bring about change.

Gardner updated his predictions in 1974 in an article entitled *Action Training and Research: Something Old and Something New.* He describes it as achieving two objectives—change and training—with one process. Action training and research increases the capability of the people involved while bringing about a change the organization needs.

McGill and Horton (1973) recommend the use of action research designs for training and development in organizations. They see training as an active rather than a passive process for the trainees, one in which they learn what they do. They feel that the organization is the appropriate context for training and development, as it is there that they must ultimately be put into effect. Further, administrators can learn to act effectively while acting and learning. They describe six examples of using action research to solve training and development problems.

The appropriate role of a training staff, then, is to stimulate line management to participate in all aspects of the management training and development program, including establishing goals, planning, operating, and evaluating. Action research can be used for creating and improving specific management courses as well as for establishing a comprehensive training and development program.

HOW CAN ACTION RESEARCH BE USED FOR ORGANIZATIONAL DEVELOPMENT?

The preceding section indicates the close relationship between training and development when the action mode is used. It is a short step to using it for bringing about organizational change as the primary purpose. The first significant example of action research for organizational change actually began a decade before Lewin first wrote about the process. John Collier (1945), U.S. Commissioner of Indian Affairs from 1933 to 1945, described using action research methods to bring about change in agricultural practices with the three southwestern Indian tribes—all in the 1933-45 era. The key element he noted in bringing about change was giving research information to tribal decision makers, discussing its meaning with them, and working with them on developing plans to overcome the problems indicated by the research.

Collier also used the process for trying, sometimes with success and sometimes not, to bring about change in the Bureau of Indian Affairs and existing or new government organizations with which the bureau interacted. Using the phrase *action research,* Collier identified the essential elements of the process we still call by that name. He reported on a failure in order to highlight the importance of involving those affected in the decision processes. In 1935, he created an organization within the bureau, called Technical Coopera-tion. It had temporary funding from the Department of Agriculture, with competent direction and staff. It conducted many excellent studies, but, because of the temporary funding, felt it did not have time to involve Bureau of Indian Affairs administrators or Indians in its studies. As a result, valuable information went unused. That failure led the newly formed Soil Conservation Service to involve those affected in its research and understanding of the meaning of its findings, and led to the creation of many thousand soil conservation districts to implement plans developed to overcome problems discovered by research.

Shepard and Blake (1962) describe changing behavior through cognitive change, a process very much like action research for bringing about major organizational changes. The purpose of this process is to use participative methods for dealing with the organization's major problems—those that are related to its reason for being. The process, as well as the purpose, is different, primarily in that it involves all levels of management in any part of the organization (usually all of it) that is involved in impending changes.

Shepard and Blake point out that in centralized, mechanistic organizations, all learning is at the top. Even though all parts of the organization have some contact with the environment outside the company, they will not learn if all important decisions are centralized. The purpose of the change toward a more organic organization is to stimulate learning at all levels and units in the organization.

Shepard and Blake describe a five-step process. First is creation of interpersonal openness and a problem-solving climate among those to be involved. This is accomplished through a series of meetings, away from the work environment, of organizational subgroups, starting with top management. These meetings explore personal and subgroup interactions and communications. The second step is organizational diagnosis, through an applications laboratory or a series of them. These laboratories "assess the present organization and its systems more objectively to plot the changes required in order to achieve key organizational or subgroup objectives in a more efficient manner. Such organizational variables include climate, concepts, structure, policy, procedure, personnel, operations, and environment to serve as a check list of the items to be considered."

The third step is implementation of agreed-upon changes and follow-up on their efforts. The fourth involves an intervention in the organization's ongoing activities to keep the organization from slipping back to its earlier, mechanistic ways of operating. This phase must deal with problems of the adjustment of individuals to the new organizational climate and to problems both in and between groups.

The fifth step is reorganization of the organization, so that its structure corresponds to the networks of interdependence required for its success, and so that its procedures facilitate intercommunication within and among the networks.

Holmberg (1958) described an action research approach to community development in Peru. In five years, a group of U.S. scientists changed an ancient hacienda, completely dependent upon its *patron* (leaseholder), into an independent community with sufficient strength and capital to assist another hacienda on its march toward independence. In this case, the scientists attempted to conduct 130 specific action research projects—both testing hypotheses and bringing about change—each matched to a specific developmental goal, such as diversification of agriculture, development of community leadership, and increasing educational opportunities for both children and adults. Each research intervention strengthened the community for larger steps.

Jenks (1970) reported on restructuring the personnel department of a large Midwestern manufacturing corporation through action research techniques. The personnel director, urged by his group vice-president and assisted by Jenks, began a process of reevaluating his own organization, decentralizing parts of his responsibility, and increasing his effectiveness. He divided his organization functionally into four parts and selected managers for each. The director, the four managers, and the consultant began to call itself the Personnel Planning Group (PPG) and together undertook to increase the internal effectiveness and efficiency of the department members. They also hoped to provide a methodological consulting model that would be useful in the PPG's work with others in the company.

A 41-item Q-sort was developed, using items describing ways of dealing with problems and people. For each specific problem the PPG decided to work on, each PPG member sorted the questions twice—first describing his own and then describing the personnel director's approach or behavior on that kind of problem. All members of the group, including the director, then received feedback on which items people agreed were most characteristic of themselves, which were least characteristic, and the items on which there was a discrepancy between how the personnel director saw himself and how his subordinates saw him. This process cleared up perceptual differences and provided a basis for deciding what problems should have highest priority in completing the department reorganization. They also considered ways of solving problems by using the Q-sort to determine an ideal way for the department to deal with a problem. Feedback identified differences of opinion on desirable approaches as well as areas of agreement, all of which were helpful in problem solving.

Koprowski (1972) described the general procedure of using action research teams to improve organizational effectiveness. He challenges the effectiveness of typical "management development" programs by pointing out the difficulties of transferring classroom learning into appropriate job behavior. He follows Gardner in viewing education as an instrument of change and suggests starting a management or organizational development process by asking questions like, "Why do we want to change?" "What and whom do we want to change?" "What are the best strategies for getting us there?" and, "How can we tell if we accomplished what we set out to do?"

Koprowski describes a five-step process. The first step is the original contact between the client and the consultant, who is usually called in as an "expert" to solve some specific organizational problem that may be only a symptom of an underlying problem. The consultant discusses the problem with members of the client organization to determine whether its value system is open, whether it values people more than things, whether there is pressure for change, and whether the people in this organization and he can work together.

The second phase is joint exploration of needed change, which involves more people and time than the original contact. This is done primarily to see them at different levels and places in the organization. The process for obtaining information is considered as important as the content obtained. The most revealing method consists of interviews with open-ended questions about job activities, clarity, likes and dislikes, and problems being faced. Other methods used include observing meetings, reading memos and documents, and, occasionally, questionnaires.

Phase three is feedback—the packaging and delivery of information. This includes a written report to the person who engaged the consultant, constructed to provide an educational experience as well as to report information and provide alternatives for the organization. Feedback is then given to the people who must change; otherwise, they will have little commitment to its validity. The fourth phase is joint development of action programs. This follows the feedback and begins with joint identification of problems by all people concerned. Possible solutions are suggested by all, and solutions are chosen and given priority for attention by different people and groups. The team then conducts pilot projects with the people affected. This process assures that ". . . no organizational units are forced to use any strategy that does not work for them, no matter how appealing that strategy sounds in the literature or to top management."

The fifth phase is process evaluation, using criteria and methods agreed upon during the joint action planning. One or more meetings to discuss evaluation findings lead to an understanding of what works, as well as what does not work and why. Note that the emphasis on this evaluation is on the process, not the content-oriented outcomes of the process. It often leads to identifying additional problems to be approached by the same process, which will spread to other units of the organization, helping them to see their problems clearer and to get the will and insight to start action.

A somewhat different model of action research, also applicable to government and private organizations, was developed by the Unitarian-Universalist Association of America, which in 1976 completed three years of its "Sharing in Growth" program for its member churches (Goodwin, 1976). The unique aspect of this model was that it used a two-part self-renewal team, half from within the affected congregation and half from other congregations.

The process typically begins with a goal-setting meeting of the congregation, facilitated by an outsider familiar with the process. Then a "home team," usually of six people, diverse in interests and backgrounds, is selected. A "visiting team" is selected by the district committee, along with two facilitators who assist with the first meeting. The facilitators' roles are similar to those described for other action research consultants, except that they ordinarily work only with the two-part team for its first meeting. The teams meet four times, usually at about one-month intervals, to discuss the congregation's goals and to develop ways of meeting them. Resources both within and outside the congregation are sought and used. The joint team meetings usually occupy a weekend, or at least a day and a half. To keep the necessary people informed and involved, there is usually a potluck dinner or similar party each weekend involving the whole congregation. The team or some of its members meet regularly with the board of trustees of the congregation to report progress, request additional resources, or whatever else is appropriate.

Forty-eight congregations participated in the first three years. They reported achieving an average of 45 percent of their goals during the Sharing in Growth process. Congregations participating showed more growth in both members and income following the process than did churches not involved in it. A valuable by-product of this process is the learning the visiting team members get from the home team and each other, which stimulates more activity in their own congregations. It seems to be highly applicable to other organizations with multiple similar units. Each unit wanting to tackle some of its problems and opportunities in this new way would be given help from similar units in the organization. Facilitators to start and perhaps to continue to monitor the process would be provided from outside the affected unit.

HOW CAN ACTION RESEARCH BE USED FOR
INDIVIDUAL DEVELOPMENT?

The use of action research methods for self-study of both individuals and groups is another variation from the more standard processes. Nevitt Sanford (1969) reported on research with students studying themselves. He pointed out that student activism then had major implications for those who study students as well as for those responsible for education. Investigators are part of the "Establishment" they were criticizing. Information is obtained from students without their awareness of the implications of what they are revealing. It is used in a decision-making system that usually does not include students and may not have their interests at heart. Sanford says that we need a new model based on three principles: Research is self-study. Teaching is inquiry. Research is action.

The student activism has subsided, at least for the present, but the same questions may be raised in the future by the increasingly well-educated labor force. Workers may protest providing information to a stranger or computer for decision-making processes in which they do not participate. We can expect that part of the worker participation movement will include action research rather than management (or consultant) research on worker needs, attitudes, activities, and problems.

Wolf (1976) recently reported on a program in which incoming or applicant doctoral candidates in the University of Southern California's Washington Public Affairs Center spend a semester examining their own goals, backgrounds, characteristics, and capabilities. The product of this research is a report discussed with other students and the program director. The use of this process has convinced some students that their motivation was insufficient for completing the program and has reinforced the goal of a doctorate for others. Similar programs are used in psychology departments, schools of business administration, and others.

We see action research used, then, for solving specific problems, for designing evaluation research, for management training and development, for bringing about organizational changes of various scopes, and for self-study of individuals and groups. As more people and groups learn to use it effectively, it will contribute to making organizations more fulfilling for the people who work in them and will help them adapt to changes in their technologies and environments.

REFERENCES

Chein, Isador, Stuart W. Cook, and John Harding, "The Field of Action Research," *American Psychologist,* Vol. 3 (1948), 43-50.

Collier, John, "United States Indian Administration as a Laboratory of Ethnic Relations," *Social Research,* May 1945, pp. 275-76.

French, Wendell, "Organization Development: Objectives, Assumptions and Strategies," *California Management Review,* Vol. XII, 2 (1969), 22-26.

Gardner, Neely, "Action Training and Research: Something Old and Something New," *Public Administration Review,* March-April 1974, pp. 106-15.

————,"Mr. Training Director—His Job," *Journal of the American Society of Training Directors,* August 1960.

————,"Training as a Framework for Action," *Public Administration Review,* January 1957, pp. 39-44.

Goodwin, Joan, "Sharing in Growth: Has It Been a Success?" *Unitarian Universalist World,* October 1, 1976, p. 1.

Holmberg, Allan R., "Values in Action," *Human Organization,* Vol. 17 (1958), 12-16.

Jenks, R. Stephen, "An Action-Research Approach to Organizational Change," *Journal of Applied Behavioral Science,* Vol. 6 (1970), 131-50.

Kirkhart, Larry, "Organization Development in a Public Agency," doctoral dissertation, University of Southern California, 1974.

Koprowski, Eugene J., "Improving Organizational Effectiveness through Action Research Teams," *Training and Development Journal,* June 1972, pp. 36-40.

Lawler, Edward, "Workers Can Set Their Own Wages—Responsibly," *Psychology Today,* Vol. 9, 10 (1977), 109-12.

Likert, R., *The Human Organization.* New York: McGraw-Hill, 1967.

McGill, Michael E., and Melvin E. Horton, Jr., *Action Research Designs for Training and Development.* Washington, D.C.: NTDS Press, 1973.

Rapoport, Robert N., "Three Dilemmas in Action Research with Special Reference to the Tavistock Experience," *Human Relations,* Vol. 23, 6 (1970), 499-513.

Sanford, Nevitt, "Psychology in Action—Research with Students as Action and Education," *American Psychologist,* Vol. 24 (1969), 544-46.

Seashore, Stanley E., and Rensis Likert, "Action Research for Better Community Programs in International Affairs," *Adult Leadership,* Vol. II (1953), 23-26.

Shepard, Herbert R., and Robert R. Blake, "Changing Behavior through Congitive Change," *Human Organization,* Vol. 21 (1962), 88-96.

U.S. Department of Health, Education and Welfare, *Evaluation in Mental Health,* Public Health Service Publication No. 413. Washington, D.C.: U.S. Government Printing Office, 1955.

Wolf, James, "Self Assessment and Career Planning—A Case Study," dissertation, University of Southern California, 1976.

Index